Setting Limits with Your Strong-Willed Teen

# Setting Limits

## WITH YOUR

# Strong-Willed Teen

*Eliminating Conflict by Establishing*
*Clear, Firm, and Respectful Boundaries*

Robert J. MacKenzie, Ed.D.

HARMONY
BOOKS · NEW YORK

Copyright © 2015 by Setting Limits: Educational
and Psychological Consulting, P.C.

Published in the United States by Harmony Books, an imprint
of the Crown Publishing Group, a division of Random House LLC,
a Penguin Random House Company, New York.
www.crownpublishing.com

Harmony Books is a registered trademark, and the Circle
colophon is a trademark of Random House LLC.

Library of Congress Cataloging-in-Publication Data is available upon request.

ISBN 978-0-8041-3876-5
eBook ISBN 978-0-8041-3877-2

Printed in the United States of America

Book design by Jennifer Daddio/Bookmark Design & Media Inc.
Cover photography: John Rensten/Getty Images; Ron Levine/Getty Images;
Tom Fullum/Getty Images; jpique/Getty Images; boy in striped shirt/Getty Images

1 3 5 7 9 10 8 6 4 2

First Edition

# Contents

# Introduction

This book reflects my developing interest in two topics: parental limit-setting practices and individual differences in children's temperament and learning styles over a twenty-year period. In 1993, I wrote my first book, *Setting Limits: Raising Responsible, Independent Children with Clear Boundaries.* The book provides parents with the basic tools they need to set clear, firm limits with children of all ages. The methods work with all kids—compliant kids, difficult kids, and those in between—but in 1993 I didn't fully understand why.

When I shared the methods with parents and teachers at my workshops, I heard the same reports over and over again. Some kids tested a lot. Others kids tested much less. A small percentage of kids were off the charts and tested constantly. Everywhere I went, I heard the same stories. It was always the same small group of kids that caused 90 percent of the problems at home, in the schools, and in the community.

Most of the parents in my workshops enjoyed very positive outcomes with their new limit-setting tools—less testing, fewer power struggles, better cooperation, and more satisfying relationships—but some had to work a lot harder than others to get there. I suspected this had more to do with their kids and less to do with their limit setting. That's when I became very interested in individual differences in children's temperaments and learning styles.

My intended target audience was all parents, but that's not the way it turned out. Few parents came to my workshops overwhelmed by the problems they faced with their compliant, easy-to-raise children. The majority came looking for answers for the problems they were having with their strong-willed, difficult-to-raise kids. They were my true target audience, and their stories inspired my interest in differences in children's temperaments.

As fate and good fortune would have it, I had a strong-willed child of my own. My second son, Ian, is a wonderful guy, but he is very strong-willed, and he was challenging to raise. His older brother, Scott, is more compliant. My wife and I used the same limit-setting approach with both boys and got the same results, but we had to work a lot harder with Ian to get there. His temperament and learning style were very different from his compliant brother's.

My experiences with Ian and the consistent stories parents shared in my workshops confirmed my suspicions. I had overlooked a very important factor in the guidance and discipline equation: differences in children's temperament. Limit setting is about teaching. Temperament is about learning. Child guidance is a continual interaction between the parents' limit-setting methods and the child's temperament through all stages of the child's development. These appeared to be the two big variables in the equation. It was time to get back to the drawing board and do some more research.

In 1998, I revised *Setting Limits* and incorporated current research on children's temperaments and learning styles with the material I already had on limit setting. I refer to this book as my "regular-strength edition" because it focuses on the full range of children's temperaments and learning styles. Finally, the two big pieces of the equation came together. The revision was well received, which inspired my next writing project for my real target audience.

In 2001, I wrote *Setting Limits with Your Strong-Willed Child*, which I affectionately refer to as my "extra-strength edition." This book addresses the limit-setting challenges parents face during early and middle childhood with strong-willed, difficult-to-raise kids. The book was a huge success. It helps parents understand their child's unique individual temperament and learning style and gives them the tools they need to set limits and teach their rules more effectively.

When your limit-setting methods are well matched to your child's temperament and learning style, amazing things begin to happen. Communication improves. Limit testing and power struggles decrease. Cooperation and learning improve dramatically.

You can't change the blueprint for your child's temperament and learning style. These traits have already been determined, but you can get to know that blueprint and learn to work with it effectively. Now the really good news! Your child's temperament and learning style are only half of the overall equation. The other half of the equation, your limit-setting methods, is solidly within your control. You can improve the match, and when you do, you get to enjoy the rewards that come with this special connection—better communication and cooperation, fewer power struggles, and more satisfying relationships. The goal is within your reach.

What happened during the thirteen years since I wrote

*Setting Limits with Your Strong-Willed Child*? The kids in the book grew up, and so did their parents' need for effective limit-setting tools during the adolescent years. I became overwhelmed with parent requests for help with their strong-willed, difficult-to-raise teens. *Setting Limits with Your Strong-Willed Teen* expands the themes of temperament and learning style into adolescence and addresses the limit-setting challenges parents face during this difficult period.

The focus and scope of this book are very narrow. *Setting Limits with Your Strong-Willed Teen* is about the basics: understanding your teen's temperament and learning style and adjusting your limit-setting practices accordingly. The goal is to help you improve the match. When you do, good things happen. The teaching-and-learning process goes much more smoothly. It's not magic. It's just the power of a good match.

This book will help you improve the match. *Setting Limits with Your Strong-Willed Teen* provides you with the information and tools you need to understand your strong-willed teen, stop unacceptable behavior and power struggles, and teach your rules in the clearest and most understandable way. You can say goodbye to all the ineffective methods that wear you down and get you nowhere. No more repeating, reminding, reasoning, explaining, arguing, debating, lecturing, threatening, punishing, or cajoling. Your teen will understand what you mean when you learn to set clear, firm limits and support your rules with natural and logical consequences. This book will show you how to do that. The methods should be a refreshing change to the ineffective extremes of punishment and permissiveness.

This book is divided into two sections to help you answer two basic questions: What's going on? and What do you do about it? Chapters 1–7 are designed to help you understand the dynamics that operate between you and your teen and recognize the things you're doing that aren't working for you. Without this awareness, it will be difficult, if not impossible, to avoid repeating your old mistakes, because most of them are made unconsciously.

Chapter 1 will help you understand your teen's temperament, as well as your own, and learn how temperament affects behavior. In Chapter 2, you'll discover how your teen's temperament and the forces of adolescence collide to create a confusing picture of who your teen is trying to become. In Chapter 3, you'll develop a better understanding of your changing role as the parent and why your teen needs you to coach from the sidelines and stay off the playing field.

In Chapter 4, you'll understand why teens need limits and the important role limits play in guiding teens down the path toward healthy development. In Chapter 5, you'll discover how teens learn your rules based upon individual differences in their temperaments and learning styles. You'll see that aggressive research is a normal and natural process for many teens. In Chapters 6 and 7, you'll identify your limit-setting approach and determine whether your limits are firm or soft.

With an understanding of what's not working for you, you'll be ready to add some important new tools to your parenting toolkit. Chapters 8 through 16 form the core of your skill-training program. In Chapters 8–11, you'll learn how to give clear, firm, limit-setting messages with your words, how to stop power struggles before they begin, how to support your rules with natural and logical consequences, and how to manage the next wave of resistance you'll likely encounter.

Determining your teen's readiness for new freedoms and

privileges is one of the most challenging issues parents face during adolescence. It's also one of the biggest sources of conflict and power struggles. In Chapters 13 and 14, you'll understand why teens and parents approach the topic of readiness from such different perspectives, and learn an easy procedure for determining your teen's readiness with the least amount of conflict and acrimony.

Trust is the underpinning of all good relationships and one of the best measures of character development. In Chapter 15, you'll learn about the Trust Bank Account that exists between all parents and teens and how to use this important tool to teach valuable lessons about relationships and character. In Chapter 16, you'll learn how to fix an overdrawn Trust Bank Account and help your teen get pointed in the right direction.

The primary focus of this book is on improving the match between your limit-setting methods and your teen's temperament and learning style. Effective limit setting will help all teens stay on a healthier path, accomplish their developmental tasks, and move safely into adulthood, but limit setting is not a panacea for all teen problems. Some teens need more. Chapter 17 will help you determine when professional help is needed and where to go when it is.

Learning the methods in this book will be relatively easy. Most are clear and fairly straightforward. The hardest part, for many of you, will be to overcome your compelling desire to revert to your old bad habits and do things the way you did in the past. On an intellectual level, you may recognize that the methods will lead to the type of change you desire, but the methods may not feel comfortable to you or your teen in the beginning. You'll likely encounter resistance from many sources, including from within yourself. If this happens to you, I encourage you to refer back to Chapter 11 to help restore the broader perspective and stay focused on your goals.

Expect to make mistakes when you begin practicing your new skills. Mistakes are okay. They're part of learning. If you're the kind of parent who's hard on yourself, write yourself a forgiveness slip. Your goal should be improvement, not perfection, and you will improve the more you practice. I didn't develop a sense of confidence with my limit setting until my boys left the house. I think that's the way it's supposed to be when you're raising teens.

Parents frequently tell me that the examples in the book resemble their own teen or family circumstances. That's a good thing. Often, it's easier to see yourself through the experiences of others. Most of the examples in this book reflect actual cases from my family counseling work. In all cases, the names have been changed to protect the privacy of those involved.

When you complete the book, refer to the suggestions for getting started in the Appendix. These tips will help you start off at a comfortable pace and provide a schedule for adding new tools to your toolkit.

Guidance for teens is a broad topic encompassing many important subtopics, such as building positive relationships, peer group influences, decision making and problem solving, family communication, puberty and physical health, sexual identity, adjusting to divorce, stepfamilies, blended families, friendships, dating and sexuality, character development, morals and values, financial responsibilities, leisure time, curfews, and school issues. Although this book overlaps with many of these subtopics, they are not the central focus of this book. In the Suggested Reading section, I've included references for those desiring more information on some of the important subtopics.

The guidance tools in this book have helped thousands of parents and teachers enjoy more satisfying and cooperative relationships, not only with strong-willed teens but with all teens. If you're willing to invest the time and energy needed to learn the skills and add the new tools to your parenting tool-kit, you too can share the rewards. Enjoy *Setting Limits with Your Strong-Willed Teen.*

## CHAPTER 1

# Who Is This Strong-Willed Teen?

Does your teenager challenge your rules and authority on a regular basis? Do you feel frustrated and worn down by the constant testing, arguments, and power struggles? Does your teen's behavior seem so extreme that you question if it's normal? If so, you're not alone. Consider the following.

Fourteen-year-old Corey is a workout! He doesn't hit the pillow on school nights until after 1 a.m. and gets up twenty minutes late each morning. The time would be later if his mother didn't prod him every five minutes after his alarm goes off. Corey usually functions on five to six hours of sleep. *No wonder he's getting D's in two classes,* his father thinks to himself. *He's running on empty.*

When Corey arrives at the breakfast table, he snarls at his two sisters, grumbles in his father's direction, then turns up his nose at the meal his mother prepared and complains that there is never anything good to eat. *This is not a battle I want to fight,* his mother says to herself as she prepares Corey his own special meal. She tells her husband that she worries about Corey's nutrition, but what she really worries about is all the grief Corey will dish out if he doesn't get his own way.

"I'm out of here," says Corey, as he gulps down his last bite and heads for the door.

"Wait a minute," says his mother. "You forgot to clear your dishes."

"I'll do it when I get home!" he shouts as the door shuts. Her husband thinks she's too soft on Corey, and so do his two sisters.

"It's not fair!" they complain in chorus. "He never has to do his chores."

By the time Corey leaves the house in the morning, his mother is ready for a nap, but she knows this is only the beginning. Round two begins in the afternoon, when Corey returns from school and the homework battles begin. She wonders how long she can take it.

Sixteen-year-old Kristal is sweet and cooperative one moment, angry and defiant the next. Little things set her off—unexpected changes, departures from routine, a misplaced hairbrush, a puzzled look from her parents, or simply not getting her own way. Emotional storms and meltdowns are common.

"Living with Kristal is like riding an emotional roller coaster," says her mother. "It's exhausting!" Kristal's parents alternate between punishing and giving in, depending upon how volatile Kristal appears or how worn down they feel; but nothing seems to make any difference. They wonder if Kristal's behavior is normal and question whether they did something to cause her to behave this way.

Thirteen-year-old Alex has a short fuse and often acts before he thinks. When things don't go his way at home, school, or in the neighborhood, Alex gets loud, uses profanity, calls

names, threatens, and sometimes hits others. He's been suspended from school three times for fighting and talking disrespectfully to his teachers. It's only October.

"When we ask him why he behaves this way, Alex says he
doesn't know," says his mother. "How can he not know?"

"It's too bad they don't spank kids at school anymore," Alex's father laments. "When Alex acts like that at home, we give
him an earful, then we whip his ass. He has to learn. We've
threatened to take away his TV, Internet, and cell phone privileges for the rest of the year if he's suspended again."

Lynn, age fifteen, is destined to be a great trial lawyer.
She's bright, intense, and very persistent. Lynn will argue with
anyone about anything if she thinks there's a chance of getting things to work out her way. Sometimes she just argues for
the sport of it. In fact, Lynn has been known to change her
position midway through an argument and argue the opposite
position even more tenaciously. She's willing to use any tactic
to win her case—anger, drama, rudeness, even dishonesty.

"I never would have imagined talking to adults the way
Lynn talks to us," her father complains. "We reason with her
every way we know, but everything turns into a heated argument."

Do any of these teens sound familiar? If your son or daughter resembles one of these, you're not alone. I see many teens
each year that parents and teachers describe as challenging,
difficult, spirited, stubborn, hell-raising, defiant, or just plain
impossible. Although no single term adequately describes all,
or even most, of the teens I see, the one that comes closest
is "strong-willed." These are normal teens with extreme behavior. They are harder to raise, difficult to discipline, and at

greater risk for behavior problems at home, at school, and in the community.

Strong-willed teens are not part of some conspiracy to make life difficult for others. They just do what strong-willed teens do. They test harder and more often, resist longer, protest louder, use more drama, take more risks, and carry things further than most of us would imagine. They are the supercharged versions of normal teens, the "movers" and "shakers" of the teen world who bring out strong reactions in others.

Teachers and principals know them as the 10 percent that cause 90 percent of school discipline problems. Parents know them as their biggest challenges. I know them affectionately as "my kids" because I spend a lot of my time with them. Yes, I'm the proud parent of a strong-willed son. My youngest son, Ian, is a delight, but during his childhood and teenage years, he also was a workout. He wasn't the least bit impressed by the fact that I write books on this subject. At home, I got no breaks or professional immunity. Ian pushed hard against my rules and authority. At times, I wondered whether his behavior was normal, especially when he became a teen.

Do you sometimes question whether your teen's behavior is normal? Perhaps you worry that you've done something to cause your teen to behave this way. If so, you'll be relieved to know that the problem, in most cases, is not parents. Most are doing the best they can with the information and guidance tools in their toolkits. The problem is not the teen, either. Most strong-willed teens are just being themselves and doing what strong-willed teens do.

The real problem is the parents' inadequate understanding of adolescence and a bad match between the teen's temperament and the parents' limit-setting style. The parents' information and guidance tools are not well suited for the job. The predictable result: conflict, miscommunication, and power struggles.

When parents arrive at my office looking for help with their strong-willed teen, one of my first tasks is to assist them in understanding their teen's temperament and this crazy time we call adolescence. Then we examine how the parents' limit-setting styles match up with their teen's temperament and discuss the predictable conflicts and friction points that develop around a bad match. That's what we're going to do in this chapter. A new perspective awaits you. You're not the problem, but you're a big part of the solution. A better understanding and improved match are well within your control.

## Understanding Your Strong-Willed Teen

My youngest son, Ian, is a great force in our family and a great source of pride and joy. He's bright, adventurous, sensitive, a risk taker, and very determined. Sometimes I think he was more determined to train his mom and me than we were to train him. He kept us on our toes. If we were unclear, inconsistent, or indecisive when we asked him to do something, he would let us know. He'd continue testing and wait for a clearer signal.

Like most strong-willed individuals, Ian didn't wait until his teenage years to show his cards. He started out as a strong-willed infant. He was strong-willed throughout early and middle childhood, and he was a strong-willed teenager. Today he is a strong-willed adult. He's still the bright, intrepid, determined risk taker I've always known and loved, except now he directs his energies into triathlons, scuba diving, skydiving, and his career. His extreme temperament traits have served him well, but Ian was not easy to raise.

From the time he was a very young child, Ian always understood the "bottom line," and he knew how to get there. He pushed hard until he found it, and when he did, he pushed a little harder to see whether it would hold up. If it did, he stopped pushing, at least for a while, and accepted the limit or boundary. But Ian always pushed a lot before he got there. It was wearing! The pattern became even more intense during his teenage years. My older son, Scott, usually cooperated for the asking without all the pushing.

How would you react if you asked two teenage boys to cooperate in the same respectful manner and got two consistently different responses? Would you become upset? Confused? Would you question whether something was wrong?

The persistent testing that is so characteristic of strong-willed individuals, children and teens, is also what drives most parents crazy. *Why would anyone do this?* I'd ask myself. *Is this normal? I would never push anyone as hard as Ian pushes me.*

Does your teen push hard against your rules and authority? Has he or she done so from an early age? Do you react in extreme ways and question whether he or she is normal? Join the club. Now it's time to get better acquainted with your teen. The following are some basic facts about strong-willed teens that will help you better understand his or her behavior and your reactions to it.

- *Strong-willed teens are normal.* You've probably worried about whether your teen is normal when teachers or relatives point out that your teen's behavior seems extreme. They're probably right, but "extreme" does not mean "abnormal." Most strong-willed teens are normal with extreme temperament traits that magnify and intensify during adolescence. They're supercharged, but that doesn't mean they are brain-damaged, emotionally disturbed, or defective. Most have no diagnosable problems at all, though some do. There is no rule that says you can only have one thing going on in your life at a time. Some strong-willed teens also have learning disabilities, hyperactivity, emotional problems, and other special needs, but a strong will does not mean they are abnormal.

- *Strong-willed teens are not all alike.* Each strong-willed teen is a special individual with his or her own unique temperament. No two behave in exactly the same way. Sure, they all test parents and behave in extreme ways, but they don't all do it to the same degree. Some are easier. Others are more difficult. Some are almost impossible.

- *Strong-willed teens are hard to understand.* Our individual temperament shapes the way we think, learn, and behave. When others think and behave as we do, we can readily identify with them and better understand their experience. When others think, learn, and behave differently from us, however, it is not easy to understand them or to identify with their behavior. *Why would anyone do that?* we ask ourselves. From our perspective, the behavior is confusing and makes no sense.

  Teens today grow up in a very different world

from that of their parents. When temperament and adolescence are thrown into the mix, we can appreciate the strong potential for confusion. Strong-willed teens, and most teens for that matter, are hard to understand for exactly this reason. As you learn about your teen's temperament and how that temperament shapes the way your teen behaves, behavior that once seemed confusing begins to make sense.

- *Strong-willed teens require a lot of guidance and discipline.* Of course, this statement seems obvious. Teens who test a lot require frequent limit setting. When you accept this statement as a fact of life rather than a source of annoyance, your attitude and perspective change. Mine did. I began to see my son's behavior more clearly and stopped taking things personally when he tested me. I realized that his job was to test, and my job was to set clear, firm limits and guide him in the right direction. My improved perspective did not change his behavior, but it sure made my life less stressful.

- *Strong-willed teens do not respond to discipline methods that seem to work with other teens.* Why do some teens respond so differently to the same request? One cooperates, while the other resists. Is the problem the resistant teen? Or the request? Most parents feel confused when their best guidance efforts work with one teen and not with another. The issue is less confusing when we consider the individual temperaments involved. Teens with compliant temperaments will cooperate with most discipline approaches, even ineffective ones, because their underlying desire is to cooperate. They permit parents a wide range for ineffectiveness. Strong-willed teens do not respond cooperatively to ineffective discipline. They require clear, firm, and consistent limit setting to make an acceptable choice to cooperate. Ineffective limit setting is the fast lane to power struggles with a strong-willed teen.

- *Strong-willed teens learn differently from their peers.* Strong-willed teens do much of their learning "the hard way." That is, they need to experience the consequences of their poor choices and behavior repeatedly before they learn the lessons we're trying to teach. It's not enough to announce your rule that playing music loud in the house is not okay. Strong-willed teens need to repeatedly experience having their music turned off or having to use their headphones each time they decide to test the rule and blast their music. Their learning style can be frustrating and confusing because it is so unlike that of compliant teens, who will cooperate the first time for the asking. "Hard-way learning" is still good learning. It's just harder on parents.

- *Strong-willed teens bring out strong reactions in others.* How do you feel when your teen challenges or defies your rules and authority? Angry? Frustrated? Confused? Threatened? Intimidated? Embarrassed? Guilty? Inadequate? Discouraged?

Resentful? Exhausted? All of the above? These are all normal reactions to extreme behavior. Strong-willed teens often place strain on marriages, cause sibling conflicts, and create other problems within the family. Learning to temper your responses will be one of your greatest challenges in getting through the storm of adolescence. There is plenty of truth in the old adage that teenagers were put into our lives to teach us patience.

- *Adolescence is temporary, even for strong-willed teens.* Now, here's a piece of good news! Adolescence doesn't last forever. Yes, your teen will have to go through the physical and emotional maturation process like all other teens, and he or she will have to complete some important developmental tasks along the way. But the most intense part of the process is temporary. This fact is hard to appreciate when you're immersed in the turbulence, but it does subside and get easier. Teens are movies, not snapshots. They grow and change, and most often for the better. You'll see that the temperament your teen brings into adolescence is the same temperament that will reemerge when he or she completes adolescence.

- *With proper guidance, strong-willed teens can develop into responsible, cooperative, dynamic, and very successful adults.* Once you discover that your teen has a strong will, the next question is: How are you going to deal with it? Your options are clear. You can fight it and try to control it. You can give in to it and let it control you. You can try some of both. Or you can accept your teen's temperament as a fact of life, make peace with it, and learn better ways to guide it in the right direction. The choice is yours. The traits that drive so many of us crazy can actually become strengths when we give our teens the understanding and guidance they need to head down the right path. As you will see throughout this book, you have a powerful influence on your teen's development.

## Discovering Your Teen's Temperament

Based upon what you've read so far, do you still think your teen has a strong-willed temperament, or is he or she just a teen behaving in a strong-willed manner? The answer may surprise you because it was already there before your son or daughter became a teen. The most difficult part for parents is trying to answer this question when you're mired in the turbulence of your teen's adolescence. Adolescence is probably the worst time to try to sort out your teen's temperament. It's too confusing. There's too much going on.

Most teens behave in a strong-willed manner at some point during their adolescence. This is normal. But acting strong-willed and having a strong-willed temperament are different things. How do parents distinguish between normal strong-willed behavior and a teen with a strong-willed temperament? We need to rewind the tape of our child's life to find the answer.

Temperament reveals itself early in a child's life, and the research shows that the traits remain fairly stable throughout an individual's life span. I've met pediatricians and obstetricians who claim they can accurately identify a child's temperament in early infancy. I've also met moms who claim they knew during pregnancy. You've probably had your suspicions.

When my son Ian was born, there was no tag attached to him that said, "Caution! Strong-willed child. Handle with care." There were no warnings at all. I discovered his temperament the way most parents do. I watched it emerge as he grew up.

I had clues about his temperament from the beginning. He was colicky and screamed a lot during the first few months. He was picky and finicky when we introduced solid foods. Mornings were hardest. He was slow to get going and cranky. For some reason, his schedule never seemed to match up with the rest of ours.

But Ian didn't put his cards on the table until he was eight and a half months old. One Saturday morning while I was sitting on the couch reading the newspaper, I saw Ian pull himself up to a standing position. *Watch out!* I thought to myself. *We're entering the furniture-walking phase.* His older brother went through this phase, and I thought I knew what was ahead. But to my amazement, Ian let go of the furniture and walked all the way across the living room! When he got to the other end, he plunked down, then pulled himself up and did it again. Wow!

I called my wife in the other room to come see Ian walk. When she arrived, I tried my best to get Ian to do it again. I pleaded, begged, coaxed, and cajoled, but Ian wouldn't budge. He just sat there with this look on his face that said, *Watch out. I'm Ian.* Nearly two weeks passed before he walked again; but when he did, he did it the way he prefers to do most things—on his terms. Looking back, I realize this was one of those defining moments.

Ian revealed an important part of his temperament well before I had the opportunity to influence him with my limit-setting or guidance efforts. He has been this way ever since. This is part of his unique style of behaving. I didn't cause it. It was already there. I just discovered it.

Reflect back on your teen's earlier development. Did he or she show some traits or unique styles of behavior that stick out in your mind? Have these traits remained stable and consistent throughout your child's life and into the teenage years? Do you recall some defining moments?

All children and teens have their own unique temperaments or inborn style of behaving. This preferred style of behavior is innate. The parents' actions, lifestyle, values, or beliefs did not cause their child to behave this way. Temperament is not caused by environmental factors, but it does interact and interplay with these factors.

Does this mean your teen's behavior is set and unchangeable? No. Temperament is not rigid in the sense that it's fixed in cement. It can be shaped and molded with your guidance and limit setting, but the underlying tendency to behave in certain ways remains the same. For example, consider the teen who persistently resists doing his chores or homework. By the time he becomes an adult, he will likely have learned not to resist carrying out his responsibilities, but he's more likely to take a strong stand on issues that affect him, both at work and at home. He will always be temperamentally persistent, but he will learn to express his persistence in more appropriate ways.

Much of what we know about temperament is credited to the pioneering research by Drs. Alexander Thomas, Stella Chess, and Herbert Birch of New York University. Their research, which began in 1956 and continues to the present, followed 133 individuals from infancy to adulthood and examined individual differences in the way they responded to the world around them. These differences, or characteristic ways of responding, revealed the unique temperament of each child. Thomas, Chess, and Birch identified nine important temperament traits that are present, in varying degrees, in all children. These traits proved to be stable predictors of how an individual will respond at different times and in different situations. Let's briefly examine each of these nine traits that make up our unique individual temperament.

1. *Persistence.* Children show individual differences in how long they persist with tasks or resist the limits they confront. The positive side of persistence is reflected in the strong determination to stay with a task even when the task is challenging or difficult. The negative side of persistence is reflected in stubborn resistance to rules, limits, or authority. How long does your child stay with a task? A long time? A short time? How stubborn is your child when he or she wants something? How resistant is your child when he or she confronts limits? Nearly all strong-willed children are high in the trait of negative persistence.

2. *Intensity.* Some children react in mild and quiet ways when they are happy or upset, while others react intensely. How does your child react when happy or frustrated? Does he or she smile and cry softly? Laugh and cry with animation? Or squeal and shout with glee and wail in frustration? Children with a flair for drama are often high in the trait of intensity.

3. *Regularity.* Some children settle into routines quickly and maintain regular patterns. Others show more variability and irregularity. How regular is your child in his or her eating, sleeping, toileting, and other daily habits? Does your child adjust well to schedules and routines?

4. *Distractibility.* Some children can sustain the focus of their attention for long periods of time. Others have very brief attention spans and are easily distracted. How long can your child stay focused on a task such as performing a chore or completing homework? Is his or her attention easily diverted? Does your child shift from one uncompleted task to another?

5. *Energy and Activity Level.* General energy and activity levels vary from child to child. Some are energetic and highly active. Others are passive and subdued. Most children fall somewhere between the two extremes. How active is your child? How energetic? Does the motor always seem to be in high gear? Can your child downshift into lower gears when the task requires it?

6. *Sensitivity.* Children show differences in the way they respond to sensory stimulation. Some are highly sensitive and reactive. Others are less affected by the sensory stimuli around them. How does your child respond to sensory stimulation? Is he or she overly sensitive to bright lights, sudden movements, loud sounds, odors, tastes of certain foods, changes in temperature, or the texture of clothing?

7. *Adaptability.* Some children adapt easily to changes and new situations, while others find change stressful and upsetting. Transitions in the day, such as leaving home for school or entering the classroom after recess, or ending a play session, are difficult for some children. Others seem unaffected. How does your child handle change? Are transitions in the day easy or stressful?

8. *Reactivity.* Some children move into new situations without hesitation or reluctance, while others stand on the sidelines, take time to get their bearings, and join in gradually. How does your child respond to new situations or people? Does he or she join in willingly or show hesitation and reluctance? Does your child withdraw and avoid new or unfamiliar situations?

9. *Mood.* Mood or emotional disposition also varies from child to child. Some tend to be positive and cheerful. Others tend to be serious and analytical. Still others tend to be cranky, negative, and stormy. How would you describe your child's basic emotional disposition?

All children and teens show these traits in varying degrees. Some show only a few traits to an extreme degree and are easier to manage. Others show many traits to an extreme degree and are quite difficult to manage. Some show no extreme traits at all. These nine traits are the puzzle pieces that make up your teen's unique temperament.

Let's rewind the movie of your teen's life back to early or middle childhood and rate your son or daughter's behavior on the scale shown in Table 1, which is a modified version of the rating scale designed by Stanley Turecki in his book *The Difficult Child*. Circle the rating that best describes your son's or daughter's characteristic ways of behaving prior to adolescence.

| TABLE 1. YOUR CHILD'S TEMPERAMENT PROFILE | | | |
|---|---|---|---|
| TEMPERAMENT CHARACTERISTIC | EASY TO MANAGE | | DIFFICULT TO MANAGE |
| NEGATIVE PERSISTENCE | LOW | MODERATE | HIGH |
| INTENSITY | LOW | MODERATE | HIGH |
| REGULARITY | REGULAR | VARIABLE | IRREGULAR |
| DISTRACTIBILITY | | MODERATE | HIGH |
| ENERGY/ACTIVITY LEVEL | LOW | MODERATE | HIGH |
| SENSITIVITY | MILD | MODERATE | EXTREME |
| ADAPTABILITY | LOW | MODERATE | HIGH |
| REACTIVITY | LOW | MODERATE | HIGH |
| MOOD | MILD | MODERATE | EXTREME |

## Your Teen's Unique Temperament Profile

Any surprises? Does your teen show a high rating in the area of negative persistence? If so, there is a high probability that you have a strong-willed teen. You probably guessed this when you picked up this book, but now you can state it with confidence. Negative persistence is the defining characteristic of children and teens with strong-willed temperaments. Only 10 percent show this trait to this degree.

Now let's see what else is going on. How many other traits does your strong-willed teen have under the "Difficult to Manage" column? One? Several? Many? The more he or she has, the harder your job becomes. Are you beginning to understand why you feel so worn down? It's a roller-coaster ride!

If your teen does not fit the strong-willed temperament profile, then let's see what other temperament profile fits best. Approximately 65 percent of all children fit one of three basic temperament types or profiles: easy or flexible, difficult or feisty, and cautious or slow to warm up. Forty percent make up the category of easy or flexible. Fifteen percent make up the category of cautious or slow to warm up, and 10 percent make up the category of difficult or feisty. The remaining 35 percent show a combination of the three basic temperament types.

Temperament types or profiles are most apparent in classroom settings, where we group students by age and grade level. Most teachers and school administrators report that 10 percent of students cause 90 percent of school discipline problems. These students fit the "difficult or feisty" profile. In this book, we'll refer to them as "strong-willed." These are the same students who are rated as "highly persistent" and "difficult to manage" by parents.

The remaining 90 percent fall into two distinct groups that generally correspond to the temperament research. The 40 percent of easy students and the 15 percent of cautious students make up the 55 percent majority we refer to as "compliant." They don't do a lot of testing. Their underlying desire is to please and cooperate. If your teen falls under the "Easy to Manage" column for Negative Persistence, there is a high probability your teen has a compliant temperament. They may have other difficult-to-manage traits, but his or her underlying desire is to cooperate.

The 35 percent of individuals that show a combination of temperament traits I call "fence sitters." As the name implies, fence sitters can go either way depending upon what the market will bear. If your teen has a moderate rating in Negative Persistence, he or she likely fits the "fence sitter" temperament profile. Fence sitters are sometimes hard to distinguish from strong-willed teens.

How is this information useful? The first benefit is your new perspective. Once you understand your teen's temperament, you can see how your son or daughter compares to other teens on the "difficult-to-manage scale." Many of you will realize that your teen is not as strong-willed as you thought and that adolescence, not temperament, accounts for much of the extreme behavior. Remember, the temperament your teen brings into adolescence is the same temperament that will reemerge when your teen completes adolescence. The chaos is temporary. Your challenge is to weather the storm of adolescence.

The second benefit is the insight you get into your teen's learning style.

Whether your teen is strong-willed, compliant, or a fence

sitter, nearly all teens show some extreme or difficult-to-manage behavior during their adolescence. You're still going to have to deal with it, and you'll need the right limit-setting tools in your toolkit to do so. A better understanding of your teen's temperament will help you adjust your limit-setting methods to your teen's learning style and teach your rules more effectively.

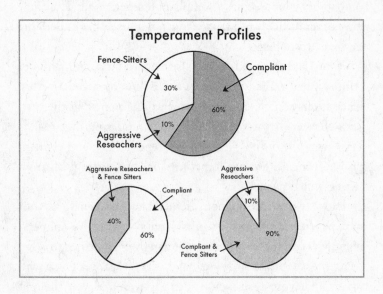

## How Temperament Affects Behavior

Temperament is a blueprint for behavior. Nature provides the blueprint when your child is born, but the plan is not fixed. It's waiting for the architect to shape it and guide it and help it take form. Parents are the architects. It's our job to work with the plan nature gives us.

Once you identify your teen's temperament, you can begin to understand the blueprint and predict your teen's behavior. Behavior that once seemed confusing begins to make sense. The question no longer is: Why does he do that? The new question becomes: What will I do to guide him when he does what he does? Based upon what you know about your teen's temperament, you can predict his or her behavior and develop more effective strategies for dealing with it.

For example, if I were to ask my son Ian, at age fourteen, to clean up his mess at the counter after finishing his snack, I can predict, from experience, that he will test and resist my request. He'll probably say, "I will," but make no effort toward getting started. What he really means is, *I will if I have to,* but Ian is not convinced he has to, so he holds out for a clearer signal. He'll dawdle and try to wait me out.

If I take the bait and ask him when he plans to pick up his mess, once again, I can predict his response. He'll likely say, "Soon," and continue to dawdle. To Ian, soon can mean hours or possibly never if he thinks there's a chance he can avoid the job. So I have to stay in the area long enough for him to be convinced he can't avoid the job. When he's convinced, he cleans up his mess.

Does this seem like a lot to go through just to get a kid to pick up his mess on the counter? It does to me, so I get to the bottom line quickly. I know what he's likely to do, and so does he. The first time I notice the mess on the counter, I say, in a clear, firm, and respectful tone, "Ian, please clean up your mess at the counter before you do anything else." Then I might have to temporarily collect his cell phone or turn off the TV to make sure he doesn't have any distractions, and I usually have to stay in the immediate area so he doesn't sneak off. He usually cleans up his mess.

Most parents can predict, with good accuracy, how their teen will respond in specific situations, but many parents feel confused and frustrated by the predictable response. They choose to fight with it or give in to it, rather than shape and guide it. When we accept our teen's temperament or strong-willed behavior as a fact of life, the behavior is much easier to understand and manage.

## How Your Teen's Behavior Affects You

Aaron, age fifteen, is like many of the strong-willed teens I see in my counseling work. He's bright and capable, but also intense, distractible, and very persistent. He can be loud, and he's not afraid to argue with adults if he thinks he can get what he wants. Yes, Aaron shows a number of those difficult-to-manage temperament traits. He arrived at my office with his parents following his third school suspension during the fall semester.

"Every year, it's the same story," complains Aaron's father. "It was like this in elementary school and middle school, and now it's happening again in high school. It begins with the phone calls from his teachers, the notes home, and finally the conferences and suspensions. By the middle of the year, Aaron wears out his teachers. They send him to the office, and the office sends him home. His teachers don't realize we're just as worn out as they are." By the look on his face, I could see Aaron's father meant what he said.

At home, family life revolves around Aaron's difficult behavior. He constantly argues and fights with his younger sister, who resents all the attention he receives. He argues and resists his parents whenever they ask him to do something he doesn't want to do. Chores and homework are daily battles. Aaron's mother is so exhausted at the end of the day that she has little energy left for her daughter or husband, who feel resentful and left out. Aaron's parents are doing the best they can with the guidance tools in their toolkits, but their tools are not working.

Like most strong-willed teens, Aaron brings out strong feelings and reactions from the people in his life. His teachers feel angry, burned-out, and resentful. "I've had all I can take," says Aaron's third-period English teacher. "When he's absent, the whole atmosphere changes in my classroom." She hopes Aaron's counselor will move him to another room.

Aaron's mother alternates between feelings of inadequacy and depression and feelings of guilt and overprotectiveness. "It's crazy!" she says. "When Aaron misbehaves at school or out in public, I feel responsible. I take his side and defend him against his father, the school, and even strangers." She would like to believe that Aaron's unruly behavior is just a stage or phase that will pass with time. She worries about the strain Aaron's behavior places on her marriage and fears others will think she's a bad parent.

Aaron's father feels confused, frustrated, and resentful. He can't imagine how things became so out of control. Before Aaron was born, he envisioned a happy family life and a warm, loving relationship with his son. Nothing turned out the way he expected.

Like many parents of strong-willed teens, Aaron's father has battled with his son for so long that the battles have become a way of life. He feels stuck and has personalized much of his son's difficult behavior. *Why is he doing this to me?* Aaron's father wonders. He blames Aaron for their turbulent family life.

To complicate matters, Aaron's parents don't agree on discipline. His mother takes a very gentle approach. She repeats, reminds, warns, cajoles, reasons, explains, negotiates, and even bribes. These methods work with her compliant daughter, but not with Aaron. He digs in his heels and resists until his mother gives in.

*I must be doing something wrong,* his mother thinks. *This approach always works with my daughter. She's such a joy and so easy to like. I wish I had two like her.*

Aaron's father tries to balance out his wife's leniency by being extra strict. He yells, blames, criticizes, and argues until he can't take it any longer, then he threatens to take away all of Aaron's favorite privileges and possessions for long periods of time. The louder he yells and threatens, the more intense and resistant Aaron becomes. The ineffective discipline actually increases Aaron's unruly behavior and intensifies their power struggles. Aaron can hold out for hours.

When things become too heated, Aaron's mother steps in and rescues him. She doesn't intend to undermine her husband's authority, but she can't stand listening to their battles. Aaron's father understands how she feels but doesn't know what else to do. He worries that Aaron will ruin the marriage.

Strong-willed teens have a wearing effect upon others. When I first met him, Aaron had exhausted his parents, burned out several teachers, and exasperated his school guidance counselor. His sister resented him, and his parents were on the verge of marital counseling. The ripple effect of his extreme behavior extended beyond his immediate family into the school, neighborhood, and community.

How has your life been affected by your strong-willed teen? Do you sometimes feel exhausted? Overwhelmed? Lonely? Confused? Depressed? Discouraged? Inadequate? Embarrassed? Responsible? Guilty? Protective? Frustrated? Angry? Resentful? Stuck in power struggles? Do you worry about the strain your teen's behavior places on your marriage and other family relationships? If so, you're not alone. These are common experiences reported by parents of strong-willed teens.

## What Role Does Your Temperament Play?

Parents bring their own unique temperaments into the interaction with their teens. How does the parent's temperament affect this interaction? Let's look at the matchups.

When parent and teen share similar temperaments, parents have a much easier time identifying with and understanding their teen's behavior. The behavior makes sense from the parents' point of view. When parent and teen temperaments are very different, however, parents have a much more difficult time understanding their teen's behavior. The behavior makes no sense from the parents' perspective. Let's look at how these dynamics play out in Aaron's family.

Aaron's parents and his younger sister have compliant temperaments, with few, if any, difficult-to-manage traits. In most situations, they cooperate and get along. Because they share similar styles of behaving, Aaron's parents can readily identify with their daughter and understand her behavior.

The dynamics between Aaron and his parents are much different. Aaron is a strong-willed individual with several difficult-to-manage traits. His tendency, in most situations, is to test and resist his parents' requests. Because Aaron has such a different style of behaving, his parents cannot easily identify with or understand him. His behavior makes no sense from their point of view. Their combined temperaments are like mixing AC and DC currents with no adapter.

Are you ready to add an adapter to your perspective? You've discovered your teen's temperament. Now it's time to get better acquainted with your own. Return to page 25 and rate yourself on each of the nine temperament traits. How do your temperaments match up?

## Good Matches and Bad Matches

Most parents carry a picture in their mind, a set of hopes and expectations about how they want their teens to behave. When the teen's behavior matches the parents' picture, the relationship develops smoothly and naturally. Things just seem to fit.

What happens when the teen's behavior does not match up with the parents' picture? It's time to introduce the concept of *fit* and discuss the grieving process parents go through when their teen's behavior and the parents' picture don't match up. "Fit" is a term mental health professionals use to describe the match between a child and the important people in the child's environment, particularly the parents. Fit or match is usually evaluated on two levels: the emotional level, or how the parents feel about the teen; and the behavioral level, or how acceptable the teen's behavior is to the parents.

In the earlier example, you recall that Aaron's mother felt a warm, positive connection with her compliant daughter, whom she described as "a joy and easy to like." Mother and daughter enjoyed a good emotional and behavioral fit. In most families, a good match develops naturally between compliant children or teens and their parents. Easy-to-manage teens are easy to like. Their behavior invites our love and affection.

But Aaron's parents have a difficult time feeling positive toward Aaron. They love him, but they don't like his behavior much of the time. Aaron's parents are quite distressed over the poor emotional and behavioral fit they have with their son.

"Sure, I'm disappointed," Aaron's father confessed. "I wish we could do fun things together, but Aaron never wants to do the things I enjoy. I wish we could be close, and sometimes I feel guilty that we're not."

Aaron's father doesn't realize it, but he is grieving the loss of the ideal son he wanted but never had. Letting go of the dream or fantasy of your ideal child can be very painful. As a result, Aaron's father will need to let go of his ideal picture and accept the real picture before he and his son can have a satisfying relationship.

Letting go of the ideal picture you hold for your strong-willed son or daughter may be one of the hardest things you'll ever do, but it's a very important task. Your teen needs you to do this before you and he can build a real relationship. If this means shedding tears, saying goodbye to unfulfilled fantasies, or creating new dreams for you and your teen, then that's what you need to do. Holding on to what isn't real will keep you both stuck in misunderstanding and conflict.

## Improving the Match: The Goal of This Book

Thus far, we've looked at four very important factors in guiding strong-willed teens: your teen's unique temperament and learning style, and your unique temperament and limit-setting style. Parenting is a continual interaction between these factors.

The problem many parents experience is that they invest too much time and energy trying to change the one thing they can't change—their teen's temperament. We can't change temperament, but we can understand it, shape it, and guide it in positive directions.

Now the really good news! The other two factors are solidly within your control. You can improve your limit-setting methods and learn better ways to manage your own temperament. That's what this book will show you how to do, but before we tinker with your toolkit, we need to discuss that stage of development we call adolescence, the context within which all your guidance and limit setting will be taking place.

## CHAPTER 2

# Understanding Adolescence

Your teen's unique individual temperament does not disappear during adolescence and magically reappear during early adulthood, but it sure seems that way. Adolescence is such a tumultuous period! It's so easy to lose perspective. Gradually, the familiar person we knew and loved in early and middle childhood reemerges in a more mature, adult form. Sound crazy? It is.

Adolescence is often described as a period of "normal craziness," "normal" because all teens go through it, "craziness" because their behavior can be so erratic and confusing. The one constant seems to be change, and change occurs at an accelerated pace. There are physical changes that come with sexual maturation, emotional changes that accompany the physical changes, and changes in thinking and behavior that come with the need for greater independence. With all this change going on, it's easy to get lost in the details.

Two developmental forces in particular have a major impact on the ways teens think and behave. The first involves a change in thinking and brain development, the ability to think and reason abstractly. The second involves a striving for an independent identity separate from the family, a process called *individuation*. In this chapter, we'll examine how both of these forces shape the emerging adult your teen is struggling to become.

## Changes in Thinking and Brain Development

Jean Piaget's pioneering research on children's intellectual development shows that an important change occurs about the time of adolescence. Some children experience the change as early as 11 or 12 years of age. Others experience it as late as 14 years. Most experience the change during middle school. What is the change? Children entering adolescence acquire the ability to think and reason abstractly. They can consider logical possibilities in future time (the way things could be), and they can evaluate the pros and cons of hypothetical situations. Unlike children in middle childhood (7–12 years), who live and think largely in the present, teens and preteens are often concerned about the future and what's possible beyond the present moment.

What does this mean in practical, everyday terms? It means that young adolescents acquire some powerful intellectual equipment to explore their world, and they're eager to test it out. They are better equipped to participate in the decision-making and problem-solving processes that affect their lives. For the first time, they are capable of testing limits with their intellect rather than with their behavior.

Does this mean they're ready and able to do this on their own? No. They've acquired the equipment, but they don't know how to use it yet. They need our coaching and guidance to figure this out. Let's examine some of the research that explains why.

When Piaget's findings were published, research on human brain development was based primarily on size and volume measurements. Early research showed that 95 percent of the brain was developed by age five years. The popular assumption was that the "hard wiring" or circuitry was already fixed in place by the time teens entered adolescence. The popular assumption proved to be wrong.

In the early 1990s, a group of researchers using brain imaging technology were able to look directly inside the brains of children and adolescents to see what's happening when they think. These researchers studied more than a thousand "normal children" between the ages of 3 and 18 over a nine-year period, at intervals ranging from several weeks to 4 years. Their findings completely revised our understanding of adolescent brain development.

Their research revealed that the brain, particularly the corpus callosum and prefrontal cortex, goes through a huge growth spurt beginning in early adolescence that doesn't end until the early twenties. The prefrontal cortex is the part of the brain that is responsible for mature judgment and decision-making skills. Also known as the "executive center," this part of the brain is most active when we are planning, evaluating options or alternatives, considering dangers, calculating risks and rewards, and making decisions. By the time we finish adolescence, the prefrontal cortex is more efficient in communicating with other parts of our brain that determine how we perceive emotion, regulate impulses, and make decisions.

Does the adolescent brain flick a switch and go from concrete thinking to mature abstract thinking overnight? No. The shift is gradual and uneven, but the process has a beginning and an end. It begins in early adolescence and extends into the early twenties. The flip-flopping back and forth between concrete and abstract thinking is very common. You've probably heard other parents of teenagers say, *One moment I'm talking to a young adult. The next moment I'm talking to a ten-year-old.* That's because the teenage brain is "a work in progress" and not fully developed. Teenage thinking is all over the map—imaginative, unrealistic, erratic, astute, dense, penetrating, insightful, simple, childish, and mature. Their new intellectual equipment does not come with an instructional manual. It's a "learn-as-you-go" process.

At the same time the adolescent brain is going through a wild growth spurt, there's another change going on in the brain that causes teens to do impulsive, risky, and sometimes dangerous things. During adolescence, there is an increase in the release of a chemical in the brain called dopamine, which leads to a heightened sense of pleasure or reward.

All of us seek rewarding or pleasurable experiences. This is natural. The sensation energizes us and drives us to do wonderful things, but the urge to do this during adolescence is very intense, so much so that teens often ignore the risks involved in pleasurable activities such as drinking, unprotected sex, drug use, Internet chat rooms, and driving fast. In the passion of the moment, their urge to follow their impulses overrides their immature reasoning capabilities. This explains why we see bright, capable teens do foolish things such as shoplifting a case of beer from a supermarket and speeding off in a car because one of their friends thought it was a good idea at the time.

Until teens finish their growth spurt, their impulses are so far ahead of their rational thinking that they can't make consistent rational decisions. This can be as confusing for teens as it is for parents. I've heard countless stories from parents who report having rational discussions with their teen during calm moments about serious topics such as turning down a ride from a friend who has been drinking. In calm, rational moments, when teens can actually access their cortex, often they say the right things and present a coherent plan. As a parent, you think, *Wow! He actually gets it. He's showing some maturity.* Then, when your teen is actually in that situation, he decides to accept the ride and puts himself in a risky situation.

When you ask why *he* did what he did, he can't tell you. He just looks at you dumbfounded. Why? Because he really doesn't know. It just seemed like the right thing to do at the time. This is common. Many teens are unaware of their internal decision-making process. In the moment, they are so driven by the urge to seek pleasure and follow their impulses that the rational course of action simply doesn't occur to them. What's the predictable result? Of course, they make an impulse-driven decision. Most teens won't have the maturity to consistently override these impulses and make thoughtful, circumspect decisions until they finish adolescence. That's why they need our help to repeatedly walk them through the process. They have the right equipment. They just don't know how to use it on a consistent basis. The parent who recognizes this is in a much better position to offer the kind of guidance their teen really needs.

## Individuation: A Self-Discovery Process

The second developmental process that has a major impact on the way teens think and behave is *individuation*. What is it?

Developmental theorist Erik Erikson describes it as a search for identity as an emerging member of society. This is a time when teens begin to assert their independence from their parents and family in an attempt to discover who they are, what they believe, and who they want to become.

Exploration and experimentation are integral parts of the self-discovery process, and this is where the teen's new intellectual equipment and urge to seek pleasure come into play. Teens want and need to try out new possibilities—new roles, new values, new beliefs, new relationships, new commitments, new dress styles and appearances, new ways of talking and behaving, and all the new feelings that accompany these experiences. They need to explore what it's like to be devoted to causes and beliefs and to have intimate relationships with boyfriends or girlfriends. The commitments are usually brief. Exploration is the most important part. When something has been explored, they change course and try something new.

Self-discovery is teen research on an almost unimaginable scale. They begin their research with no systematic plan, little or no awareness of what they're doing, but a strong sense of urgency to get the mission completed. At times, they become so absorbed in the complexity and intensity of their research that their whole world seems to be about them. Once again, this is typical of teens. Most teens believe that their individual quest is so unique that no one, especially an adult, could possibly understand what they're experiencing.

Does this sound crazy to you? If thinking and behaving erratically and not knowing why meets your definition of craziness, then you probably nailed it. But as crazy and disturbing as this process seems, this is a normal, healthy, and absolutely essential part of adolescent self-discovery. In fact, it would be abnormal if teens didn't experiment. Their identity as an emerging adult hangs in the balance. With each new experience they collect a new piece of information about who they are, what they believe, and who they want to become. Gradually, the pieces of the puzzle come together.

Symbols play an important role in your teen's quest for independence. What are they? Symbols are expressions, and I prefer the word *statements,* about your son or daughter's independence. They come in a wide variety of forms: dyed hair, pants so baggy you could hide a second person in them, blouses so skimpy they resemble the top piece of a two-piece bikini, pierced tongues, pierced navels, pierced nipples, spiked hair, shaved heads, nose rings, blasting car stereos, and outfits that would stand out at the Mardi Gras. Most are harmless expressions of your teen's quest for independence, and not worthy of your limit-setting attention.

But what are the first things parents react to when their teen enters adolescence? Of course, those symbols of independence, and your reaction, are exactly what your teen wants. The symbols send a message: *I'm different. I'm not you. I'm growing up.* Simply acknowledging the statement is usually enough to satisfy them. Just see it for what it is and keep the big picture in view. It's not worth going to battle over something that embarrasses you and won't last long anyway.

Does this mean parents should not set limits on symbols of independence? Don't some symbols go too far? How far is too far? When should parents take a stand and set limits? There is no universal standard. These are questions you need to answer for yourself based upon your values, morals, and beliefs. In my house, symbolic statements that involved self-injury, body disfiguration, abuse of others, sexual degradation of women, glorification of violence, or illegal stuff were not on the acceptable list. That's where my wife and I drew the line. To the ire of my sons, we had to veto a few clothing selections, pull down offensive posters from their bedroom walls, and confiscate items that made the "unacceptable list." But even my oldest, compliant son wore blue hair to school on more than one occasion.

How can we help our teens through this necessary developmental process without losing our minds? We can help by understanding what they are going through and by supporting their self-discovery rather than resisting it. The process is temporary. Teens don't experiment and behave erratically forever. Again, teens are more like movies than snapshots. The way they appear at a particular point in time, as disturbing as that may seem, is not the way they will always be. Try to hold on to the big picture.

Teens need to the explore rules that accompany increased freedom and independence. They need to test our limits, bump up against our walls, and answer their pressing research questions. The answers provide pieces of information to complete the puzzle about who they are. We can't help them when we're stuck in power struggles or chasing after unimportant symbols that are temporary.

## Recognizing When Limits Are Not Needed

Limits support self-discovery when they provide the firm walls that teens need to guide their exploration. But limits can also be roadblocks to self-discovery when they are used for purposes of control or in situations when they are not needed. To ensure that our limits have their intended effect, we need to ask ourselves some questions before we use them. What are we trying to achieve with our limits? Are they really necessary? Are we trying to guide exploration or suppress it? If our goal is to suppress exploration, the likely result will be a deteriorating relationship and power struggles.

This is what happened with Stacey, a bright and capable thirteen-year-old who enjoyed wearing black. She and a group of friends at school wore black outfits every day. Most of the time it was black pants, black tennis shoes, and a black T-shirt or hooded sweatshirt. The black outfits were accompanied with generous helpings of black eye shadow and makeup. The black outfits and makeup were their individual and collective statements of identity and independence.

At first, Stacey's parents went along with it. They didn't like it, but they didn't see any harm in it, either. After all, Stacey was doing well at school. She had good grades, belonged to several clubs, and had friends who were generally polite and friendly. *What can it hurt?* her parents thought. *It's just a fad. It will pass.*

But weeks and months went by, and Stacey continued to wear black—every day. Her parents were becoming concerned. *What's going on?* they wondered. *I hope she isn't involved in some type of cult.* Comments began to slip out in the mornings, like, "Stacey, you have so many nice outfits. Why don't you wear something different?"

"I'm happy the way I am," Stacey would say with a smile, but the comments continued. As her parents became more concerned and embarrassed, the comments became more critical and sarcastic.

"Going to a funeral today?" her father chided one morning. Stacey felt she had taken enough.

"I don't tell you how to dress or make sarcastic comments about the way you look," she snapped. "Why do you have to do that to me? Why can't you just leave me alone?"

"If you dressed and used makeup like a normal person, we would," said her father, "but you look ridiculous. I've had enough of this foolishness. You can wear your funeral attire once a week. The rest of the time, you're going to dress normal like everyone else." Stacey shot him an angry look and stomped out of the room.

Stacey's father succeeded only in driving her underground. The next day, she brought two black outfits to school to keep in her locker. When she arrived at school, she changed into her black outfits, then changed again before she went home.

Stacey's mother had a clue to what was going on when she noticed Stacey washing two of her black outfits with her gym clothes one weekend. "Are you wearing those outfits at school?" asked her mother.

"What would it matter if I did?" Stacey shot back, defiantly.

"Your father and I said once a week is enough," said her mother, angrily. "Since you deliberately disobeyed us, all of those outfits are going in the garbage." She put all of Stacey's black outfits in a trash bag and took them away.

For the next few weeks, Stacey did her best to avoid her parents. She seldom spoke at meals and spent most of her time in her room. When her parents made comments about how nice she looked in the mornings, Stacey just glared at them. Things were only getting worse. That's when her parents decided to call for an appointment, but Stacey was not included in the first visit.

Her parents filled me in on the events that had taken place over the black outfits. We discussed how experimentation was a normal part of the self-discovery process and how teens need to try out new roles and ways of doing things.

"But this has been going on for months," said her concerned mother. "It's so unlike her. I'm really worried that something serious is going on."

"I am, too," added her worried father. "She seems different."

"What do you think might be going on?" I asked.

"I'm afraid she's involved in some type of cult or satanic group," said her father. Stacey's mother nodded.

"What did she say when you asked what her black outfits meant to her?" I asked. Each parent looked at the other. They never asked. They were just guessing about what was going on in Stacey's world.

Stacey joined us for our next session. I encouraged her father to share his concerns. When Stacey heard him talk, she rolled her eyes in disbelief.

"Oh sure, Dad!" she said. "Do I look like a Satan worshipper? Get real."

"Well, you've been acting very different since you've been wearing those black outfits," he replied. "You've been sulking around the house and spending a lot of time by yourself."

"Do you think it might have anything to do with the fact that you've been treating me like a little girl and trying to run my life?" Stacey responded. "I don't need anyone to tell me how to dress. My friends and I aren't hurting anybody or doing anything wrong. It's our thing right now." Her father didn't know what to say.

The more her parents heard, the better they felt about what she was doing. They realized their fears were unfounded. Stacey was experimenting the way teens are supposed to. The problem was not the black outfits. The problem was their fear and suspicions about what those outfits represented. Like many parents, they got all worked up over Stacey's symbol of independence and lost perspective. This can happen to any parent.

Stacey's parents apologized for the way they treated her and offered to replace the outfits they had thrown away. Stacey took them up on their offer, but the new outfits weren't needed for long. In a matter of weeks, Stacey and her group had given up wearing black and were on to something new.

Are you ready to guide, rather than fight, your teen's journey through adolescence? Can you hold on to the big picture of what's going on and avoid overreacting to your teen's symbols of independence? To the extent that you can, your limit-setting efforts will be rewarded.

## CHAPTER 3

# Your Changing Role
# as Parent

During early and middle childhood (ages 3–12), children expect us to take an active role as the primary authority figure in
their lives. They need our active guidance and support on the
playing field of life. When adolescence begins, this changes.
The child who depended upon us to play an active role for so
many years now wants us to coach from the sidelines and stay
off the playing field.

*What happened?* we ask ourselves. *Who flicked the switch?*
*The same child who sat in my lap at public events three years ago*
*doesn't want to sit anywhere near me now. Some days, he acts like*
*he doesn't even want me in his life.* The emotional distance we
feel is our cue that our role as parent is changing.

Adolescents want, and are ready for, increased freedom,
independence, and privileges. They're eager to redefine the
ground rules of early and middle childhood, which they feel
they've outgrown, and assert more control and authority over
their lives. Does this mean we should relinquish our authority
and learn a new system of training? No. The basics still apply.

Adolescents need our clear, firm limits to guide their

testing and exploration even more than they did before. They need our encouragement, our guidance in problem solving, and our instructive consequences when they choose to learn their lessons the hard way. This won't change. But we'll need to adjust our role and our methods to meet the needs of an older and more capable young person—an emerging adult. That's what this chapter will prepare you to do.

## Coaching from the Sidelines

The shift your adolescent wants you to make, from an active role as a primary authority figure (rule maker and rule enforcer) to a seemingly less involved background figure, can be disturbing. After all, you've probably developed a comfort level with the role you've played for most of your child's life. Suddenly your child wants to shake things up, but the change to a less involved background figure is not as dramatic as it seems. I use the word *seemingly* because your adolescent's wants and needs are full of contradictions.

Do they really want us to give up much of our parental authority? Yes and no. The "yes" applies when teens want the space to explore and try out new privileges without adult interference. The "no" applies when things don't go well, when they get into trouble and recognize they're not ready to handle the freedom and privileges they were so eager to take on. In short, they want you to be strong and involved when they need you to be strong and involved, and they want you to be passive and less involved when they need you to be that way. How do you know when they need you to be one way or the other?

Often, you don't know. Confusing? You bet, because what they want and need varies with the circumstances.

They want you to be a strong authority figure when they need you to be that way, but they don't want to think of you as such. Adolescents prefer to see themselves as free agents who direct their own affairs. You have to be a strong parent to play along with this fantasy, but it's a fantasy your teen needs you to preserve. As long as you know the truth, you can navigate through these murky waters with less confusion.

Perhaps the term that best describes the role your teen wants and needs you to take is "supportive coach." Coaches have to shift between taking an active role during practices and a passive role during games, but when the game is in progress, the coach stays on the sidelines. That's where they exercise their leadership. They know their players belong on the playing field as much as possible, but coaches are prepared to step in and make the tough calls when that's needed and support players when they get hurt or in trouble.

Coaches have to keep sight of the fact that their main goal is to help players improve their skills and become successful. To achieve this goal, coaches must provide the ground rules players need to stay on course, the guidance they need to improve their skills, and the support players need to perform their best. When the game is over, coaches celebrate their players' successes and console them for their defeats. In Chapter 10, you'll see how neatly the strong, supportive coach role dovetails with the democratic limit-setting approach that is ideally suited for teens.

Are you ready to coach from the sidelines? If you are, both you and your teen will enjoy an easier transition into adolescence.

But you'll still need to adjust some of your guidance practices to meet the needs of an older and more capable young person. Let's look at what your teen needs most from you.

## What Your Teen Needs Most from You

Consider all the possible roles your teen needs you to play: taxi service, cooking service, cleaning service, activities planner, fashion consultant, relationship adviser, personal tutor, educational planner, disciplinarian, banking service, health adviser, etiquette consultant, sounding board, spiritual adviser, financial planner, risk manager, birth control adviser, driving trainer, time manager, counselor, referee, job supervisor, career planner, probation officer, rescue service, shoulder to cry on . . . A complete list would take many pages.

How do parents juggle all of these roles effectively? We can't. The job description is nearly impossible. All we can do is our best, and our best should begin with focusing on the tasks that are most important. Successful coaches concentrate on the basics, the fundamentals. I recommend you do the same. The following tasks should be at the top of any parent's list of fundamentals.

### A POSITIVE, RESPECTFUL RELATIONSHIP

The research shows that teens who respect their parents are much less likely to experience significant adjustment difficulties during adolescence. But developing a positive, respectful relationship with someone who wants to create distance from you is no easy task. Hang in there. The research shows it's well worth the effort.

How do you create a respectful relationship with someone who wants less of you in his or her life? Stick with the basics. One of the best ways to get respect is to role-model respect. You can do this in a number of ways: through your limit-setting and problem-solving practices and in your day-to-day communication. In Chapters 8 and 10, you'll learn how to gain your teen's respect through respectful limit-setting and problem-solving practices.

The importance of building a positive, respectful connection with your teenager cannot be overstated, particularly in your day-to-day interactions. There are many excellent books on the topic. One of the best is Michael Riera's book *Staying Connected to Your Teenager.* I particularly like the emphasis he places on taking short car trips together and joining your teen for late-night snacks. Other books on this topic are referenced in the Suggested Reading section.

## CLEAR, FIRM LIMITS TO GUIDE THEIR TESTING

All teens test limits. Limit testing is one of their most important jobs during adolescence. Teens need to test to discover what they are and are not ready to handle and who they want to become. How can we help?

We can help by providing a clear, firm path to guide their exploration. The clearest path is always the easiest to follow. The respectful path is the one that's most inviting and the one most teens prefer to travel. In Chapter 6, you'll learn how to create a firm and respectful path for your teen. In

Chapters 10–17, you'll learn how to keep them on that path and guide them safely through the gauntlet of adolescence.

## ASSISTANCE WITH READINESS TESTING

Limit testing is your teen's job. Readiness testing should be one of yours. Your teen's age and abilities are not the most important factors to consider when deciding whether to increase his or her freedom and privileges. The most important issue is readiness. Many teens are old enough and capable of handling increased freedom and privileges, but they may not be ready to do this on a consistent basis because they lack the judgment or impulse control to make consistently good choices.

How do you determine your teen's readiness? There is no universal set of standards. Readiness varies from teen to teen. Parents must make their determinations on a case-by-case basis. In Chapter 14, you'll learn a proven method for determining your teen's readiness. The process is as easy as conducting a fourth-grade science experiment. You simply set the question of readiness up and test it out. Your teen's behavior will show you what he or she is ready to handle. The process is cooperative, not adversarial. You get to learn along with your teen what he or she is ready to handle.

## SUPPORT FOR INDIVIDUATION

Limits support individuation and self-discovery when they provide the walls teens need to guide their exploration. Limits also can be roadblocks to self-discovery when they are used for purposes of control or in situations when they are not needed. Do you recall the example of Stacey and her black outfits in

Chapter 2? What happened when Stacey's parents overreacted to her black outfits and placed limits on her expression of independence? Stacey and her parents became embroiled in a needless power struggle.

To ensure that our limits have the intended effect, we need to ask ourselves some questions before we use them. What are we trying to achieve with our limits?

Are they really necessary? Are we trying to guide our teen's exploration or suppress it? If our goal is to suppress exploration, then we should expect a deteriorating relationship and power struggles. Limits should foster growth, not inhibit it.

## ASSISTANCE WITH PROBLEM-SOLVING SKILLS

Teens have the intellectual ability to plan into the future, to consider their options, and to make informed choices. Does this mean they will automatically do so? No. Having the ability and mastering the skill are two different things. There's still an important step that needs to happen. Teens need to be taught how to use their intellect to solve problems. If you enjoy a positive, respectful relationship with your teen, he or she may tolerate, even welcome, your help in this area. If not, you're likely to encounter more resistance than cooperation. You'll need to work on the relationship before you'll be much help.

Exploring choices is an effective method for helping teens look ahead and discover what lies in their path: obstacles, choices, courses of action, and the consequences associated with various choices and actions. Your role is to be a guide and a sounding board. You ask questions, provide feedback, and encourage further testing and exploration. The goal is to help teens discover their best choices on their own.

Wouldn't it be easier just to tell them what to do? Yes, it would, but that's the last thing most teens want. Telling teens what lies ahead and what choices they should make doesn't require much thinking ahead on their part. Why? Who's doing all the thinking and problem solving? Parents. Our goal should be to help teens think for themselves and make decisions on their own.

The procedure is most effective when carried out in an atmosphere of trust and mutual respect. This is not a time for lectures, criticism, value judgments, or strong emotion that will derail the process. Let's look at how Allen's father uses this procedure to help him prioritize his commitments.

Allen's parents were surprised to receive an academic progress report informing them that their fifteen-year-old was receiving D's in two classes. His GPA had dropped below a 2.0, the minimum required for participation in school sports. His eligibility was in jeopardy.

Allen had always been responsible for his studies in the past. His parents knew how much sports meant to him. They also knew he had been distracted the last few months with a new girlfriend and a part-time job.

"Are you aware of how you're doing in two of your classes?" his father asks one evening.

"I knew I was a little behind, but I didn't think it was that bad," says Allen. "It's been hard to fit in study time with my new job."

"I know your job is important to you," says his father. "Do you think you may be taking on too much?"

"I can handle my job and get my grades up," insists Allen.

"Have you thought about what might happen if you don't?" asks his father.

"What do you mean?" asks Allen. His father hands him the progress report. Allen reads the section about losing his eligibility for spring baseball if his grades don't come above a 2.0 GPA. The seriousness of the issue was beginning to sink in.

"I forgot all about that!" Allen says. He didn't imagine the rule would ever apply to him.

"There's another thing we need to discuss," says his father. "What is our agreement about getting your driver's permit?"

*Oh no!* Allen says to himself. Now he's really worried. He remembers their agreement requires a minimum of a C average at school and doing his part at home.

"What do you think you need to do to get those grades up?" inquires his father.

"I can talk to each of my teachers to see if I can make up some of the missed work," Allen replies. "I can also study hard for the final exams."

"That should help, but do you think your job commitment will leave you enough time to do that?" asks his father.

"I'll have to quit my job," Allen announces. "I can't risk losing my baseball eligibility or my driver's permit."

Exploring choices helped Allen look ahead and make better choices about his commitments and responsibilities. He had taken on a lot, and he never considered the consequences of not being able to manage all of his commitments.

Allen's father was probably tempted, like many of us would be, to tell his son what to do and save Allen the disappointment of learning from his mistakes. Allen's father also realized that if he continued to make decisions for his son, Allen would not learn to think ahead or make good decisions for himself.

Now let's consider the alternative scenario to this story. Let's say that Allen decides to continue working and try to pull his grades up at the same time. Would this decision lead to less learning? No. This decision might decrease the likelihood that Allen would play sports and get his driver's permit, but either way he would learn to be responsible for his own choices. Easy-way learning and hard-way learning are two paths to the same conclusion. Both lead to good learning.

## Chapter Summary

When children enter adolescence they want and need us to shift from a direct and active role as primary authority figure to a seemingly less involved background figure that coaches from the sidelines. The role they want us to play is full of contradictions. Most teens want, and still need, us to be the central authority figures in their lives, but they don't want to think of us as such. They prefer to think of themselves as free agents who can manage their own affairs.

But the vast majority of teens are not ready to be the "free agents" or to manage their own affairs. They still need our firm limits to guide their testing and exploration, our encouragement, our assistance with problem solving, and our instructive consequences when they choose to learn their lessons the hard way. They still need us to be strong, but they want us to exercise our strength from the sidelines. Are you ready to coach from the sidelines? To the extent that you are, both you and your teen will enjoy a smoother transition into adolescence.

Where should you focus your energy in your new coaching role? Take the advice of other great coaches and focus on what matters most, the basics: developing a respectful relationship, setting clear, firm limits, and assistance with readiness testing and problem-solving skills. The basics won't let you down.

## CHAPTER 4

# Why Teens Need Limits

When teens and some preteens enter adolescence, they know they're smarter and more capable than they were before, but how smart? How capable? They're eager to test out all that new intellectual equipment they've acquired and get some answers. Limits help them measure their growth, but the lessons parents intend those limits to provide often break down when our limits are unclear or ineffective. Stephen is a good example.

Fourteen-year-old Stephen knows he's supposed to be off the phone by ten on school nights, but it's ten thirty, and he has been talking for nearly two hours.

"It's time to finish your call," says his concerned mother. "You know the rule." Stephen gives her an annoyed look and continues talking. Ten minutes tick by.

"Stephen! I thought I asked you to finish your call," his mother says again.

"I will," Stephen insists.

"When?" she asks.

"Soon," Stephen replies. Another fifteen minutes go by. His mother is fuming.

What does *soon* mean to a fourteen-year-old who doesn't

want to get off the phone at all? Ten minutes? Twenty minutes? Thirty minutes? And who decides? Do you think Stephen and his mother are likely to repeat this scene? They will if she continues to use unclear and ineffective limits to guide his research.

Does any of this sound familiar? If it does, you're not alone. All teens, strong-willed and otherwise, need to test and explore their world, but they also need clear, firm limits to guide their exploration. They depend on us to provide this information. In this chapter, you'll understand why, and you'll discover the many important functions limits provide for exploring teens.

## What Are Limits?

It's time to define terms. What are limits? *Webster's Dictionary* defines a limit as "a point or line beyond which something cannot or may not proceed." Limits are boundaries that specify how far something can or should go. Limits are essential for communicating our rules to others. This leads us to the next term we need to define.

What is a rule? In the context of parent–child relationships, a rule is an expectation you have for how you or others should think or behave and how things should turn out. All of us carry around rules in our head about how others should behave and how things should turn out. We have rules for nearly everything: how people should talk, how people should dress, how people should eat, appropriate hygiene habits, appropriate language, how our friends should treat us, how our family members should treat us, how people should behave at church, in the workplace, in libraries, at the mall, at sporting events, at parties, at school, at the theater . . . The list is endless.

Reflect on some of the rules you hold for others and how things should go in your world. Your rules or expectations will usually involve the words *should* and *must*. Here's a brief sampling from my personal list: *People should treat me fairly. My friends should be honest with me. My wife should never leave me with an empty gas tank. Friends and family members should thank me for gifts. People should turn off lights when they're not using them. My wife should consult me before making plans for us. The weather should cooperate during my vacations. People shouldn't tailgate me on the freeway. The newspaper should be in my driveway by 6:30 a.m. My wife should leave enough coffee for me to have a second cup. My kids should replace the roll of toilet paper when it's done.* I could fill a book with my rules. I'll bet you could, too.

Now ask yourself: *How much power and control do I really have over my world and whether others cooperate with my rules?* Not much, I bet. Neither do I. Why? Because many of the rules we expect others to follow are unenforceable; that is, we have a very limited capacity to make them happen. We can wish and hope others will cooperate. We can do our best to influence them, but the choice to cooperate belongs to them, not us. Enforceability, or the capacity to influence the choices people make, is the key issue here.

How does this apply to parents and teens? Consider some of the typical rules and expectations parents hold for teenagers: *My teen should treat me respectfully. My teen should keep me informed of his comings and goings. My teen should do her homework regularly and get good grades. My teen should get a full night's sleep. My teen should stay away from drugs and alcohol. My teen should practice safe sex. My teen should drive responsibly.* Most parents would consider these to be good rules, and I agree, but our rules are not the problem. The problem and biggest source of conflict between parents and teens is the ineffective methods that parents use to enforce their rules. Many parents rely on limit-setting methods that carry little enforceability. In Chapter 6, you'll gain a deeper understanding of the methods you've relied on in the past to enforce your rules and the methods teens respond to best.

The rules we can realistically expect our teens to follow are the rules that we can enforce with a high degree of consistency. All those other rules that carry a low degree of enforceability are not really rules at all. They're just theories about how we want our teens to behave. If we take those theories too seriously and regard them as rules others should follow, we run the risk of making ourselves a little crazy. In Chapter 7, you'll learn what type of rules you've used in the past. With a better understanding of what limits and rules are all about, let's look at the many important functions limits serve.

## Limits Help Teens Do Research

Have you ever thought of teens as researchers? Well, they are, and they are remarkably well equipped for the job. They are astute observers of people and behavior. They know how to conduct experiments, test out hypotheses, collect research data, and form conclusions based upon the data they collect.

It's a natural and normal process. All teens do it, but some do it more aggressively than others.

Sixteen-year-old Courtney is a good example.

Courtney wants to use the family car to visit a friend. "Return the car by seven p.m.," says her mother. "I have a meeting I can't miss." But Courtney doesn't return until eight thirty. When she does, her annoyed mother launches into a long lecture about respect. "I really don't appreciate your lack of consideration," she says, but other than the lecture, nothing happens.

What kind of research data does Courtney collect from this experience? Is compliance required or optional? She knows what her mother prefers, but Courtney also knows from experience that she doesn't have to comply with the request if she is willing to tolerate her mother's annoying lectures. Do you think Courtney and her mother are likely to repeat this scene? Of course, without firm limits to guide her research, Courtney knows she can do what she wants.

Now let's replay this scene, but this time, when Courtney shows up late with the car, her mother says, matter-of-factly, "The car is off-limits for the rest of the week. When I say I need it back by seven, that's what I mean." No lectures or drama or lengthy appeals for cooperation.

Did Courtney receive the firm limit she needs to guide her future research? Yes. Does the data she collects support the conclusion that compliance is expected and required? Based upon this experience, do you think Courtney will regard her mother's request more seriously next time?

Brianna's mother also understands what her fifteen-year-old needs when she decides to test her mother's rule about borrowing clothing without permission. "Is that my new belt you're wearing?" her mom asks when Brianna shows up for breakfast. "You know you're supposed to ask first."

"Please, Mom . . ." pleads Brianna. "The belt looks so good with this outfit. I didn't think it would hurt anything. I'll be sure to ask next time."

"Then that's a good choice for next time," says her mother, matter-of-factly, "but this time you didn't ask, so please take it off and put it back in my closet where you found it." Brianna rolls her eyes, lets out a big sigh, but returns the belt.

Did Brianna receive a clear, firm limit when she decided to test her mother's rule? You bet. Is compliance optional or required? Brianna will probably think carefully before deciding to wear her mother's clothing without permission.

## Limits Define Acceptable Behavior

Have you tried to hike a trail with few trail signs or markers? It's confusing. You're not sure which direction to travel. Without clear signals to keep you on course, you're more likely to make wrong turns and get into trouble. That's the way it is for teens as they try to navigate the path of acceptable behavior. At home, it's the parents' job to post the trail markers and help teens stay on the right path. When our limits are clear and consistent, the path is easier for teens to follow. When our limits are unclear or inconsistent, teens are more likely to steer off course and lose their way. Fourteen-year-old Andy is a good example.

Andy has been suspended from school three times for

interrupting class and talking disrespectfully to his teachers. It's still October. When he does this at home, his parents usually stop whatever they're doing and give him their undivided attention. Sure, they're annoyed with his behavior, but they consider it to be a phase that will pass with time.

One evening, while Andy's parents are in the middle of a conversation, he bursts into the room and announces he won't join the family on a visit to their neighbor's home for dinner. "Please," pleads his mom. "We told the Jansens you're coming."

"Screw that!" says Andy. "The Jansens are a bunch of assholes."

"I wish you'd reconsider," says his dad, trying to ignore Andy's rudeness.

"I bet you do," says Andy. "Well, forget it." He rolls his eyes and walks away.

Andy's mom and dad have a picture in their minds about how they expect their son to behave, but Andy is not a mind reader. He lives in the real world, and he knows what he experiences. What does he experience? He experiences that interrupting and talking disrespectfully to adults is okay because he's allowed to do it time after time with no consequences to guide his research. What other conclusion can he reach? Do you think Andy is heading for even more conflict at school?

Andy needs the same signals fourteen-year-old Jessica receives when she interrupts or talks disrespectfully. Each time this happens, her parents tell her that interrupting and talking disrespectfully is not okay, then they tell her what they expect her to do.

"Wait for a pause in the conversation, please," says her father, matter-of-factly. "Then say 'excuse me' and wait to be recognized before you speak." If Jessica rolls her eyes or says something disrespectful, her parents end the conversation and ask her to try it again when she's ready to do it the right way. When she handles it respectfully, they tell her how much they appreciate it and give her their undivided attention. Their expectations are clear, and so is the path they want her to stay on.

## Limits Define Relationships

How do teens know how much power, authority, and control they should have in their relationships with adults? Often, they don't, but they do know how to find out. They do the research. They just go ahead and do whatever they want and observe the outcome. The outcome reveals where they stand with others.

When teens experience clear, firm limits, they get answers to their most pressing research questions: Who's really in charge here? How far can I go? What happens when I go too far? When our limits are unclear or inconsistent, teens often develop an exaggerated sense of their own power and authority, which sets them up for testing. Thirteen-year-old Collin is a good example.

Collin knows he's supposed to finish his chores early on Saturdays before he does anything else, but he dawdles and avoids most of the day. When his friends arrive at the door and ask if Collin can join them, his mother holds firm on the chores.

"Collin can join you in about forty-five minutes after he

finishes his chores," his mother says. "Would you like to come inside and wait?"

"Oh, come on, Mom," Collin pleads, but his mother holds firm. So Collin appeals to his father, who seems more sympathetic.

"Come on, dear," says Collin's father. "His friends are already here. I don't see what it hurts to let him go now. He can finish them when he gets back." Collin's mother isn't pleased. She doubts that will actually happen.

"Thanks, Dad," says Collin as he hurries out the door.

What did Collin learn from this experience about power and authority in his family? Are his parents a united front? No. Who calls the shots? Dad. How much authority does Collin's mom have in their family? This is unclear. What will Collin have to do to answer this question? Of course, he has to test.

What will Collin likely say to his mom next time this situation arises and his dad is not around? Sure, he'll say, "Dad says I don't have to do it." What will happen if his dad decides to hold firm next time and insists that Collin do his chores first before leaving? Collin will likely respond, "Last time, you said I didn't have to do it." In either case, inconsistent limit setting sets up all family members for testing and conflict.

How could Collin's parents handle this situation more effectively? Let's replay the scene at the point where Collin's friends arrive at the door and his mother holds firm on the issue of chores. But this time, when Collin appeals to his dad, his dad says, "What did your mother say? If she said 'no,' then the answer is 'no.' Your friends are welcome to wait while you finish what you have to do."

This time Collin collects some very different research data.

He knows his parents are a united front. They share power and authority, and he can't undermine their authority or play one against the other. He also knows, based on his experience, that completing chores early on Saturdays is expected and required, not optional. If his parents respond this way consistently, Collin will know what's really expected.

## Limits Provide Security

Fifteen-year-old Kaitlyn tells her parents that she's going to Abbey's house for a sleepover but goes to an unsupervised party instead and gets caught. The police break up the party and call parents to pick up the underage teens. When Kaitlyn's parents arrive, they see three police cars in front of the house and beer cans and liquor bottles strewn all over the lawn. An officer greets them at the door. The heavy odor of marijuana permeates the house. Kaitlyn waits at a table with several other underage teens. She looks scared and relieved at the same time. The officer explains what happened.

"The parents are away on a trip and left their sixteen-year-old daughter in charge," he says. "The neighbors called us when things got out of control. Most of the kids were eighteen or older. Several were arrested for drug possession." Kaitlyn's parents thank him and leave.

"I didn't know most of the kids would be older or that there would be drugs there," says Kaitlyn. "Abbey didn't know, either. We thought it would be a fun party, but we got scared when we saw what was going on. I'm really sorry."

"We're really glad you're safe," says her concerned father,

"but we're really disappointed that you deceived us. You told us one thing and did another. We'll need to agree on some new ground rules before we're comfortable extending this privilege again." They suspend Kaitlyn's sleepover and party privileges for the next eight weeks. The next evening, Kaitlyn and her parents have a family meeting to discuss how Kaitlyn can restore her sleepover and party privileges.

"We need your word that you're willing to follow our ground rules before we're comfortable restoring your privileges," her mother begins. "You need to ask our permission before going to any parties or sleepovers. There must be adult supervision, and we need the parents' phone number so we can verify the arrangements. We also need to agree on drop-off and pick-up times. If any changes come up, we expect a phone call to get our permission. Most importantly, if you find yourself in a risky or unsafe situation, use us as your big excuse for backing out. Just tell them your parents will ruin your life if they find out. Is that clear?" Kaitlyn nods. "If you agree to follow these ground rules, then we're willing to give you another chance in eight weeks to show you're ready for this privilege."

Now Kaitlyn has some clear, firm limits to guide her research. Will she decide to test her parents' expectations again? She might. Kaitlyn and her parents may have to repeat this lesson several times before she learns it, but her parents are doing the right things to keep her safe and secure during her research.

## Limits Teach Problem-Solving Skills

Teens need to experiment and test limits. That's their job, but can you accept the logic that we should help them test limits more effectively? We can do this, and we should. Why? Because teens are ready to begin testing limits with their intellect, but they're not likely to do this on their own. They'll need our help, and they're not likely to ask for it.

So how do parents offer guidance that's needed but not wanted or requested? The low-key approach works best. We'll talk more about this more in Chapter 9, but the essential point is that teens want to feel like they are in charge of the process, not us. Our job is to serve as an impartial guide and sounding board and walk teens through the problem-solving process. We ask the questions. They do the thinking, and they reach their own conclusions.

Wouldn't it be easier just to tell them what to do? Yes, but that's the last thing teens want. On an intuitive level, teens understand that being told what to do, what choices to make, and what obstacles lie in their path do not require much exploration or thinking on their part. This is their journey, their research, and they want to do it on their own as much as possible. If you recall, you've been through this with your child once before.

What did your two-year-old say to you when you offered your well-intended but unsolicited help? *I can do it myself.* Well, it's the same process all over again with teens. The research, discovery, growth, and sense of accomplishment belong to them. They don't appreciate our interference.

Let's preview coming attractions by looking at what

Connie's mom does when she receives a call from her daughter's high school counselor. Connie, an eleventh grader, has been suspended from her English literature class twice for being disrespectful. If it happens again, she'll be dropped from the class. It's too late in the semester to consider a transfer, so Connie will have to make up the credits during summer school. Connie's mom says she'll discuss the matter with her daughter when she gets home.

"I got a call from your counselor today," Connie's mom begins.

"I thought you would," says Connie. "I got suspended again from Mr. Beckner's class. He's such a jerk. I really hate him. I want out of his class."

"Your counselor says that will happen if you're suspended one more time," her mom replies.

"Good!" says Connie. "I'm tempted to tell him off tomorrow."

"I can see your feeling angry, but what do you think will happen if you are dropped from his class?" asks her mom.

"I'll transfer into another literature class," Connie replies, "and I'll be rid of him."

"Your counselor says it's too late to transfer," says her mom. "There are only three weeks left in the semester. You have a B in the class now. What will happen to your credits if you get an incomplete?"

"I guess I'll lose them," Connie replies, "but it's worth it."

"It might seem that way now, when you're angry, but when would you make them up?" asks her mom.

"Summer school?" replies Connie, a little less enthused.

"Right, for six weeks. Do you have other plans for the

summer?" asks her mom. Connie was looking forward to visiting her favorite aunt in Philadelphia for three weeks. The trip would have to be canceled. Connie realizes it, too.

"What am I going to do?" asks Connie.

"What do you think your best choices are?" replies her mom.

"I can try to keep my mouth shut and follow his stupid rules for three more weeks, but it will be torture. I'm not even sure I can do it," says Connie.

"That's one choice," her mom replies. "What's another?"

"I could tell him to go to hell," says Connie with a big smile, "but I would miss Philadelphia and have to spend my summer making up credits." The sensible choice is clear.

"So what are you going to do?" asks her mom.

"I'll try to hang on for another three weeks," says Connie. "I'm not going to let Mr. Beckner ruin my summer, too."

Connie may not realize it, but she just received a valuable lesson in how to test limits with her intellect. With her mom's help, Connie walked down the path in front of her. She examined her choices, considered the consequences associated with those choices, and reached her own conclusion about the best thing to do. Isn't this what we want our teens to do on their own? Connie's mom understands the process that helps them get there.

## Limits Clarify Readiness

Most parents recognize that 3–6 p.m. on weeknights is a "danger zone" for unsupervised teens. When Aidan began eighth grade, his parents thought he was ready for the privilege of having friends in the house after school, but things didn't work out. There were stains on the carpets, cigarette butts in the sink, broken furniture, and a missing cell phone charger. Aidan assured his parents he would talk to his friends and promised it wouldn't happen again, but the messes continued for several more weeks. His parents had seen enough and suspended the privilege altogether.

"You've shown us you're not ready for this privilege," says his dad. "We'll try it again next year."

"It won't happen again," Aidan promises. He pleads for another chance, but his parents hold firm. He decides to go underground and try extra hard not to get caught. *What are you going to do? Lock my friends out of the house?* Aidan says to himself. His parents are suspicious. The next afternoon, his mom leaves work early and pays a visit to the house. She catches Aidan in the act with three friends. That evening, Aidan and his parents have a family meeting.

"We've decided to hire a college student to help out from three to six p.m. each night until we get home," says Aidan's father. "His name is Dennis, and he starts tomorrow."

"You hired a babysitter!" exclaims Aidan. "I'm thirteen years old!"

"No, we hired an adult to be in charge during our absence," says his mom. "We'll continue with Dennis through August, then reevaluate. The same rules apply when Dennis is here as when we are. Is that clear?"

Did Aidan's parents provide the firm limits he needed to guide his research? You bet. Is it clear what he needs to do next time to demonstrate his readiness? Aidan will think carefully if he wants another shot at this privilege in the fall. In Chap-

ter 14, you'll learn a simple and effective procedure for determining your teen's readiness for new freedoms and privileges.

## Limits Teach Lessons About Trust

Jake, age sixteen, is sure he's one of the smartest people on the
planet. He gets A's in all of his classes and devotes minimal
time to study and homework. His parents are proud of him,
and they should be. They trust him.

But lately, Jake has been behaving strangely. He tallied up
seven late slips at school, served after-school detention on two
occasions, and has one day marked "truant" on his attendance
record, which he claims is a mistake. His parents believe him.

When Jake's best friend invites him to spend the night,
Jake readily accepts the invitation. He tells his parents that he
and Kyle will be staying up late studying for a science test, but
their real plan is to skip another day of school and hang out
together.

"It's easier for me to spend the night at Kyle's house and go
to school with him in the morning," Jake says to his parents.
They nod their approval and don't give it a second thought.
They have no reason to doubt him.

*Wow! My parents are really stupid,* Jake thinks to himself.
*They didn't ask any questions or anything. I'll just tell them the
truancy is another clerical error. They'll believe it.* He can't wait
to skip another day of school and hang out with his best friend.

What Jake doesn't realize is that his research is about more
than his parents' intelligence and gullibility. He's about to em-
bark on a much larger research study about the meaning of
honesty and trust.

Jake's parents don't think limits are necessary because they trust him and have no reason to doubt him. All that is about to change. Do you think they will repeat this mistake once they discover what's really going on? Soon Jake will have a new set of limits to guide his research.

Have you been in this position with your teen? Jake made a significant withdrawal from the "Trust Bank Account" he shares with his parents. At some point, most teens conduct this type of research, and when they do, parents need to help them learn to rebuild the trust that has been lost. In Chapters 15 and 16, you'll learn how to help teens rebuild trust by making deposits, not withdrawals, from their Trust Bank Account.

## Limits Are Yardsticks for Measuring Growth

After school, fifteen-year-old Lisa likes to hang out with her friends, but she has a habit of not being where she says she will be. Her parents consider this a trust issue and insist that Lisa follow some basic ground rules so they can feel comfortable extending the privilege.

"You need to ask for our permission before you go," says her dad. "We need to know where you will be and how long you will be there. If there are any changes in your plans, we expect a call so together we can decide what to do. You have a cell phone, so there are no excuses. Are you willing to follow our ground rules?"

Lisa promises she will, but things don't work out that way during the first few weeks. Each time, she has a ready excuse, such as "I forgot," or "I lost track of time," or "My cell phone wasn't charged," and each time, her parents review the ground rules and suspend the privilege for three days. They question her readiness.

On the fourth week, Lisa asks permission to visit a friend and says she'll be home by five. Her father arrives home at five thirty. Lisa isn't home. He gives her a call, but she doesn't answer. At six, he drives to her friend's home and discovers that the girls left hours before without specifying their destination. It's dark. Her frantic parents call around, but no word from Lisa. She arrives home after seven.

"It's not my fault," pleads Lisa. "My friends wanted to go somewhere else. I meant to call, but it's embarrassing to do it in front of my friends. They don't have to call their parents. I didn't think it would hurt anything." Her parents suspend the privilege for a full month.

When the month is over, Lisa is eager to resume her time with her friends. Her parents review the ground rules once again and ask the same question they asked the first time: "Are you willing to follow our rules?" She promises she will. Her parents hope she's ready this time.

Things go well for the first few weeks. Each time, Lisa asks permission, keeps her parents informed, and returns at the agreed-upon time. *Maybe she's ready,* her father thinks to himself. On the fourth week, Lisa calls to inform her mother that her plans have changed and asks permission to go to a nearby park with her friends. Her mother agrees but drives by the park on her way home from work to verify Lisa's story. Lisa sees her.

"You don't trust me!" says Lisa as she enters the house.

"I really want to," replies her mom, "and today you helped me get there. Thank you. I'm beginning to feel like you're ready for this privilege. I love you too much to take chances with your safety."

## Limits Should Grow with Your Teen

Would you extend the same dating privileges to a thirteen-year-old that you would for a seventeen-year-old? Probably not. Would you set the same curfew for a thirteen-year-old that you would for a sixteen-year-old? Again, probably not.

Teens grow and change, and as they do they become ready for increased freedom, privileges, and responsibilities. They need opportunities to explore their world, practice their skills, test out their new intellectual equipment, and develop competence and independence. That's their job. Our job is to provide them with limits and boundaries that support, not hinder, this normal developmental process.

How do we provide limits that support healthy development? We do so by expanding and adjusting those limits as our teen demonstrates readiness for increased freedom and privileges. The process is one big balancing act. Limits should be broad enough to encourage healthy testing and exploration, restrictive enough to provide safety and security, yet flexible enough to allow for growth and change.

How do parents know when teens are ready for more freedom and control over their lives? Often, we don't know, and neither do they. Readiness varies from teen to teen. There is no single standard that applies to all, but there is an easy way to find out if your teen is really ready. We simply set up the readiness question as a research experiment and test it out. Your teen's behavior will answer the question. Chapter 14 will show you how to do this. You'll be surprised how easy this process is to set up and carry out. Best of all, we get to learn along with our teens what they're really ready to handle.

## Chapter Summary

Teens want and need to understand the rules of their world. They want to know what's expected of them, who's really in control, how far they can go, and what happens when they go too far. They want to know where they stand with others, and they want to measure their increasing skills and capabilities as they grow. Limits provide answers to these important questions. Limits should grow along with your teen. They should be firm enough to provide safety and security and guide healthy testing and exploration, yet flexible enough to permit growth and learning. Limits are crucial for healthy development.

## CHAPTER 5

# Limit Testing:
# How Teens Do Research

Fourteen-year-old Sean and his sixteen-year-old bother, Daniel, know they're supposed to remove their snow gear before entering the house on snowy days, but hanging up their gear in the cold garage is a hassle. Sometimes, when they think they can get away with it, they make a dash for their rooms. Their mother suspects this is one of those times and greets them at the front door.

"Hi, guys," she says. "Please hang up your gear in the garage before you come in the house. Is that clear, Daniel?" She directs the question to him because she expects him to test.

"Oh, all right," says Daniel, reluctantly. Both boys head toward the garage, but as they do, they hear the phone ring and know their mother will be distracted. "Now is our opportunity," says Daniel, as he bolts for his bedroom. Sean remembers his mother's words and decides to play it safe. He heads to the garage.

When their mother gets off the phone, she heads to the garage to see if the boys' snow gear is hanging on the hooks. She sees Sean's gear, not Daniel's, and confronts him in the kitchen.

"Did you hang up your snow gear?" she asks. Daniel knows he's busted.

"You owe me twenty minutes of housecleaning before you do anything else," says his mother matter-of-factly. Daniel pleads for another chance, but his mother holds firm. He's not happy about it, but he knows he'll have another chance tomorrow.

Like most strong-willed teens, Daniel chose to learn his lesson the hard way. He decided to test and see if his mother really meant what she said. She did. Daniel and his mother will probably have to repeat this lesson a number of times before he's convinced that her rule is firm, but his mother's limit-setting approach will certainly lead him to the desired conclusion.

Daniel's mother understands that her sons have different temperaments and learning styles, and she's prepared to teach her rules however the situation requires—the easy way or the hard way. Daniel is strong-willed. She expects him to test, and she's ready to follow through with an instructive logical consequence to help him learn the lesson. Like most aggressive researchers, Daniel requires repeated consequences before he's convinced his mother's rules are required, not optional. Daniel's temperament and learning style make him a challenge to raise.

Sean, on the other hand, has a compliant temperament. He doesn't do much testing because his underlying desire is to please and cooperate. His mother expects him to cooperate in most situations, but she's ready to follow through with instructive consequences when he doesn't. Like most easy-way learners, Sean doesn't require much discipline. His temperament and learning style make him easier to raise.

Notice how Sean and Daniel's mother doesn't waste her time with ineffective discipline. No yelling or threats. No arguing or debating. No lectures or sermons. No angry dramatic displays. She simply gives them a clear message with her words and supports her words with an instructive logical consequence. Her researchers get all the data they need to arrive at the desired conclusion. The message is clear, and so is the rule behind it. She makes learning the hard way look easy. In this chapter, you'll understand why the hard way is the clearest way for strong-willed teens or any teen who chooses to conduct their research aggressively.

## Temperament and Limit Testing

All teens test limits. This is normal, but not all teens test limits or learn rules in the same way. Temperament has a lot to do with how they conduct their research.

In the opening example, Sean and Daniel responded differently to the same limit-setting message from their mother. One continued to test and challenge his mother's rule. The other didn't. Why?

Sean is a good example of a compliant teen. Compliant teens don't do a lot of testing because they don't require a lot of hard data in the form of consequences to be convinced to accept and follow our rules. Their underlying desire is to please and cooperate. Most are willing to accept our words as all the data they need and cooperate for the asking. Sean is easy to teach because he does most of his learning the easy way. Compliant teens don't require a lot of consequences to complete their research. This is good news for parents and teachers because compliant teens account for approximately 55 percent of temperament profiles.

Strong-willed teens, on the other hand, are much more aggressive in the way they conduct their research. They test frequently, and they require a lot of data in the form of consequences before they are willing to accept our authority and follow our rules. Although they constitute only 10 percent of the temperament profiles, parents and teachers agree they cause 90 percent of guidance and discipline problems in homes, schools, and community settings. Strong-willed teens push hard against adult rules and authority.

Daniel is a good example of a strong-willed teen. To him, the word *stop* is just a theory or a hypothesis. He's more interested in what will happen if he doesn't stop, and he knows how to find out. He continues to test. Daniel's mother knows, from experience, that she will have to use a lot of consequences to help Daniel stay on the right path. This isn't right or wrong, good or bad. It's just the way it is. Strong-willed teens are difficult to teach because they do much of their learning the hard way. Parents have to be at the top of their limit-setting game to work with this challenging group.

There is no one right way to learn. Of course, most parents prefer that their teens learn the easy way. Who wouldn't? Easy-way learning is less work for us and less wear and tear. The lessons are usually brief. Hard-way learning, on the other hand, is a lot of work for us and very stressful. The lessons can take weeks and months to play out. When the choices are "easy way" versus "hard way," what parent would choose hard?

Unfortunately, we don't get to choose how our teens learn.

That's their job. Our job is to support the lesson however they choose to learn it. When we discover that they've chosen to learn the hard way, the next question is: How are we going to deal with it? We can fight it and make it harder. We can give in to it and make it longer. We can try some of both and get nowhere. Or we can accept it as a fact of life, make peace with it, and support the learning process by helping our teen complete his or her research. Hard-way learning is still good learning.

Although the opening example did not include a fence sitter, they are a formidable group that accounts for the remaining 35 percent of temperament profiles. Fence sitters, as the name suggests, are a mixed group who can go in either direction depending upon what the market will bear. They cooperate most often when they encounter clear, firm limits to guide their research, and they will test rules and authority aggressively when limits are unclear or when they see other teens getting away with something. Fence sitters also require generous helpings of consequences to complete their research.

Let's look at how the dynamics of temperament and learning styles play out in family situations. Imagine you're the parent of three teenage girls: Terri, age seventeen; Brittany, age fifteen; and Jenna, age thirteen. Each has a different temperament and learning style. Terri is a fence sitter. She tests intermittently and can be aggressive in her research. Brittany is strong-willed. She tests frequently and is always aggressive in her research. Jenna is compliant. Her underlying desire is to cooperate, but she doesn't miss the things her older sisters get away with.

It's Friday evening. All of you are sitting at the dinner

table, and Brittany asks if she can go to the mall with a friend on Saturday afternoon. The girls know trips to the mall are a touchy subject for their mother. The local newspaper runs frequent stories of assaults, shoplifting, and teens loitering in the food court. Brittany points out the advantages of the trip.

"Erica's mom will pick us up and drop us off, so you won't have to do any driving," says Brittany.

Without giving it much thought, you respond, "Sure, but don't be late for dinner. I want you back on time."

The next afternoon, Brittany heads to the mall but doesn't return until eight. "We just lost track of time," she says. "Erica didn't even call her mom to pick us up until seven thirty."

"I was worried about you," you say with concern, "but I'm glad you're home and safe," and that's all that happens.

What did Brittany learn from this experience? Does it matter if she is late for dinner? Not this time. Were there any clear ground rules or expectations to guide her research? No. You said, "Don't be late, and I want you back on time." What do these words mean to a strong-willed fifteen-year-old who wants to hang out with her friends at the mall? Based upon this experience, what conclusions does Brittany reach? Of course, it's okay to hang out at the mall as long as you like. Nothing happens when you return late. What do you think Brittany will do next time she's offered an opportunity to hang out at the mall?

Brittany's sisters observed everything that took place. What did they learn from this experience? Terri, the fence sitter, is skilled at watching other people do her research for her. She learned the same lesson Brittany learned. Terri can't wait to stretch out her next trip.

What did Jenna learn? She learned that her mom doesn't ask many questions about trips to the mall and doesn't have clear expectations about how the outing should go. Although Jenna is the least likely of the three to take advantage of her mom's vagueness, she knows she can get away with a late return if the opportunity arises. In any case, the lack of clear, firm limits to guide their research sets up everybody for testing and conflict.

Now, let's replay the scene from the point when Brittany asks permission to go to the mall, but this time you are clear and firm about your expectations. "Brittany, I'm comfortable with the trip if you agree to return no later than five thirty and call me if anything comes up that affects where you'll be or when you'll return. Is that clear?" Brittany nods. "Will you agree to that?" Again, Brittany nods.

But Brittany doesn't return at the agreed-upon time. No phone calls. When she walks in the house at nearly eight, she offers a feeble excuse. "We just lost track of time," she says. "I know I said I'd call, but I wasn't paying attention."

"I understand," you say, matter-of-factly, "and that's why you're not ready for this privilege. We can try it again in a few months." No lectures. No shaming or blaming. No drama. Your message is clear and so is the rule behind it.

What did Brittany learn this time? She learned that compliance is expected and required, not optional. She'll probably think carefully next time she's offered the opportunity. Based upon what her sisters observed this time, do you think Terri and Jenna will be testing this issue anytime soon? Not likely. Your clear, firm message helps everyone know what to expect.

## Aggressive Research

How do teens like Brittany know that our spoken rules are really the rules we practice? Often, they don't know, but they do know how to find out. They test. They simply do what we asked them not to do and wait to see what happens. This is limit testing, or how teens do their research. The data they collect helps them form conclusions about our rules and answer some very important research questions: What's really okay? What's not okay? Who's in charge? How far can I go? What happens when I go too far?

Devon, age fourteen, is a good example of the many hard-way learners I see in my family counseling work. He's bright and capable but resists doing what he's asked, both at home and in the classroom. He arrived at my office with his parents because he was at risk of failing three of his classes during the fall semester of his ninth-grade year, largely because he refused to write down his assignments in his weekly lesson planner.

During elementary school, Devon seldom wrote down his homework assignments but still managed to get mostly A's and B's. In middle school, the task of keeping track of books, assignments, long-term papers, and projects is more challenging. Middle schools strongly encourage students to keep track of all their assignments by using their weekly lesson planner. Devon never used his. He tried to keep track of everything by memory, and as a result, he missed many homework assignments and failed to prepare for tests and long-term projects. His grades dropped to B's and C's. When I met him, Devon was midway through the first semester of his ninth-grade year and at risk of failing three of his seven classes.

"Devon pushes everything to the limit," his father complained. "He challenges and defies most of our requests and doesn't seen satisfied until everyone is upset. He spends more time with his friends, cell phone, and video games than he ever does with his schoolwork." I had a hunch I was about to meet a very aggressive researcher.

As his father talked, I could see Devon was sizing me up. Then he went right to work on me. He interrupted his father in mid-conversation and directed his comment toward me. "I don't care what anybody says," Devon began. "Lesson planners are stupid and a complete waste of time. My grades have always been good. I don't need anybody telling me how to do my schoolwork, and I don't need to here." When he finished, he slumped in his chair, crossed his arms, and scowled at his parents.

"You're at risk of failing three classes!" his father exclaimed. "Something is not working. Can't you just try the planner and see if it helps?"

"No way!" replies Devon. "I just got a little behind. I can bring up those grades anytime. I don't need any stupid lesson planner to get my grades up." I had barely spoken a word before Devon introduced the essential research question on his own. I was about to capitalize on the opportunity when Devon's cell phone rang. Without hesitating, he answered the call and began a conversation during our session! His mother had an incredulous look on her face. Devon's father was seething.

"That is so rude!" says his father. Devon gives his father an annoyed look, rolls his eyes, but ends his conversation. His dad reaches for the phone, but Devon holds it out of his reach.

This is limit testing. When it happens, I know I'm going to learn a great deal about how the family communicates about limits. I watch the teen, the parents, and the cell phone for five to ten minutes, and I get all the data I need.

Devon's parents reacted to his cell phone antics the way many parents do. They gave him a look of disapproval, expressed their annoyance, but didn't remove the phone. Devon knew what they would do next. They continued complaining.

While Devon's parents complained, he pulled out his cell phone and began texting one of his friends. I watched to see what his parents would do next. His mother shot him a stern, disapproving look, and his father reached over to grab the cell phone once again. Devon acknowledged their gestures, stopped texting, and put the phone in his pocket.

Devon's parents were trying their best to say "Stop!" but Devon knew from experience that stopping was not really expected or required. The data he'd collected over the years convinced him that compliance with his parents' requests was optional, not required. All their words and gestures were meaningless steps in a well-rehearsed drama. We were fifteen minutes into our session, and Devon had still not received a clear, firm message from his parents. Finally, his exasperated mother turned to me and said, "See what he does? This is the same thing he does at home and at school!"

At this point, I intervened and attempted to get us back on track. In a matter-of-fact voice, I said, "Devon, clearly you're a bright and capable student who got good grades for years without using a planner. Maybe lesson planners are stupid and not helpful. Would you be willing to participate in an experiment to test out that question?" He looked at me suspiciously.

"Are you some kind of expert on homework and planners?" he asked in a less than respectful manner. The bait was skillfully presented. His parents bit first.

"It's not okay to talk to any adult like that," said his father. "Dr. MacKenzie is here to help us."

"Well, I don't need his help," said Devon in the same surly tone. They were about to start an argument when I tried once again to get us back on track.

"Devon has a right to be suspicious," I said, trying to shift things back to neutral. "He doesn't know me. He's the only teenager in the room surrounded by adults." On the inside, I wanted to throttle him. I took a couple of deep breaths and posed the question about our experiment once again.

"What do I have to do?" Devon asked.

"For the remaining four weeks of this semester, you won't have to do anything different than you're already doing."

"Nothing?" he asked.

"Not a thing," I replied. "Are you willing?" He nodded.

"Good," I said. "Here's how the experiment works. For the rest of this semester, you don't have to use your lesson planner. This will give us a full semester to see if you can bring your grades up on your own without a planner. If you do, then we'll know that all this talk about planners is a waste of time, and we can drop this topic for good. Sound good?" Devon nodded.

"But in the event that your grades don't improve to at least B's and C's at the end of the semester, we'll need comparison data the following semester to determine how much difference the planner really makes. Are you willing to use your planner to write down all assignments and keep track of all your tests and quizzes next semester?" I asked.

"That won't be necessary," said Devon. "I know I can bring my grades up." He skillfully evaded the question. So I posed the question again.

"You're probably right," I said, "but if the unlikely occurs, we need comparison data to answer our research question—Do planners help? Are you willing to write down all of your assignments in your planner the following semester so we can complete our experiment?"

"Okay," said Devon, still insisting the planner wouldn't be needed. I directed my next question to Devon's parents.

"Are you willing to hold him to his agreement?" I asked. Both parents nodded. They liked the plan.

"We're even willing to suspend his cell phone and video game privileges on the days he arrives home without his completed planner," offered his father. With our experiment in place, we set a follow-up appointment at the end of the semester.

What do you think happened? Of course, Devon couldn't bring his grades up. The answer to the first semester's research question was clear, but things didn't go smoothly during the next semester. Despite his agreement, Devon's compliance with the planner was about 60 percent. Some days he didn't write down all of his assignments. Some days he didn't use it at all. Each time this happened, his parents revoked his cell phone and video game privileges for that day. No yelling or complaining. No threats. No drama.

Gradually, his grades improved. Midway through the second semester, he had B's and C's in all of his classes. The conclusion of our experiment was clear. The planner helped, but it took nearly two semesters of hard-way learning for Devon to reach this conclusion on his own.

## Aggressive Research Tactics

No discussion of aggressive research is complete without addressing the tactics teens use to wear us down while they do their research. Most of these tactics are not new. You saw them during early and middle childhood, and these tactics are not unique to strong-willed teens, either. Most teens do this at some point. I'm talking about arguing and debating, lying and deception, and attacks on our character.

What is new is the level of sophistication with which teens carry out these tactics, and this all relates back to those changes in thinking and brain development we discussed in Chapter 2. Teens know they've become smarter during adolescence, but what they don't know is how smart they really are in relation to parents, teachers, and others. But teens do know how to find out. They test. They push hard against our rules and authority and hit us from many angles.

The wear and tear on adults is huge. At times, it makes us crazy, but that's exactly why they do it. Their intent is to overwhelm us and wear us down. That's how Devon's parents felt in the previous example, and that's how many of us feel when this happens to us. Sometimes the process is so intense and emotional that it feels more serious than simply limit testing, but in most cases, that's exactly what it is. This is still aggressive research with an added layer of resistance. In Chapter 15, we'll discuss how to manage these tactics. For now, let's get better acquainted with the tactics so you can see what's coming your way. Buckle your seat belt.

## Arguing and Debating

Have you noticed that some teens argue for the sheer pleasure of arguing? Sometimes they don't even care about the issue. The pleasure is in the process. Arguing is a great way for them to show off their new intellectual powers. They are serving notice that they can match wits with us and hold their own in an intellectual discussion whether they believe in the issues or not. Sometimes they're even better at this than we are. Fifteen-year-old Lindsey is a good example.

Lindsey knows she's expected to rinse the dishes and load the dishwasher each night after dinner, but tonight she's not in the mood and makes her best pitch to avoid the job. "I have a huge amount of homework tonight," says Lindsey. "May I do the dishes after homework?" Lindsey's mom is suspicious. She gave in to this excuse before and discovered Lindsey on her cell phone with one of her friends.

"The dishes only take a few minutes," says her mom. "You'll be done in no time. Then you won't have to worry about dishes for the rest of the evening."

"But Mom," Lindsey pleads in a whiny voice. "That's not fair! I have a really important test in Biology. It's my hardest subject. I need to put in all the time I can. Do you want me to get a lousy grade?"

"I'm sure you'll do just fine," says her mom. "You're a good student." Her mom doesn't budge. Lindsey rolls her eyes, lets out a big sigh, and tries again.

"When you and Dad have something really important that you want to do really well, don't you try to put your best efforts into it?" asks Lindsey.

*That's logical, well thought out, and persuasive*, her Mom thinks to herself. *I wonder if she really means it this time?* Lindsey can sense her mom softening and tries again.

"I'll even wipe down the counters if you let me do the dishes later," Lindsey adds. Her mom is tempted but still suspicious.

"That's a nice offer," says her mom, "but the counters are in good shape. Thanks for the offer." Lindsey tries a different approach.

"When Jeff has soccer or baseball after school, you don't make him do his chores until after his homework is complete," she says. "Why aren't you willing to do the same thing with me? Biology is more important than sports."

Jeff is thirteen, very compliant, and a hard worker. Completing chores is never an issue with him. Lindsey's mom recognizes the inconsistency and the logic in her daughter's argument. Once again, she's tempted to give in. Then she realizes how much time they've spent discussing the issue and holds firm.

"You could have finished the job twice during the time we've been discussing it," says her mom, matter-of-factly. "We're done talking about it." She leaves the room. Lindsey follows her.

"I'll bet Grandpa and Grandma cared more about your grades when you were a kid than you care about mine," says Lindsey.

*I'm not going to respond to this*, her mom says to herself. She seeks refuge in the bathroom and locks the door. Reluctantly, Lindsey heads to the kitchen to do the dishes. When her mom checks on Lindsey twenty minutes later, she's on her cell phone with one of her friends.

## Lying and Deception

Seventeen-year-old Dylan shares time between two homes in a fifty-fifty custody arrangement. His dad is going out of town for the weekend, and Dylan is supposed to stay at his mom's house. Dylan sees this as a big opportunity. He asks his mom if he can go bowling with his friends Friday night. She agrees.

The next day at school, Dylan rounds up a group of his friends and announces he's having a party Friday night at his dad's house. "I have some really good weed," says Dylan. "You guys bring your own booze and anything else you want. Please keep it quiet and don't tell anybody else. I told my mom I'm going bowling, and I don't want her to get suspicious." His friends all agree. Everything is set.

On Friday evening Dylan makes a brief stop at the bowling alley just to say he did so, then heads to his dad's house. Five girls arrive together at about eight thirty. Two were uninvited. When Dylan asks one of the invited girls, Glenda, why she brought two friends, she replies, "It's just Debbie. She's my best friend, and you know Tracy. She's cool. I didn't think you'd mind."

Dylan's buddies arrive next with a story of disappointment. Their attempt to buy beer at a convenience store didn't work out. It's not a total loss. One of them stole a bottle of gin from his parents' home.

"Does your dad have any alcohol?" asks one of his friends. "We'll replace it before he gets home." They investigate the liquor cabinet. It's well stocked.

"Don't touch my dad's wine collection!" warns Dylan. His dad has a separate wine cabinet with dozens of bottles of expensive wines.

More friends arrive, some invited, several uninvited. *This is getting out of control*, Dylan thinks to himself. The party moves into high gear. Some kids are smoking weed. Others are drinking. Each time the music gets too loud, Dylan turns it down, but someone else turns it up again. Dylan fears the neighbors might discover what's going on.

One buddy and his girlfriend approach Dylan and ask to use one of the bedrooms. He points them to the middle bedroom. "Don't use my dad's room or my sister's," Dylan warns. He doesn't realize it, but his sister's room is already in use.

As the party starts to wind down, Dylan notices that several bottles of wine are missing from his dad's collection. *Oh shit!* He says to himself. But things get worse. One of the uninvited girls is passed out on the couch and can't be awakened. Her best friend, Glenda, is really worried and agrees to take Debbie home. Several boys stuff her in the backseat of Glenda's car.

Monday, at school, things begin to unravel. Glenda is first to share the news. "When I dropped Debbie off at home, her parents freaked out and took her to the hospital. She had alcohol toxicity. Her parents were furious and wanted to know what happened."

"Did you tell them?" asks Dylan.

"No, but I don't know if Debbie said anything," says Glenda.

When Dylan arrives home from school, his mother informs him that his father's home was burglarized over the weekend. Several items were stolen.

"Well, Dad is terrible about locking his doors," says Dylan.

Later that same evening, Dylan's mother receives a call from Debbie's parents, who share the incident about their daughter's trip to the emergency room. "Debbie said she was at a party at Dylan's house. Debbie's best friend, Glenda, said the same thing."

"I'll talk with my son and get back to you," Dylan's mother assures them. When she confronts Dylan with the news, he denies knowing anything about it and insists he was at the bowling alley with his friends. So Dylan's mother confronts him with another piece of information. "Your friend, Glenda, also told Debbie's parents she was at your father's house." Finally, Dylan comes clean. "We need to call your father and tell him what's really going on," says his mother.

Abstract thinking and deception are a powerful combination of tools that many teens need to test out for themselves. Dylan's research provided a lot of valuable information. What did he learn? He discovered that he isn't as smart or skillful in the art of deception as he thought he was, that his parents and other adults are not as dumb as he thought they were, and that his friends are not as trustworthy as he believed. As difficult as this hard-way learning experience appears, Dylan collects valuable information about himself, others, and the importance of honesty and trust in his relationships.

## Parent Bashing

Fourteen-year-old Aidan and a group of his friends eat lunch together in their high school cafeteria and enjoy one of their favorite pastimes—parent bashing. To many teens, parent bashing is an indoor sport. They take turns trying to outdo one another.

"My dad dresses like such a geek," Aidan begins. "He wears the same white shirts to work every day with this stupid plastic pen holder in his pocket so he won't get ink stains on his shirts. Then he hikes his slacks about a foot above his waist and holds them in place with a thick belt. He looks like a penguin. I can't stand to be seen with him outside our house." His friends laugh at the image.

"Oh yeah, you should see my dad," says another teen. "He's bald, has a big pointy nose, and bushy eyebrows. He bobs his head up and down when he listens to his country music station on the way to school in the mornings. It's the stupidest thing you've ever seen." He does an imitation. His friends howl with laughter.

"That's nothing," says another teen. "My mom farts all the time, and moms aren't supposed to do that." Everybody erupts with laughter. "She has some kind of stomach problem." He makes a farting sound and everybody erupts again.

Parent bashing often continues when teens arrive home. "How was your day today, Aidan?" his dad asks at dinner.

"Okay," says Aidan.

"Did you do anything fun or exciting?"

"No," Aidan replies.

"How are your classes going?" asks his dad.

"Okay," says Aidan.

"Are you keeping your grades up?" asks his dad. Aidan snaps.

"Dad, why do you always ask the same lame questions? Every day, I go to the same boring classes with the same boring teachers, and nothing ever happens," says Aidan. "Don't you get it?" He rolls his eyes and gives his dad a look of disgust as though he's the stupidest person on the planet.

"You're my son. I'm interested in how you're doing," says his dad.

"Well, I'm doing fine," says Aidan in an irritated tone. "Can we drop it now? I don't grill you with the twenty-questions routine during dinner."

Sound familiar? You have to develop a tough skin to be a parent of a teenager. It's hard to believe that this is the same child you've loved all the way through early and middle childhood, the same one who jumped in your lap and incessantly peppered you with "why" questions about everything. Now your child is a teenager. You ask a simple question, and you can't get a direct answer without attitude, hostility, or an argument.

To make matters worse, your teen has intimate knowledge of your bad habits, eccentricities, character flaws, and imperfections, and he or she enjoys pointing these things out to you each time the opportunity arises. Ouch! Even the most loving parents have a difficult time not taking the message personally because it hurts so much on an emotional level.

Is this hitting below the belt? Maybe. But what feels like a personal attack is really part of something much larger. These are the unpleasant side effects of that identity quest we discussed in Chapter 2. Your teen is trying to separate from you emotionally and psychologically, and there's no instruction manual on how to do it. So they do what comes naturally. They act on their feelings and impulses and send messages that say, *Back off. I'm me. I'm different from you, and I need space to be me.*

## Chapter Summary

Limit testing and experimentation are important tasks of adolescence. All teens do it, but they don't all do it in the same way. Temperament has a lot to do with how they conduct their research. Compliant teens do a lot of their learning the "easy way"; that is, they don't require much hard data in the form of experience to reach their conclusions. Often, they cooperate for the asking. Supporting their learning process is not hard on parents.

Strong-willed teens, on the other hand, are much more aggressive researchers. They require a lot of hard data in the form of experience before they're convinced that cooperation is required, not optional. Instructive consequences play an important role in their research. Strong-willed teens are a major workout for parents and others. You have to be at the top of your game to work with this group.

Fence sitters are a versatile group. They can go either way depending upon what the market will bear or what they see others getting away with. Fence sitters are astute observers of their strong-willed counterparts, who are more willing to take risks. Fence sitters don't need to learn the "hard way" if they see that it's not working for others. But if it is, fence sitters can be very aggressive researchers.

Parents don't get to choose how teens learn rules or conduct their research. Those jobs belong to them. We can, however, choose to support their research, rather than resist it, and we can teach our rules however our teens choose to learn them—the easy way, the hard way, or some of both. You just need the right tools in your toolkit. Chapters 8–16 will show you how to do that.

Now it's time to examine the guidance tools you've been using up to this point. Is your limit-setting approach a good match or a poor match to your teen's temperament and learning style? You're about to find out.

## CHAPTER 6

# Limit Setting: How Parents Teach Rules

We know how teens learn our rules. Now it's time to examine your limit-setting style or the methods you use to teach your rules. Is your limit-setting approach a good match or a bad match to your teen's learning style? You're about to find out. In the pages that follow, I'm going to hold up a mirror for you to look into so you can identify your limit-setting style and the current set of tools in your toolkit. Without this awareness, you'll just be repeating old mistakes and expecting different results.

When it comes to setting limits, most parents operate somewhere on a continuum of limit-setting approaches. On one extreme is the autocratic or punitive approach. The limits are firm, but the methods are not very respectful. On the other extreme is the permissive approach. The methods are respectful, but the limits are not very firm. Some parents use a mixed approach and flip-flop back and forth between these two extremes. Still others have managed to find the right balance between the two extremes and use an approach that is both firm and respectful. The balanced approach is the key to winning your teen's respect.

What is your limit-setting style? Have you struggled to find the right balance between firmness and respect? Is your approach well matched to the temperament of your teen? This chapter will help you answer these questions. By examining the methods used by other parents, you'll gain a better understanding of the limit-setting approach you've used up to this point and discover how well that approach is matched to the temperament and learning style of your teen. Let's begin by looking at the punitive approach.

## The Autocratic or Punitive Approach (Firm but Not Respectful)

Imagine the following scene. Austin's mother gives her sixteen-year-old permission to use the family car on the condition that he return it by 7 p.m. She has an important meeting to attend. Austin returns home with the car at eight thirty.

> Mom (in a loud voice, almost yelling):"Where were you? Didn't I tell you I needed the car back by seven?"
>
> Austin: "I was playing video games at Reggie's house. I guess I lost track of the time. I'm sorry."
>
> Mom: "You are one of the most selfish, inconsiderate, irresponsible people I've ever met! I thought you would at least have given me the courtesy of a phone call. I missed a really important meeting. I knew I shouldn't have trusted you."

Austin: "I said I'm sorry. What more do you want?"

Mom: "I want to see some responsibility for a change, but I guess that would be asking too much from you."

Austin (hurt and angry): "What a bitch!"

Mom (yelling): "Nobody talks to me like that! You're grounded to the house for a full month."

Parents who use the punitive approach often find themselves in roles of police detective, judge, jailer, referee, and probation officer. They investigate the misdeeds, determine guilt, assign blame, and impose penalties that tend to be harsh and drawn out. The problem-solving process is often loud, angry, and adversarial. Cooperation is achieved through threats, fear, and intimidation.

The belief underlying this approach is that discipline needs to hurt to be effective. Methods include investigation, interrogation, accusations, threats, criticism, shaming, blaming, and taking away favorite possessions or privileges for long periods of time.

How do teens respond to punitive limit-setting methods? Compliant teens usually cooperate out of fear. Strong-willed teens often rebel and retaliate. Fence sitters do a little of both. Most teens feel angry and resentful and perceive the methods as hurtful and humiliating. The punitive approach is poorly matched to the temperaments of all three groups.

### Examples of Punitive Limit-Setting Practices

- Spanking, slapping, whipping, and other forms of corporal punishment

- Taking away favorite privileges or possessions for long periods of time
- Shaming and blaming
- Threatening, intimidating, and humiliating
- Grounding for excessive periods of time
- Calling them names to show them how it feels
- Using sarcastic or demeaning language

As a limit-setting approach, the punitive model has few advantages and many limitations. It does permit a degree of enforceability by stopping unacceptable behavior initially, but it doesn't teach positive lessons about communication or problem solving or earn your teen's respect. Why? Because the methods encourage hurtful communication and disrespect. Is this the lesson we really want to teach? If it is, then disrespect is what we should expect to get back.

Can you imagine what it would be like if our traffic laws were enforced with this approach? Visualize yourself driving through a stop sign or red light. A cop sees you and pulls you over. As he approaches your car, he shouts insults and angrily writes out a ticket. But, before he returns to his car, he smacks you with his nightstick.

How would you respond to this kind of treatment? Would you turn to the officer and say, "Thanks, I needed that. I understand your point, and I'll try harder to stop in the future"? Probably not. Would you feel like cooperating with someone who treated you so disrespectfully? Not likely. When it comes to humiliation, teens respond much like adults. They understand the rule, but they don't respect the person teaching it. Cooperation is at the expense of the relationship.

The punitive approach is poorly matched to the temperaments and learning styles of strong-willed teens, and fence sitters in particular. It makes them angry and resentful and incites them to retaliate. The brief cooperation parents achieve comes at a high price—injured feelings, damaged relationships, and angry power struggles. Is this any way to earn your teen's respect?

### Table 2 The Punitive Approach

| | |
|---|---|
| Matchups | Poorly matched to temperaments and learning styles of all three temperament profiles |
| Parents' Beliefs | If it doesn't hurt, teens won't learn.<br><br>Teens won't respect my rules unless they fear my methods.<br><br>It's my job to solve my teen's problems. |
| Problem Solving | Persuasion by force, fear, or intimidation<br><br>Adversarial<br><br>Win-lose (parents win)<br><br>Parents do all the problem solving and make all the decisions. |
| Enforceability | At the expense of the relationship |

| What Teens Learn | Hurtful methods of communication and problem solving<br><br>Parents are responsible for solving teen problems.<br><br>Disrespect for parents |
|---|---|
| How Teens Respond | Anger, hurt, resentment, stubbornness, revenge, rebellion, withdrawal, fearful submission |

If the punitive approach has so many limitations, why do so many parents continue to use it? Most parents who use punishment were raised that way themselves. It feels natural and familiar, and they don't question its effectiveness. When things break down, they assume the problem is with their teen, not their methods.

# The Permissive Approach (Respectful, but Not Firm)

Permissiveness emerged in the 1960s and 1970s as a reaction against the hurtful and autocratic nature of the punitive approach. Many parents were looking for a more respectful method of raising children based upon democratic principles of freedom, equality, and mutual respect.

Putting these principles into practice, however, was not as easy as it sounded. This was uncharted territory for those of us who grew up with the punitive approach. How do you do it? Is it a simple matter of relaxing your rules and expectations and giving kids more freedom and control? That's what many parents tried. The plan seemed respectful to kids, but the experiment often backfired. Why? Because an important ingredient was left out—firm limits.

Freedom without limits is not democracy. It's anarchy, and kids raised with anarchy don't learn respect for rules or authority or how to handle their freedom responsibly. They tend to think of themselves first and develop an exaggerated sense of their own power and authority.

Let's return to the example of Austin and his mom and see how this situation plays out with the permissive approach. Austin borrows the car and returns an hour and a half late.

Mom: "Austin, where were you? I've been worried."

Austin: "I was playing video games at Reggie's house and lost track of time."

Mom: "This is the second time this week you've arrived home late with the car. Did you remember that I had an important meeting tonight? We need to be considerate of each other when we share the car."

Austin: "Oh, yeah. I forgot. I won't do it again."

Mom: "Okay. I'll let this one go with a warning. I hope you try harder next time."

Austin: "I will."

Did you hear a clear message that returning the car on time is expected and required? Austin didn't. Based upon his experience, do you think he will take his mother's warnings more seriously next time? Not likely. Austin understands that cooperation is optional, not required. Do you think Austin and his mom are likely to repeat this scene? Of course.

Permissive parents constantly shift gears and use different verbal tactics to convince and persuade kids to cooperate. The underlying belief is that kids will cooperate when they understand that cooperation is the right thing to do. The assumption generally holds for compliant kids, who do most of their learning the easy way. But the assumption does not hold for strong-willed kids and fence sitters, who do much of their learning the hard way. They require more than words to be convinced.

Permissive methods involve a lot of repeating, reminding, warning, second chances, reasoning, explaining, pleading, cajoling, bribing, begging, arguing, debating, negotiating, and other forms of persuasion. Consequences or actions, if they are used at all, are typically late and ineffective. Basically, it's lots of talk and very little action. The methods are certainly respectful to kids but not very firm.

How do teens respond to permissive limit-setting methods? Compliant teens usually cooperate, not because the signals are clear, but because their underlying desire is to please and cooperate anyway. Compliant teens give parents a wide margin for ineffectiveness.

The opposite is true for strong-willed teens and many fence sitters. When they encounter signals that lack firmness or clarity, they usually test to see what the market will bear. They tune out, ignore, challenge, defy, argue, debate, dawdle, procrastinate, or dig in their heels. They know from experience that if they resist long enough, there's a good chance their parents will compromise away their limits or give in altogether.

*Examples of Permissive Limit-Setting Practices*
- Ignoring or overlooking unacceptable behavior
- Allowing your teen to misbehave when you're in a good mood
- Giving warnings, second chances for unacceptable behavior
- Arguing, debating, and negotiating with a disrespectful teen
- Repeating, reminding, giving long explanations
- Offering bribes and special rewards for cooperation
- Pleading and begging for cooperation
- Giving in to drama
- Cleaning up messes for your teen
- Making excuses for your teen's unacceptable behavior
- Using lectures and sermons as consequences
- Inconsistent follow-through by a parent
- Inconsistent follow-through between parents

As a training model, permissiveness is poorly matched to the temperaments and learning styles of strong-willed teens and fence sitters, and it provides ineffective role modeling for compliant teens. Permissiveness doesn't accomplish any of our basic training goals. It carries very little enforceability. It doesn't stop misbehavior. It doesn't teach respect for rules or authority, and it doesn't teach the lessons we intend about responsibility, respectful communication, or cooperative problem solving. The methods inspire testing and power struggles. Permissiveness is humiliating to parents.

Can you imagine what things would be like if our traffic laws were enforced with permissiveness? Visualize yourself driving home once again. You approach a red light, but there isn't another car in sight. So you run it. Each time you approach an intersection with no cars around, you do the same thing. Eventually, a cop sees you and pulls you over.

He approaches your car, smiles, tips his hat, and informs you that you ran four stoplights. Then he proceeds to lecture you on the importance of obeying traffic laws.

"Those signals are there for your safety," he says, "and the safety and protection of other motorists. If everyone ran stoplights, we would have accidents all over our streets, injuries, and higher insurance rates." Then he pleads with you to try harder to follow those signals in the future. When the lecture is over, he gets in his car and drives off. If our traffic laws were enforced in this manner, do you think people would take them very seriously? Not likely.

Permissive parents are a lot like the cop in my example. They give lots of warnings, reminders, second chances, and persuasive reasons why their teens should cooperate. Parents may threaten to write tickets, and sometimes they actually do, but most of the time teens talk their way out of it, and parents let things pass with a warning.

Is a warning a sufficient deterrent to stop you from doing something you really want to do? Let's test it out. When you approach an intersection and the light is yellow, but you can safely make it through, do you always stop at the yellow light, every time? Most drivers don't, and neither do teens when parents hold up these signals to stop their unacceptable behavior.

Teens don't stop, for the same reason adults don't. Stopping is optional, not required. Most of us wait for the signal that really matters, the red light. Why? Because we associate this signal with a consequence that matters—a ticket, a collision, higher insurance rates, or something worse.

Teens are no different. They respect the signals that matter, the ones that have a direct and meaningful effect upon them. Without tickets (consequences) to hold them accountable, teens have little cause to take their parents' rules seriously.

Permissiveness is a limit-setting approach based on yellow lights. Stopping is optional, not required. Teens know it, but permissive parents are unaware that their signals do not really require stopping. They sincerely believe that all their repeating, reminding, warnings, and words of persuasion are equivalent to a red light.

Why are permissive parents so reluctant to use consequences with their kids? Most have the best of intentions. They're not trying to be vague. They simply want to teach their rules the "easy way" and avoid the conflict and temporary frustration that accompany following through with consequences.

Let's do a little reality testing. Are you accustomed to always getting your way out in the world? When you don't, do you feel good about it? Aren't we supposed to feel frustrated when we don't get what we want? Isn't that how we learn to delay gratification and adjust to reality?

## Table 3 The Permissive Approach

| Matchups | Poorly matched to strong-willed teens and fence sitters |
|---|---|
| Parents' Beliefs | Teens will cooperate when they understand that cooperation is the right thing to do. |
| Problem Solving | Problem solving by persuasion.<br>Win-lose (teens win)<br>Parents are responsible for solving the problems. |
| Enforceability | Nearly absent or late and ineffective |
| What Teens Learn | Rules are for others, not me. I do as I wish.<br>Parents should serve us and keep us happy.<br>Dependency, self-centeredness, disrespect for others |

| | |
|---|---|
| How Teens Respond | Limit testing. Power struggling.<br><br>Challenge and defy rules and authority<br><br>Ignore and tune out what parents say<br><br>Wear parents down with resistance<br><br>Develop entitled thinking<br><br>Lack sensitivity toward others |

# The Mixed Approach (Neither Firm nor Respectful)

As the name implies, the mixed approach is a combination of the punitive and permissive limit-setting styles. The mixed approach is characterized by inconsistency. It combines the worst elements of the two extremes and brings out the most extreme reactions in teens and parents.

Parents who use this approach do a lot of flip-flopping between permissiveness and punishment in search of a better way to get their message across. They know how to be respectful, but not without being permissive. They know how to be firm, but not without being punitive. The problem is they don't know how to be firm and respectful at the same time, so they flip-flop back and forth.

Try to imagine what our traffic laws would be like if they were enforced with the mixed approach. When you run a red light, sometimes the cop gives you a lecture and lets it pass with a warning. Other times, he screams insults at you, writes out a ticket, and threatens to hit you with his club. How do you know what will happen from one time to the next? You don't. How would you respond?

If you were compliant, you probably wouldn't risk running red lights very often. If you're a fence sitter, you'll decide what to do based on what you see others getting away with. If you're strong-willed, you'll probably run red lights frequently and find ways to retaliate when you get caught.

There are many variations to the mixed approach. The most common variation is the one in which parents begin permissively, then wear down, lose their patience, and resort to punitive tactics—threats, shaming, blaming, long and drawn-out consequences. Other parents begin punitively, but give in and resort to permissive tactics when they encounter complaints or resistance. Still others remain loyal to one approach for longer periods of time. They try permissiveness for weeks or months, until they can't stand being tuned out and ignored any longer, then they crack down and use punishment, until they can't stand how tyrannical they sound. Then they switch back to permissiveness. The cycle of flip-flops just takes longer to repeat itself.

Another common variation occurs when parents differ in their respective approaches. One parent might be punitive, the other permissive, but their combined approaches constitute a mixed approach. To kids, this is like living under the same roof with two governments operating simultaneously.

One government takes the hard line. The other takes the soft line. Kids figure this out and play one government against the other. If they know one parent is certain to say "no," then they'll ask the other to get a "yes." The inconsistency sets up everybody for conflict and power struggles.

### Examples of Mixed Limit-Setting Practices
- Ignoring misbehavior until you can't stand it anymore, then using harsh consequences
- Permitting your teen to misbehave sometimes
- Threatening consequences but failing to follow through
- Using different consequences for the same unacceptable behavior
- Asking your teen to be quiet, then yelling at him
- Using permissive and punitive practices under the same roof
- Giving warnings and second chances, then punishing

Let's return to our ongoing example of Austin and his mom and see how this issue is handled with the mixed approach. Let's assume that Austin returned the car late two times already this week and received only warnings and lectures.

Mom: "Where were you? Did you remember that I had an important meeting?"

Austin: "I was playing video games at Reggie's house, and I lost track of time. I won't let it happen again."

Mom (exploding with anger): "I've had enough of
   your selfish, inconsiderate crap! You can't use the
   car for the next month."

Austin: "Hey, that's not fair! I said it wouldn't happen
   again."

Mom (shouting): "Don't talk to me about fairness.
   I've been more than fair to you, and you just take
   advantage of me. I'm sick of being treated like a
   doormat. If you want to argue, I'd be happy to
   add another month."

Did Austin cause his mother to explode or did she set herself up by allowing things to go too far? Let's see. What happens the first time Austin shows up late with the car? He gets
a warning and a lecture. What happens the second time? The
same thing.

Is a warning or lecture equivalent to a ticket? Austin's
mom probably thinks so, but not Austin. He was permitted
to return the car late on two occasions with no consequences.
If Austin's mom continues to use this approach, do you think
they're headed for more of these upsetting encounters? You bet.

## The Democratic Approach
## (Firm and Respectful)

Effective limit setting requires a balance between firmness and
respect. The punitive approach is firm but not respectful. The
permissive approach is respectful but not firm. The mixed approach is neither firm nor respectful. These methods are based

on win-lose dynamics of problem solving, and faulty beliefs about learning; they are also poorly matched to the temperaments of most teens. The methods they employ invite testing and power struggles and fail to role-model respectful communication. Is there a better alternative? Definitely.

The democratic limit-setting approach combines firmness with respect and accomplishes all of our goals. It stops unacceptable behavior. It teaches responsibility, and it conveys, in the clearest way, the lessons we want to teach about respectful communication and problem solving. Best of all, the democratic approach is well matched to the full range of temperaments and learning styles: easy-way learners, hard-way learners, and those in between. The approach gets the job done in less time, with less energy, and without injuring feelings or damaging relationships.

The research shows that teenagers who respect their parents are the most likely to get through adolescence without experiencing major problems. How do parents develop this level of respect with their teens? It's not magic. This is a teachable set of skills that is well within your reach. The democratic approach to limit setting is an ideal match for all teens.

Please don't be confused by the term *democratic*. I'm not trying to politicize this issue. You can call it the republican approach if you want. I'm not suggesting decision making by consensus or problem solving by compromise or that you abdicate your parental authority. The term *democratic* is used to illustrate how freedom, choice, and limits are arranged in the limit-setting process.

The punitive approach provides limits without much freedom or choice. It's firm, but not respectful. The permissive approach provides freedom and choice without clearly defined limits. It's respectful but not firm. The democratic approach is simply the balance between the two extremes. It provides the freedom and choice teens need to test and explore but within clearly defined limits and boundaries. The approach is both firm and respectful, and because it is, it engenders respect in teens. The democratic approach is simply a healthy, balanced blueprint for teen development.

The democratic approach succeeds where others fail because it combines the right ingredients in the recipe— respectful words and respectful actions or consequences. No anger, no drama, and none of the strong emotions and power tactics that interfere with good communication and learning. The message is clear, and so is the rule behind it. The approach provides enforceability but not at the expense of the relationship.

The teaching-and-learning process is cooperative, not adversarial. Parents don't act like broken records trying to wear teens down with words, and parents don't act like police detectives, judges, or probation officers trying to force teens into cooperation. Instead, parents act like teachers and guide the learning process. They give clear, firm messages with their words, teach skills when needed, and follow through with instructive consequences when teens decide to test or challenge rules. Whether teens choose to learn the easy way or the hard way, it doesn't matter. The democratic approach will help you teach the lesson you intend however your teen chooses to learn it (see Table 4).

### Examples of Democratic Limit-Setting Practices
- Removing a privilege temporarily when teens misuse or abuse that privilege

- Expressing confidence in your teen's capabilities
- Separating teens from activities temporarily when they are disruptive
- Acknowledging your teen's cooperation and good judgment
- Removing items temporarily when teens misuse or abuse those items
- Expressing confidence in your teen's ability to make good choices
- Separating yourself from your teen when he or she is disrespectful
- Accepting your teen, not his or her unacceptable behavior
- Separating your teen from siblings when your teen is hurtful or unkind
- Showing forgiveness when a discipline incident is over

Let's return to our now-familiar scene with Austin and his mom to see how this issue is handled with the democratic approach.

Mom (in a matter-of-fact voice): "Austin, where were you? Did you remember I needed the car by seven? I had an important meeting tonight."

Austin: "I was playing video games at Reggie's house, and I lost track of the time."

Mom: "When I say I need the car back at a certain time, I mean just that. May I have your car keys, please? They'll stay with me for the rest of the week. We can try this again on Monday if you're willing to return the car on time."

Austin: (hands his mom the car keys)

Notice how short this interaction is. Effective limit setting takes less time and less energy and yields better results. This time, Austin's mom is working with a plan. No time is wasted on ineffective lectures or detective work. No yelling or threatening. No shaming or blaming. No anger or drama. She gets right to the point. She states her expectation and supports that rule by temporarily suspending Austin's driving privileges.

Can you see yourself handling problems like this? Can you imagine how much more rewarding your parenting would be if you could get your message across the first time and avoid nearly all of the power struggles? You can. The democratic approach is your ticket to respect and credibility. All you need is the right tools in your toolkit and a better awareness of the methods you've used in the past that don't work for you. Let's get started on the awareness step. Chapter 7 will help you examine the quality of your signals and determine whether your limits are firm or soft.

### *Table 4 The Democratic Approach*

| Matchups | The democratic approach is well matched to all temperaments and learning styles. |
| --- | --- |

| Parents' Beliefs | Teens are capable of solving problems on their own. Teens should be allowed to learn from their choices. |
|---|---|
| Problem Solving | Cooperative<br>Win-win<br>Based on mutual respect<br>Teens are active participants in the process. |
| Enforceability | Fully effective, but not at expense of the relationship |
| What Teens Learn | Respect for parents, rules, and authority<br>Responsibility<br>Cooperation<br>Independence |
| How Teens Respond | Less limit testing<br>More cooperation<br>Regard parents' rules and authority more seriously |

## CHAPTER 7

# Are Your Limits Firm or Soft?

When you say "no" to your teen, does it really mean no? If you ask many teens, often they'll tell you that no really means yes, sometimes, or maybe. The problem, in most cases, is unclear communication about limits. Many parents believe they're holding up a red light when they say "no," but teens see it as green or flashing yellow because stopping isn't required.

What kind of signals have you been using to get your teen to cooperate? Are your red lights really red lights? Or are they green or yellow? This chapter will help you find out. You'll discover the specific things you say and do that don't work for you, and you'll understand why your teen responds to your signals the way he or she does.

Limits come in two varieties: firm and soft, depending upon their level of enforceability. Each sends very different messages about your rules and expectations.

Firm limits send clear signals about your rules and expectations. Words are supported with effective action or instructive consequences so firm limits carry a high degree of enforceability. Compliance is expected, not optional. Teens raised with firm limits learn to tune in to our words, to take them seriously, and to cooperate more often for the asking.

Soft limits, on the other hand, are mixed messages or unclear signals about our rules and expectations. Compliance is optional, not required. Words are not supported with action. Consequences, if they are used at all, are often late and ineffective. Soft limits carry a low degree of enforceability. Teens raised with soft limits learn to tune out and ignore our words and push us to the point of action more often. Soft limits are a setup for aggressive testing and power struggles with strong-willed teens and most fence sitters.

## The Reality of Imperfect Control

Most parents would like to believe they have a high degree of influence and control over their teen's choices and behavior. It's time for a reality check. Short of placing your teen in a full-time lockup facility, the perfect control you'd like to have is not going to happen. Why not? Because perfect control requires perfect enforceability. In the real world, we seldom have perfect enforceability over our rules and expectations.

Let me illustrate this point by revisiting some of the typical rules and expectations parents hold for their teenagers, which we discussed in Chapter 3: *My teen should treat me respectfully. My teen should keep me informed of his comings and goings. My teen should do her homework regularly and get good grades. My teen should get a full night's sleep. My teen should stay away from drugs and alcohol. My teen should practice safe sex. My teen should drive responsibly.* These are good rules. Wouldn't you agree?

Now, be honest. Do you have the power and control to get your teen to do any of these things on a highly consistent basis? Most of us don't, and it's unrealistic to think that we should. Having limited control over your teen's choices and behavior is a reality for all of us. Sure, you can wish and hope your teen behaves the way you'd like, but wishes and hopes are soft limits that carry little enforceability. Without enforceability, you don't really have a rule at all. At best, you have a hopeful expectation or a hypothesis for how your teen should behave. Most teens don't take these signals seriously, and neither should you.

Unfortunately, many parents do take their soft limits seriously. Worse yet, they mistakenly believe their teen shares the same perception. Is this a setup for miscommunication, conflict, and disappointment? You bet. Believing you're teaching a rule when you're not is self-deception on a large scale, and most parents are not even aware they're doing it. Awareness is the key to breaking free.

Soft limits are like land mines in a minefield. They blow up on you and cost you endless hours of grief and disappointment. How do you clear your minefield?

First, you need to recognize them for what they are and avoid them. Soft limits sabotage your ability to influence your teen's choices and behavior.

Recognizing that perfect control is a myth and limited control is a reality, how do we maximize the limited influence and control we do have? You avoid the things that don't work (soft limits) and use the tools that have been tested and proven: firm limits. The best we can do is set up an effective learning experience for our teens with guidance tools that carry a higher degree of enforceability. Let's continue our discussion by looking at the signals you should avoid.

## Soft Limits: Yellow Lights with No Tickets

Fifteen-year-old Andrew arrives in the kitchen attracted by the aroma of freshly baked chocolate chip cookies his mother prepared for dessert. He knows he's not supposed to have sweets before dinner, but while his mother is busy on the phone, he helps himself to a handful of cookies. When she discovers what he's doing, she intervenes.

"Andrew! You know you're not supposed to have cookies or sweets before dinner," she says. "You'll ruin your appetite." Andrew looks apologetic but continues to eat the cookies. His mother continues to reason with him.

"If I allowed you to eat sweets anytime you want," she adds, "you'd never be hungry at meals and you wouldn't get the nutrition you need. If you feel like eating something before dinner, let me know first. Okay? I'll find something that doesn't ruin your dinner." Andrew nods as he grabs another handful of cookies.

"All right, honey," says his mother. "You'll ask next time, won't you?" Andrew nods again as he gulps down the last few cookies.

Andrew's mother is using soft limits to communicate her rule about eating sweets before meals. By the time she finishes talking, she believes her message got across, but has it? What did Andrew really learn about eating sweets before dinner?

Andrew understood his mother's words and gave many of

the appropriate responses, but he also finished off two hand-fuls of cookies while his mother lectured. What Andrew really learned is that eating sweets before dinner is actually okay, as long as he can endure his mother's annoying lectures. The limits Andrew's mother allowed conveyed a very different message than she intended. If she had removed the cookies or made them unavailable, she would have conveyed the message she intended.

Soft limits are rules in theory, not in practice, because they're not enforced. They invite testing because they carry a mixed message. The words seem to say stop, but the action message says that stopping is neither expected nor required. Andrew understood this clearly and responded the way many teens do when they encounter unclear signals. He acknowl-edged the signal but continued to do what he wanted.

From a teaching-and-learning perspective, soft limits are ineffective because they fail to give teens the information they need to make acceptable choices. The signals simply fail to get the message across. Worse yet, they invite testing, escalating misbehavior, and power struggles.

Soft limits come in a variety of forms. They can be ineffec-tive verbal messages or ineffective action messages. Sometimes they are both at the same time. All share the feature of being ineffective at communicating an intended limit or message. Most parents who use these signals do so without realizing their actual impact. Let's look at some typical examples.

## Wishes, Hopes, and Shoulds

Maddie, age fourteen, knows she's not supposed to play computer games on her father's expensive new computer with the large high-resolution monitor, but when no one is looking, she turns it on and does it anyway. The graphics are great. Her mother enters the room and sees what she's doing.

"Maddie, I really wish you wouldn't play with your father's new computer. Didn't he ask you not to play with it?" Maddie ignores her and continues playing. Her mother tries again.

"What are you supposed to do when you want to play computer games?" her mother asks again. "Remember what Daddy said?" Maddie ignores her again and continues playing.

"Maddie! I'm getting angry," says her mother. "I really hope you stop before I get even angrier."

*I'll bet you do,* Maddie says to herself, but she makes no move to stop.

Did you hear a clear message that Maddie is expected and required to stop playing with her father's new computer? Maddie didn't. Wishes, hopes, and shoulds are another way of saying that stopping would be nice, but you don't really have to. Compliance is optional, not required. When teens hear these messages, particularly strong-willed teens and fence sitters, they test for clarification. That's exactly what Maddie did when she ignored her mother and continued to play. Do you think Maddie and her mother are likely to repeat this scene?

## Repeating and Reminding

Jamal, age sixteen, sits in the living room watching his favorite television show with the volume cranked up high.

"Jamal! Turn the TV down!" his annoyed father yells from the other room. Jamal ignores the first request. Several minutes go by.

"How many times do I have to tell you? Turn the TV down. Are you deaf?" his father yells again. Jamal continues to ignore the request.

"The neighbors can hear your show from across the street!" his father yells. Again, no response.

Finally, Jamal's father enters the room, stands between Jamal and the TV, and, with one hand on the on/off button, says, "Turn it down or I'll turn it off." This time, Jamal gets up and turns the volume down.

What happened the first time Jamal ignored his father's request? Nothing. Jamal got what he wanted. The second and third requests followed the same pattern. If Jamal's father didn't mean what he said the first three times, why should Jamal take him seriously? He doesn't.

Jamal's father's words seem to say, "Turn it down," but what does his action message, or lack of one, say to Jamal? Of course, "I'm not going to do anything about it, at least not for a while." If you are a teen who really wants to watch your show with the volume high, which message would you follow? Like many teens, Jamal doesn't decide to turn the volume down until he has to—that is, when his father actually decides to enforce his rule. Parents who repeat and remind without following through are actually teaching their teens to tune out and ignore.

# Warnings and Second Chances

Fifteen-year-old Darryl antagonizes his younger brother and calls him "a shithead." His mother intervenes.

"Darryl, it's not okay to call your brother names, especially that name. It's not nice."

"Well, he is a shithead," Darryl insists, with a mischievous smile. He enjoys the strong reaction.

"You may not talk to your brother or anyone else like that!" says his mother in a serious tone. "Do you understand me? That's a warning." Darryl enjoys the live entertainment and decides to push it a little further.

"Shithead, shithead, Max is a shithead," says Darryl, in a singsong voice. Now his mother is really angry.

"Stop it now!" she shouts. "I really mean it. This is your last warning. If I hear that word again, you'll lose your car keys and cell phone for the rest of the day."

"Okay," says Darryl, in a less than sincere tone. "You're right. That wasn't kind. Max is really a butthead anyway."

"Give me your keys and cell phone," says his mother. "You've crossed the line."

"What line?" Darryl protests. "That's not fair! I called him something else. You're changing the rules."

"You knew what I meant," says his mother, "but I'll give you one last chance. If I hear any more name-calling, I really will take your keys and phone." Darryl has gotten about as much entertainment as he wanted and leaves the room.

How many times did Darryl call his brother a name? What happened each time he did? He got more warnings and second chances. If calling names is really not okay, why did she permit it to happen six times?

## Reasoning and Explaining

Thirteen-year-old Janice has been told she's not supposed to use her skateboard without wearing knee and elbow pads, but she decides to do it anyway and gets caught.

"Skateboards are really dangerous, Janice," says her concerned father. "Knees, wrists, and elbows take a long time to heal."

"Safety pads are stupid," complains Janice. "None of my friends have to wear them. They haven't been hurt badly."

"They've been lucky," her father replies. "Your doctor says he says sees skateboard injuries on a regular basis. Your mother and I are not willing to take those risks with you. We want you safe. I hope you consider the risks before you decide to skate without them."

Janice's father believes his reasons and explanations will convince his daughter to follow his rule and use safety gear, but what happens if Janice is not convinced? Nothing. She can still skate without the safety gear. His rule is not a rule at all. It's a hopeful theory at best. Janice may have to listen to more of his reasons and explanations. She can live with that if she can still avoid wearing the gear.

If Janice's father expects her to use safety gear when she skates, he needs to support his words with effective action and take away her skateboard for two or three days each time she decides to skate without safety gear.

## Speeches, Lectures, and Sermons

Sandra, age fourteen, knows she's supposed to come directly home after school but decides instead to hang out with her friends. She arrives home nearly two hours late.

"Where have you been?" asks her concerned mother. "This is the second time this week. You know how your father and I feel about this. We worry. I called the school, and I was about to call the police."

"I went with Meredith to get a Coke," replies Sandra. "I didn't realize how much time went by."

"This is so inconsiderate," says her mother. "What would our house be like if all of us just showed up whenever we pleased? Your brother and father have the courtesy to call me when they expect to be late. I expect the same courtesy from you. Is that asking too much? Please don't let this happen again."

Did you hear a clear message that showing up late would not be tolerated? Sandra didn't. Will her mother's lecture help Sandra arrive home on time next time she feels like hanging out with one of her friends? Not likely. Sandra understands that her parents' rule about showing up late is not one she has to follow. Sandra is not likely to take her mother's rule seriously unless her mother starts suspending Sandra's after-school privileges for three or four days each time this happens.

## Statements of Fact

Sixteen-year-old T.J. is supposed to take off his wet and dirty shoes before he enters the house, but he's in a hurry and walks in anyway. He leaves a trail of muddy footprints all the way to the kitchen.

"You make me so mad!" says his mother when she notices the mess. "This carpet is hard to clean. I'm tired of cleaning up your messes." T.J. hurries out the door while his mother cleans up the mess.

Do you think these statements will dissuade T.J. from entering the house with dirty or wet shoes next time he's in a hurry? Probably not. He knows he can count on his mother to clean up the mess. If she really wants him to take her seriously and not wear dirty shoes in the house, she needs to make him clean up his messes each time it happens. Statements of fact, without enforceability, are simply ineffective statements of annoyance and helplessness.

## Ignoring Unacceptable Behavior

Thirteen-year-old Allison enjoys the attention she receives when she brings up disgusting topics at mealtimes. Her parents ignore this behavior in the hope it will eventually go away, but Allison hasn't stopped.

"My friend Kendra had the worst case of diarrhea this morning," Allison reports as her family sits down for dinner. "She crapped her pants during her second-period class. It stunk so bad! The teacher had to call the custodian to clean up the mess." Allison looks around the table for a reaction.

"I didn't need to know that," says her older brother, disturbed by the image. Allison's parents are disgusted, too, but try to ignore her comments.

"You haven't heard the worse part," Allison continues. "I helped her clean up in the bathroom before she went home. She had it all over herself. It was so gross!"

"Would you shut up!" her brother shouts. Allison smiles mischievously. Her parents continue to ignore her. Mealtimes aren't fun for Allison's parents.

What makes us think that the absence of a green light is equivalent to a red light? At best, it's a yellow light, and we know how many teens respond to yellow lights. When we ignore misbehavior that is unacceptable, we're really saying: It's Okay to do that. Go ahead. You don't have to stop.

If Allison's parents really want her to stop saying disgusting things at the dinner table, they need to stop ignoring it and start enforcing their expectations by excusing Allison from the table each time she does this.

## Unclear Directions

Eli, age seventeen, shows up late for dinner on a regular basis. His parents are annoyed. As he heads out the door to visit one of his friends, his mother reminds him, "We're eating at six p.m. Don't be too late."

What does "too late" mean to a seventeen-year-old who wants to hang out with his friends? Six thirty? Seven? Or later? And who decides? Eli knows what the market will bear. When he's late, his parents routinely wait for him. So far, he has managed to arrive home late on a regular basis and sit down to a warm meal.

Unclear or open-ended directions invite testing and set up

both parents and teens for conflict. If Eli's parents really expect him to return home for dinner by 6 p.m., then they need to enforce their rule with effective action. They need to serve their meal at 6 p.m. and not heat it up when Eli arrives late. The most they need to say is, "Our dinners are at six p.m." He'll arrive on time if he wants a warm meal.

## Ineffective Role Modeling

Curt, age fourteen, and his brother Chris, age twelve, get into a heated argument over a video game. The quarrel disturbs their father, who decides to check it out. When he arrives on the scene, he sees the boys pushing and shoving and shouting names at each other while they wrestle for the controller.

"What the hell is going on?" their father shouts. He pushes Curt away from his brother and shoots Chris an intimidating look. "Can't you two share the game without acting like a couple of jerks?" their father says, angrily. He grabs the controller out of Chris's hand and smashes it on the floor. "That should stop your fighting for a while."

What did the boys learn from this? They were trying to resolve a conflict by yelling, shoving, and name-calling. So what did their father do? He tried to resolve their conflict with more yelling, shoving, and name-calling. In effect, he's teaching them to do the same thing he's punishing them for. If he really wants to teach them to share the game without quarreling over it, he simply needs to stop the game and put it away for the rest of the day each time it happens.

## Pleading, Begging, and Cajoling

Fifteen-year-old Cheri is fully capable of getting herself dressed and out the door at 7:45 in time for high school, but each morning she goes into a stall.

"Come on, Cheri," her mother urges. "Please hurry. We need to leave the house in the next ten minutes." Cheri is unconcerned. Her hair is still wet from her shower, and she hasn't even started to apply her eye makeup. Her mother tries again.

"Would you like to use my hair dryer?" her mother asks. "Your hair will dry faster, and you'll have more time for your makeup."

"No, thanks," Cheri replies. "I like my dryer better. I'll put my eye makeup on in the car."

"Please hurry, then," pleads her mother. "We should be leaving right now." Five more minutes tick by. Cheri's hair still isn't dry. Her mother tries another tactic.

"Cheri, I'll wait for you in the car. If I see you in the next two minutes, I'll surprise you with something nice after school." Five more minutes go by. Finally, Cheri arrives at the car.

Parents who plead, beg, and cajole their teens to cooperate are really saying: Do the job when you feel like it. Who decides when or if the job gets done at all? The teen. Cheri knows compliance is optional, not required, so she delays the job to get the maximum attention possible.

If Cheri's mother really expects her daughter to get dressed in a timely manner, she needs to state her rule clearly and firmly and enforce her words with effective action. Her message should sound something like this: "Cheri, we're leaving the house at seven forty-five and no later. If you want a ride from me, you need to be in the car at seven forty-five. If you're not there on time, then it's up to you to get to school on your own. You can walk or start riding the bus again." No pleading. No begging. No cajoling. After a few of these experiences, Cheri will likely take her mother seriously and be ready to leave by 7:45.

## Bargaining and Negotiating

Nathan, age thirteen, is supposed to clean up the dog run, comb out the dogs, and add fresh water to their drinking bowls on Saturdays before he does anything else, but decides to take off with his friends and tell his parents he forgot. As he walks out the door, his father reminds him, "Don't forget to take care of your dog jobs."

"Do I have to?" Nathan asks. "The dog run is in pretty good shape and the dogs look fine."

"Remember our agreement when we got the dogs?" asks his father. "You promised you'd do it first thing on Saturdays."

"I know," says Nathan, "but why can't I do them this afternoon or tomorrow? I'll get the job done this weekend. I promise."

"You said the same thing last weekend and never did get around to it," reminds his father. "If you get the jobs done now, you'll have the rest of the day to be with your friends without anything hanging over you."

"But my friends and I arranged a basketball game this morning. Can't we compromise? I'll add fresh water to their bowls and do the rest tomorrow. I promise." He senses his dad wearing down.

"Okay," says his father in frustration, "but I'm not going to let you do this every time. Do you understand?"

"I understand," says Nathan.

What Nathan really understands is that his father's rule about taking care of the dogs on Saturdays is negotiable. To many teens, particularly strong-willed teens, negotiable feels a lot like optional. What do you think will happen next time Nathan doesn't feel like handling his dog chores? Parents who routinely bargain and negotiate over their limits invite their teens to test and redefine their rules.

## Arguing and Debating

Lucas, age fourteen, works on his bike all afternoon and leaves tools and bike parts spread all over the garage. Lucas also hates to clean up messes. You can imagine his reaction when his mother announces, "It's time to pick up all your stuff in the garage so your father can park the car when he gets home."

"I'll do it later," Lucas replies. "I'm tired."

"I'm sure you are," says his mother, "but you know the rule. It's your job to pick up your things in the garage before your father gets home."

"Sometimes you don't pick up your things when you're done with them," counters Lucas. "I don't see why I have to pick up my things if you don't have to pick up yours."

"You know that's not true," says his mother. "I always pick up after myself."

"Not your sewing stuff," says Lucas.

"Those things are in my sewing room," says his mother. "They're not in anybody's way. Now, do what you're asked, please."

"That's not fair!" protests Lucas.

"I've had enough of your arguing," says his mother. "You know the rule. Now do it."

"Yeah, it's a stupid rule," Lucas snaps back.

What is the message Lucas's mother sends by arguing and debating over her rules? Sure, her rules are negotiable. What's not happening while all the arguing and debating is going on? Lucas is not picking up. That won't happen until the argument is over, and some arguments can go on for quite a while.

By participating in a verbal sparring match with her fourteen-year-old, Lucas's mother is really inviting a power struggle by encouraging her son to test her limits.

## Bribes and Special Rewards

Sixteen-year-old Kobe hates to do chores. When asked, he digs in his heels, protests, argues, and tries to negotiate his way out of them. His parents fear he's going to be a lousy college roommate because he's so unwilling to pick up after himself. A well-intended relative suggests bribing him.

*Perhaps she's right*, Kobe's father says to himself. *Kobe likes money*. The next day he asks Kobe to take the trash out of his room.

"No way!" says Kobe.

"I'll pay you two bucks. It'll take less than two minutes," offers his father.

"Okay," says Kobe. "Show me the money." His father hands him two bucks, and Kobe promptly takes out the trash.

*That worked great!* his father says to himself. The next day, he asks Kobe to clean up his mess in the kitchen.

"Forget it," says Kobe.

"I'll pay you two bucks," offers his Father. Kobe thinks about it.

"I'll do it for three bucks," says Kobe. His father gives him three bucks and Kobe cleans up his mess in the kitchen. Kobe's father uses this approach for the next three weeks and gets Kobe to do things he's never done before.

By the end of the month, Kobe's father has paid out nearly seventy dollars. He begins to question the wisdom of his approach.

*Nobody paid me to pick up after myself when I was a teenager,* his father says to himself. The more he thinks about it, the madder he gets. The next day he decides to confront Kobe about cooperation.

"Kobe, would you take the recycling out to the garage?" his father asks.

"What's it worth to you?" Kobe asks.

"You've shown me for almost a month that you can pick up after yourself," says his father. "I don't think I should have to pay you for doing things you're capable of doing on your own."

"Then forget it," says Kobe. "That's not fair! I'm not doing it." That's when his father realizes he's been sending the wrong message.

When parents offer teens bribes and special rewards in return for cooperation, what they're really saying is cooperation is optional and contingent upon receiving a reward. Is this the message you want to send to your teen? Often, cooperation stops as soon as the reward is withheld.

## Inconsistency Between Parents

One of the biggest soft limits of them all is inconsistency between parents. When one parent says, "yes," and the other says, "no," it's like living under the same roof with two governments operating simultaneously. Which government prevails? Who knows? But teens know how to find out. They test. Inconsistent limit setting between parents sets everyone up for testing and conflict.

For example, seventeen-year-old Megan asks to use the car to visit a friend. Her mom says, "If you finish your chores you can go." Megan appeals to her father, who says, "It's okay, dear, she can finish her chores when she gets back." He holds the door open for Megan to escape. What message does Megan receive about her parents' rules and expectations?

In effect, there are two sets of rules operating. Mom's rule says, "Do your chores before you leave," and Megan's father's rule says, "You don't have to." Whose rule prevails? Yes, Dad calls the shots.

What will happen next time Megan asks to visit a friend and her mom is home alone? What will Megan say? Of course. "Dad says I can do it when I get back." If Dad is home alone and insists that Megan finishes her chores before she leaves, she'll likely say, "Last time you said I didn't have to do it." In either event, inconsistency between parents sets everyone up for testing and conflict.

*Examples of Ineffective Verbal Messages (Soft Limits)*
- "Would you try to be nice for a change?"
- "I need you to be home on time, okay?"
- "Can't you see I'm on the phone?"
- "I don't like your attitude."
- "How would you like it if I interrupted you?"
- "Wipe that smirk off your face."
- "I don't believe it. You actually cooperated!"

*Examples of Ineffective Action Messages (Soft Limits)*
- Allowing your teen to walk away from a mess
- Cleaning up your teen's messes for him
- Ignoring unacceptable behavior in the hope it will go away
- Calling hurtful names to show your teen how that feels
- Rescuing your teen from experiencing unpleasant consequences
- Giving in to drama
- Making excuses for your teen's unacceptable behavior
- Arguing with your teen about your rules
- Relaxing your standards in the hope some work will get done

# Firm Limits: When No Really Means No

Did you see yourself in any of the examples of soft limits? If so, you just took a big step toward clearing your minefield. Keep these examples in mind as you work to improve your limit-setting skills. Most of these ineffective messages are simply bad habits we do unconsciously. Catch yourself when you're about to use them and replace them with a firm limit-setting message that really works, like the parents in the following examples.

Fifteen-year-old Lizzie and her mother plan a shopping trip to the factory outlets. Her mother sets a sixty-dollar spending limit for Lizzie's purchases. "Choose carefully," says her mother. "We're going to stay on budget."

They finish their shopping and head to the checkout counter. Lizzie lays out all of her items and the cashier rings them up. Lizzie's tab comes to seventy-five dollars.

"Where did that camisole come from?" her mother asks. "That wasn't on your list, and you're over budget."

"Please?" pleads Lizzie. "I really want it. It looks so good on me." The salesclerk looks to Lizzie's mother for a decision.

"Put it back, Lizzie," says her mother, matter-of-factly. "You remember our agreement."

"Please?" Lizzie begs. "Just this once?"

"No," says her mother once again. "Put it back, please." Lizzie decides to play her drama card. She gets teary and continues to protest. The clerk looks at Lizzie's mother once again for a decision.

"Please deduct the camisole from the total," Lizzie's mother says to the clerk. She pays the bill and leaves with her whimpering daughter. No yelling. No screaming. No threats or angry lectures. And no giving in. After five minutes of pouting, Lizzie regains her composure.

In a separate example, thirteen-year-old Clayton is eating

dinner with his family when his cell phone rings. His dad shoots him a disapproving look.

"Clayton, you know the rule: No cell phones at the dinner table," says his dad. "Please don't bring it again." Clayton checks to see who called, then quickly places the phone in his pocket. His family continues with their meal.

Five minutes later, Clayton's dad notices him texting with the phone concealed in his lap. His dad gets up, walks over to Clayton, and collects the phone. No shaming or blaming. No warnings or second chances. He simply enforces his rule.

"You can have it back after dinner," says his father, matter-of-factly. "If this happens again, I'll collect your phone before meals on a regular basis. Is that clear?"

Clayton nods.

Lizzie's mom and Clayton's dad are using firm limits to communicate their rules and expectations. Their words say stop, and their actions convey the same message when they enforce their rules with instructive consequences. Both teens receive a very clear message and collect the research data they need to make a better choice next time. Firm limits carry a high level of enforceability. Teens know that compliance is both expected and required.

Firm limits send clear signals to teens about our rules and expectations. They understand that we mean what we say because they experience what they're told. Words are consistent with actions. When these tools are used consistently, teens learn to regard our words more seriously, test less, and cooperate more often for the asking. The result—better communication, less testing, and fewer power struggles.

### *Examples of Effective Verbal Messages (Firm Limits)*
- "Turn down the TV or I'll have to turn it off."
- "Take your shoes off the sofa, please."
- "Be home for dinner by five thirty, please."
- "Finish your chores before using the cell phone."
- "Your curfew is eleven. I'll expect you home at that time."
- "Notify me if you expect to be late."

### *Examples of Effective Action Messages (Firm Limits)*
- Turning off the TV when your teen refuses to turn it down
- Asking your teen to move off the sofa when he refuses to take off his shoes
- Not warming up dinner when your teen arrives late
- Confiscating your teen's cell phone when she uses it before completing chores
- Revising a curfew time to ten thirty when your teen shows up after eleven
- Suspending visitation privileges for a few days when teens fail to inform you

## Chapter Summary

Limits come in two basic varieties: firm and soft (see Table 5). Soft limits (when no means yes, sometimes, or maybe) are rules in theory, not in practice, because they carry a low level of enforceability. They come in a variety of forms, but all invite testing and resistance as teens attempt to clarify what we really expect. Soft limits are a predictable setup for testing and power struggles.

Firm limits (when no means no) are the gold standard for guiding an effective learning experience because they carry a high level of enforceability. Teens understand that compliance is both expected and required. Firm limits are your ticket to credibility and cooperation.

*Table 5 Comparison of Firm and Soft Limits*

|  | *Firm* | *Soft Limits* |
|---|---|---|
| *Characteristics* | Stated in clear behavioral terms | Stated in unclear terms or as "mixed messages" |
| | Words supported by actions | Actions do not support rules or expectations |
| | Compliance expected | Compliance not expected |
| | High enforceability | Little or no enforceability |
| | Provides data to make cooperative choices | Insufficient data to make cooperative choices |

| | | |
|---|---|---|
| **Predictable Outcomes** | Cooperation | Resistance, noncompliance |
| | Decreases limit testing | Increases limit testing |
| | Clear understanding of rules and expectations | Escalating power struggles |
| | Tune in to parents' words | Tune out parents' words |
| **Teens Learn** | No means no. | No means yes, sometimes, or maybe. |
| | Cooperation is expected. | Cooperation is optional. |
| | Rules apply to me. | Rules are for others. |
| | I am responsible. | I'm not responsible. |
| | "My parents mean what they say." | "My parents don't mean what they say." |

## CHAPTER 8

# How to Be Clear with Your Words

A clear limit-setting message begins with your words, and most often, that's where communication breaks down because parents say and do more than is needed. Anger, drama, and strong emotion can easily sabotage the clarity of your message and reduce the likelihood of cooperation. It's not only what you say that matters; it's how you say it. Your words are an important part of your overall message.

This chapter will show you how to use your words in the clearest and most understandable way. By following a few simple guidelines, you'll learn how to give your aggressive researcher the information he or she needs to make an acceptable choice and cooperate from the beginning without inviting needless testing. Let's look at how Conner's parents do this with their fifteen-year-old.

Conner, age fifteen and a half, recently completed his driver's training classes, passed the written test, and got his driver's permit. He's eager to get behind the wheel. He asks his father if he can drive the family car on a shopping outing. His father agrees, but only blocks from the house, his father questions Conner's readiness.

"Conner, slow down," says his father. "This is a residential area, with a posted speed limit of 25 miles per hour. You're going 38."

"Are you serious?" Conner replies. "Nobody drives 25 around here."

"Well, I expect you to do that if you want to drive the car," says his father. Conner rolls his eyes but slows down. When he enters a busier street with more traffic, Conner's father notices another problem.

"Conner, you're following the car in front of you way too close," says his father. "You should allow one car length for every 10 miles per hour. We're going over 40 and you have less than one full interval."

"Dad, I'm driving, not you," Conner says in an irritated tone. He continues his speed and one-car interval.

"If you're not willing to follow the traffic laws, then you're done driving for today," says his father, matter-of-factly. "Pull the car over and park, please, at the next convenient place," says his father. "We'll try it again another day if you're willing to obey the traffic laws." No shaming. No blaming. No shouting. No drama. The focus of his message is on Conner's driving, not on attitude, feelings, or Conner's worth as a person. He simply tells Conner how he expects him to drive and what will happen if he doesn't drive that way.

Conner's father gives a clear, firm limit-setting message about his rules and expectations. Conner has all the information he needs to make an acceptable choice and cooperate. He may or may not, but either choice will lead to good learning if his father follows through. His father's clear message sets up an instructive lesson.

## Guidelines for Giving Clear Messages

The key to giving a clear, firm limit-setting message with your words is to say only what needs to be said, in a firm and respectful manner. The following tips will help you get started.

### KEEP THE FOCUS ON BEHAVIOR

Our primary goal in guidance situations is to reject unacceptable behavior, not the teen performing the behavior. Therefore, we should begin our message with the focus on the right thing—behavior, not on attitude, feelings, or the worth of your teen. Messages that shame, blame, criticize, or humiliate go too far. They reject your teen along with the unacceptable behavior and obscure the clarity of your message. The focus is misdirected.

For example, if you want your fourteen-year-old to stop poking and antagonizing his younger brother, a clear message would be "Keep your hands off your brother, please," or "Stop poking your brother," not "How would you feel if someone continued to poke you after you asked them to stop?" or "Why do you have to be such a pest?" These messages fail to provide the essential information your teen needs, namely that poking his brother is not okay and must stop.

### BE SPECIFIC AND DIRECT

A clear, firm limit-setting message should inform teens, specifically and directly, what it is you want them to do. If necessary, tell them when and how to do it. The fewer the words, the better.

For example, if you want your thirteen-year-old home to

clean up her mess at the table, before she leaves the dining room your message should be, "Clean up your mess at the table, please, before you leave. That means clearing your plate and salad bowl, picking up your silverware, and wiping off the table where you were seated."

If instead your message is "I hope you do a better job cleaning up tonight," or "Please leave the table a little cleaner tonight," who decides what "a better job" and "a little cleaner" means? You or your teen? Without a specific and direct message, your teen's interpretation of your message will probably fall short of your expectations.

## USE YOUR NORMAL VOICE

The tone of your voice is important. A raised, irritated, or angry voice shifts the focus of your request away from behavior and onto feelings. That's when teens are most likely to test your message or try to hook you into a power struggle.

Your tone should convey that you are firm, in control, and resolute in your expectations that they must do what you ask them to do. The best way to communicate this expectation is simply to state your message matter-of-factly in your normal voice.

Firm limits are not stated harshly. It's not necessary to yell, scream, or raise your voice to convince your teen that you mean what you say. If needed, your actions when you enforce your rule will convey that message more powerfully than your words. Just say what you want your teen to do in your normal voice and be prepared to move on to your action step and enforce your rule if your teen decides to test.

Sound easy? It is for some parents, but not for others,

particularly those who grew up in homes where yelling and screaming were commonplace. Over time, the feelings of anger and frustration and the urge to yell become deeply engrained habits and nearly automatic responses. Old habits don't disappear overnight just because you're inspired to do things differently. You have to work at it. Managing anger and strong emotions is a skill you can learn; but like most new skills, the learning process takes time, patience, and lots of practice. Chapters 11 and 12 will offer some tips to help you get started.

## SPECIFY THE CONSEQUENCES FOR NONCOMPLIANCE

Remember, strong-willed teens and most fence sitters are aggressive researchers. When you ask them to stop doing something, the first thought in your teen's mind is *Or what? What are you going to do if I don't stop?* They want to know the bottom line because they're planning on taking you there anyway. So get to the bottom line quickly. You can prevent a lot of testing and power struggles by simply providing your teen with all the information he or she needs to make an acceptable choice from the beginning.

If you expect your teen to test, tell him or her, in your normal voice, what will happen if he or she doesn't cooperate. This is not a threat. You're just being clear by providing your teen with all the information he or she needs to make an acceptable choice. Be prepared to follow through and enforce your rule if necessary. Your credibility hangs in the balance.

For example, if your sixteen-year-old asks to use the car but you need it back by five, and you expect her to test, your message should be "I expect you to return with the car by five o'clock or the keys will stay in my pocket for the rest of the week." Now your teen has all the information she needs to make an acceptable choice. She may or may not, but either way, you set up an effective learning experience. If you do this consistently, she'll know you mean what you say.

## Chapter Summary

A firm limit-setting message begins with our words, and most often, that's where communication breaks down. Anger, drama, and strong emotion can easily sabotage the clarity of your message. You don't need a lot of words or anger or drama to show that you mean business. You simply need to state your expectation clearly and be prepared to follow through.

A clear limit-setting message focuses on behavior, not on attitude, feelings, or the worth of your teen. Your message should be specific and direct and delivered in a firm, respectful tone. If you expect testing, inform your teen in advance what will happen if he or she decides not to cooperate. A clear guidance message reduces testing and sets up instructive learning experiences for teens of all temperaments and learning styles.

## CHAPTER 9

# Stopping Power Struggles Before They Begin

The best way to stop a power struggle is not to start one. We should begin with a clear, firm limit-setting message, resist the tempting baits teens use to hook us into power struggles, and hold firm. Hannah's father does this effectively in the following example. You can, too, but don't expect your teen to give up his or her testing quickly.

Hannah, age fifteen, can argue circles around most adults. She can argue and debate like a courtroom attorney or develop sudden hearing loss and tune out even the clearest request. She knows just the right moment to become emotional or dramatic when she thinks her parents are wearing down or close to giving in. Hannah can hook adults into power struggles faster than any student in her high school.

But Hannah's parents are catching on to her tricks. They're beginning to see her behavior for what it is, a manipulative power struggle, and they're ready to put an end to it. One Saturday morning, as Hannah begins her usual chores, she gets an invitation to join a girlfriend for a trip to the mall. "Can I go, Dad?" she asks.

"Yes," he replies, "after your chores are finished." Hannah is halfway down the hall before he finishes his sentence. *Did she hear what I said?* he wonders. *I'd better check in to make sure.*

When he arrives at Hannah's room, she's busy getting dressed for the mall. "Did you hear what I asked you to do before you go?" he asks.

Hannah looks at him blankly. She really did tune out. So he repeats his original request. "I said you have to finish your chores before you go."

"But, Dad!" Hannah protests. "My friends will be here in thirty minutes. I can do my chores when I get back." Her dad is tempted to argue the issue, then stops himself.

"We're done talking about it, Hannah," he says matter-of-factly and leaves the room.

*He doesn't mean it,* Hannah says to herself. *He'll come back and remind me a few more times, then we'll argue, then my friends will come, and he'll have to let me go. The plan has always worked before.*

As predicted, Hannah's dad returns in a few minutes, but instead of reminding and arguing, he surprises her with an announcement. "You have fifteen minutes to finish your chores," he says. "I'll set the timer if you'd like, but if they are not done, you can't go." Then he leaves the room.

*Hey! What's going on?* Hannah asks herself. *No reminders? No arguments? No pleading and cajoling? And no giving in? He's not supposed to do that.* She's in shock. Quickly, she scrambles to finish her chores before her friends arrive. Hannah's father skillfully ended this power struggle before it got started.

Your teen is unlikely to quickly give up manipulative strategies that have worked in the past. You should expect your teen to challenge even your clearest request and do everything he or she can to hook you back into a power struggle and wear you down. You might be tempted to go along with it, too. This chapter will help you resist the urge by recognizing the bait, avoiding the hook, and staying out of the power struggle. Let's begin with the baits and how to avoid them.

## When Teens Tune Out, Check In

One of the best ways for teens to hook parents or any adult into a power struggle is to tune out and ignore their requests. When this happens to parents, they wonder, *Did my message get across? Am I being ignored? Is it time to support my words with a consequence?*

The simple act of tuning out gives your teen deniability and avoidability. If you ask, "Why didn't you do what I asked?" your teen can say, "I didn't hear you say anything, so I shouldn't have to do it."

The check-in procedure is a simple and effective way to clarify whether your message was heard or understood, without getting hooked into the old repeating and reminding routine. When in doubt, check in with your teen by saying one of the following:

"Did you understand what I said?"
"Were my directions clear?"
"Tell me in your words what you heard me say."

For example, sixteen-year-old Adrian is watching his favorite show when his mother calls him from the other room.

"Adrian, it's time to turn off the TV and wash up for dinner," she says. No response. Adrian continues to watch his program.

*Did he hear what I said?* his mother wonders. *If he did, he sure doesn't act like it.* She decides to check in. She walks into the room, stands between Adrian and the TV, and looks him directly in the eyes.

"What did I ask you to do?" she asks matter-of-factly.

"Turn off the TV and wash up for dinner," Adrian replies. He heard her accurately the first time.

"Then do it, please," says his mother, "or the TV will be off-limits for the rest of the evening." Adrian turns off the TV and goes to wash up.

*What got into her?* he wonders. *What happened to all the warnings, reminders, and threats? I should have gotten at least another ten minutes.*

In this example, Adrian understood his mother's request but decided to ignore it. He was testing. He fully expected that his avoidance tactics would buy him another ten minutes. By checking in, Adrian's mother eliminated any doubt or ambiguity about her message. Her expectation was clear, and so was the cost for noncompliance.

Let's add a new twist to the example above. Let's say that when Adrian's mother checks in, he looks at her with a blank stare because he really was tuned out, completely. What should she do?

She should give him the information he missed the first time and be prepared to turn off the TV if he doesn't cooperate. When the message is clear, it's time to act.

The check-in procedure also is useful in situations where teens give you the right response but the wrong behavior.

Ruben, age thirteen, is a good example. He knows he's not supposed to put his shoes on the couch, but he wants to get comfortable and does it anyway. His father sees him.

"Ruben, take your shoes off the couch, please," says his father.

"I will," says Ruben, but a few minutes go by and his shoes are still on the couch. His father decides to check in.

"Ruben, what did I ask you to do?" his father inquires.

"I will," says Ruben as convincingly as the first time, but he makes no move to do so. His father clarifies the message.

"Your words say you will, but your actions say you won't. Let me be more clear. If you don't take your shoes off the couch now, you'll have to sit somewhere else," says his father. This message is very clear.

*Crap! He didn't go for it,* Ruben says to himself as he takes his shoes off the couch.

## When Teens Argue, Cut It Off

The time for arguing and debating is not when your rules are being tested or violated. That's the time for action. If you take the bait and engage your teen in an argument or debate over your rules, what you're really saying is that your rules are negotiable. What's not happening during the argument? The cooperation you requested. That won't happen until the argument is over, if at all.

To strong-willed teens and most fence sitters, negotiable feels a lot like optional, and optional rules invite testing. Parents who are willing to engage teens in verbal sparring matches over their rues are opening themselves up for power struggles. How do you avoid the power struggle? By ending the argument before it starts.

The cutoff procedure is simply a respectful method for ending an argument before it develops into a power struggle. When your teen tries to hook you into arguing or debating over your rules, end the discussion by saying one of the following:

> "We're done talking about it. If you bring it up again, we're going to spend some time apart." Ask your teen to leave the area. If he or she refuses, then you leave the area. Lock yourself in the bathroom or your bedroom and don't respond to the bait when they continue to try to hook you.
>
> "The time for discussion is over. You can do what you were asked or you can spend some time by yourself getting ready to do it." Then separate yourself from your teen by asking your teen to leave the area or by leaving yourself.

For example, fourteen-year-old Elliot knows he's not supposed to use his father's expensive new camera without permission, but he really wants to take some pictures of his friends doing tricks on their skateboards. He heads out the door with the camera. His mother sees him.

"Elliot, is that your father's expensive new camera?" she asks. He nods.

"Aren't you supposed to ask your father's permission before using it?" she asks. Elliot nods again.

"I forgot," he says. "Can I use it, please? I want to get some pictures of my friends doing tricks."

His mother holds firm. She knows that if she gives in, he's going to try this again. "Not today," says his mother. "Maybe tomorrow if you ask your father's permission first."

"Come on, Mom," Elliot pleads. "Can't you give me another chance? Please? I'll ask next time, I promise."

"Sorry, Elliot," says his mother. "Not this time."

"But that's not fair!" he argues. "Dad is at work, and my friends are doing their tricks now. Can't you make an exception?"

The bait was skillfully presented. Elliot's mother was about to bite and debate the issue of fairness when she remembers what she read about ending power struggles. *Oh no,* she says to herself. *We're not going through this again.*

"Put it back, Elliot," she says matter-of-factly. "If you bring it up again, we'll need to spend some time apart." Her answer is very clear. Elliot grumbles but puts the camera back where he got it.

If you've been permissive in the past, you'll probably feel compelled, like Elliot's mother, to give reasons and explanations when your teen challenges you by asking, "Why?" Feel free to have that discussion, but make sure the discussion follows your teen's cooperation. Say something like the following:

"I'd be happy to tell you why after you do what I asked you to do." (Then arrange a time for the discussion.)

In most cases, you'll find that the issue is not about why. The real issue is whether your teen has to do what you requested. If he or she can wear you down in an argument or debate, then compliance might be optional, not mandatory.

By requiring compliance before the discussion, you eliminate the potential for a power struggle.

For example, Miranda, age thirteen, knows she's supposed to finish her homework before visiting her friends but decides to visit her friends first anyway. Her mother is suspicious and intervenes.

"Have you finished your homework?" her mother asks.

"Yeah," Miranda replies.

"May I see it, please?" asks her mother. Miranda knows she's caught.

"I can do it later," she says. Her mother holds firm.

"You know the rule, Miranda," says her mother. "Homework comes first, then time with friends."

"Why?" protests Miranda. "Give me one good reason why I should have to do it now."

"I'd be happy to after you do what you are supposed to do," says her mother.

*What's going on?* Miranda says to herself. *No arguments? No debates? Not even a discussion?* She heads off to finish her homework so she can visit her friends.


# When Teens Are Disrespectful, Cut It Off

Dwayne, age fourteen, wants to attend a late-night rock concert with a friend without any adult supervision. His parents don't believe he's ready for this privilege and tell him so. Dwayne launches into an angry, disrespectful protest.

"You guys suck as parents!" he shouts. "You never let me do anything! Tom's parents are okay with the plan. You treat me like a little kid. Give me one good reason why I can't go," says Dwayne angrily. "You guys are so full of shit!"

"We're done discussing it," says his father, matter-of-factly. "You need some time by yourself to cool down. Leave the room, please. When you do cool down, we expect an apology. It's not okay to talk to us like that." Dwayne makes an obscene gesture but leaves the room. His parents were prepared to leave the room themselves if he didn't.

There is no rule I know of that says parents should stand toe-to-toe with an angry, disrespectful teen and tolerate his or her verbal abuse. The best thing you can do, under the circumstances, is end the interaction before you or your teen says or does something you'll later regret. Someone has to act like a responsible, mature adult in this situation, and it's not likely to be your teen. The cutoff achieves this goal effectively.

Sure, Dwayne's parents were probably tempted to respond angrily on his level, yell or shout, and perhaps do something worse. But what would that accomplish? They'd simply be role-modeling the behavior they're trying to stop. Dwayne doesn't need another lesson in disrespect. He already knows that. He needs to learn to manage his angry feelings in a more mature way. That's what his parents are role-modeling.

## When Things Get Hot, Use the Cooldown

Effective problem solving is difficult for anyone to do, parents or teens, in an atmosphere of anger and strong emotion. We all get angry and frustrated from time to time. This is just a normal part of family life, but feeling angry does not have to result in problems that cause ongoing conflict, hurt, or injury. Problems and conflicts occur when we handle or manage our angry feelings ineffectively by saying or doing hurtful things to others. Managing angry feelings is a skill parents can teach and role-model for their teens. The cooldown helps us to get through these stressful situations until the time is right for problem solving. In situations of anger or extreme upset, separate yourself from your teen by saying something like the following:

> (When both parties are upset) "I think we both need some time apart to cool down. Please wait for me at (select the appropriate place) and we'll talk in ten minutes or however much time you need to cool down."
>
> (When parent is upset) "I'm feeling angry, and I need some time to cool down."

This strategy works best when parents and teens are in separate rooms during the cooldown period. Allow sufficient time for both you and your teen to restore control before attempting problem solving. People recover from upset at different rates. Don't assume your teen is ready to talk just because you are. You may want to preface your problem solving with a question such as "Are you ready to talk?" If things get hot a second time, use the procedure again. Use it as often as you need it. Consider the following.

Sam, age sixteen, and his dad are both strong-willed and

very reactive. They'd become stuck in a pattern of angry, hurtful power struggles that recently turned violent. When Sam exploded at his dad with a barrage of angry obscenities, his dad responded in kind and gave Sam a shove when Sam got too close. Sam shoved back. That's when his dad realized they couldn't continue like this without someone getting hurt. He made an appointment for both of them a short time later.

When I explored each of their temperaments, I could see Sam and his dad were two peas in a pod. Both were excitable, reactive, and tended to say hurtful things before they realized it. They needed some way to interrupt their angry power struggles. I suggested the cooldown method and showed them how it worked. They agreed to give it a try.

Shortly after our appointment, Sam borrowed the family car and left a mess on the front seat. Empty fast-food containers and napkins were strewn about, and there were ketchup splatters on the seat. When Sam's dad saw the mess, he exploded.

"Sam! Get out here!" he shouted from the garage. When Sam arrived, he braced himself for what would follow, but his dad remembered what we discussed a few days earlier. To Sam's astonishment, his dad said, "I need a few minutes by myself to cool down. Wait for me in the house, please."

Sam's dad needed a full fifteen minutes to cool down, then approached Sam in the kitchen. He calmly handed Sam some fabric cleaner and paper towels and asked him to clean up his mess. No yelling, no insults, no profanity, and no injured feelings. It felt strange to be treated respectfully. When Sam completed the job, his dad thanked him.

By using the cooldown, Sam's dad role-modeled anger

management and respectful problem solving. Both had taken a big step in the right direction.

## When Parents Cross the Line, Apologize

We all get angry from time to time, and sometimes we say hurtful things we really don't intend to the people we care about. When we do, it's time to mend fences and heal wounded feelings. A sincere apology helps mend injured feelings and conveys our respect for others. Without this step, we'll just be collecting hurt and damaging relationships that are important to us. Consider the following.

Jody, age thirteen, is having a rough day. She wakes up in a bad mood, grumps at her mother during breakfast, and leaves the house without her lunch money or a warm coat, and it's fifty degrees outside. She returns home in the afternoon more grumpy than she left.

"How was your day, honey?" asks her mom as Jody enters the house. Jody just looks at her and grunts, then begins to complain that there is never anything good to eat when she gets home.

"Would you like a fruit smoothie?" offers her mom, trying to brighten Jody's mood. "You always like those." Jody nods, but when her mother delivers the smoothie, Jody grabs it without saying thanks and begins blaming her mom for allowing her to leave the house without her coat and lunch money.

"Remembering your coat and lunch money is your job, not mine," says her mom. Jody parrots back her mom's words in a very sarcastic tone. That's when her mom loses her patience.

"Damn it, Jody!" her mom shouts. "What the hell is wrong with you? I'm sick and tired of your bratty attitude! You're behaving like a two-year-old." Her mom is about to say something even more hurtful when she realizes what she's doing and stops herself.

"Please go in the other room for a while," says her mom. "I need some time to cool down."

After the cooldown, she goes to Jody to apologize.

"I'm sorry for the hurtful things I said," her mom begins. "I lost my temper. I think you're a wonderful thirteen-year-old who's having a rough day, and I love you very much. Will you accept my apology?" Jody nods and gives her mom a big hug.

Raising a strong-willed teen, or any teen for that matter, is a challenging and exhausting job. From time to time we all lose our patience, react in frustration, and say or do things we later regret. How can we repair the damage?

An apology is the best way to begin. The gesture conveys all the right messages: "I love you, respect you, and care about your feelings." An apology helps heal the little hurts that lead to bigger hurts, resentment, and angry power struggles. Most important, an apology from a caring adult gives your teen permission to be human and imperfect and the courage to try harder.

Some parents believe that apologizing to teens is a sign of weakness that diminishes the teen's respect for the parent's authority. My years of family counseling have shown that just the opposite is true. To teens, an apology is not a sign of weakness. It's a sign of emotional strength that inspires them to try harder. Teens respect adults who have the courage to take responsibility for their own imperfections and mistakes.

## Ignore Attitude, Not Unacceptable Behavior

Grumbling, mumbling, eye rolling, door slamming, and looks of impatience and disgust are tempting baits that are hard for most parents to resist. If you bite and respond on your teen's level, then you're back in the power struggle, and what have you accomplished? A lesson in disrespect? Your teen already knows that. That's why your teen is trying to hook you in the first place. Your teen's goal is to shift the focus away from their unacceptable behavior and onto you. When your teen tries to hook you with a disrespectful attitude, remember Evan's mother in the next example. Stay focused on the right issue. Ignore the attitude, not the unacceptable behavior.

Fourteen-year-old Evan knows he's not supposed to use his PlayStation before completing his chores and homework, but his mother isn't paying attention, so he decides to do it anyway. She hears him and intervenes.

"Evan, shut down your PlayStation, please, and finish your chores and homework," she says matter-of-factly. "If you don't, the PlayStation will be off-limits the rest of the evening."

Evan gives his mother a look of disgust, rolls his eyes, mumbles something under his breath, and lets out a big har-rumph. "It's not fair!" he complains. "All my friends' parents let them play video games before chores and homework. I don't see why I should have to follow your stupid rule. I'm almost fifteen. I should be able to choose for myself when I do homework."

Evan's mother holds firm. She stands next to him and waits for him to comply. *I'm the adult. He's the kid,* she reminds herself. *I'm not going to get hooked by his attitude.* Evan shuts down the system at a turtle's pace and makes one more attempt to hook her.

"You're such a tyrant," he murmurs, loud enough to be heard. "Here's what I think of your stupid rules." Evan gives her the finger.

"No one treats me like that!" says his mother. "The Play-Station is off-limits for the rest of the week. Hand over your cell phone, too. You need to finish what you were asked to do." She leaves the room.

Evan tried his best to hook his mother with his disrespectful attitude, but she didn't take the bait. Instead, she held her ground, maintained her composure, and remained focused on getting what she wanted—his cooperation. When he saw she wasn't going to budge, he decided to escalate matters by using an obscene gesture. At this point, he crossed a line. His mother moved on quickly to her action step and suspended his PlayStation privileges for the rest of the week. Evan collected the research data his mother intended.

Does ignoring a teenager's disrespectful attitude mean that it's okay? Certainly not. It doesn't feel good, and we don't like it. But if you reward it by responding to it, you'll likely see a lot more of it. This is one of the few behaviors I encourage parents to ignore. Allow them their moment of protest, and see it for what it is—an attempt to provoke you. Don't bite.

When does attitude cross the line and become unacceptable behavior that shouldn't be ignored? This is a judgment call each parent has to make for him- or herself based upon your value system. I can offer some guidelines based on my value system. Mumbling, grumbling, eye rolling, looks of disgust, yelling, screaming "I hate you," stomping, and door slamming are baits I generally ignore. Profanity, obscene gestures, hurtful name-calling, rude gestures, throwing items, and destructive behavior (for example, breaking items) cross the line. I always respond to these with a logical consequence.

## Don't Personalize Unacceptable Behavior

When your teen misbehaves and responds with a negative attitude, do you sometimes ask yourself, *Why is she doing this to me?* If so, you're probably personalizing your teen's behavior and setting yourself up for more grief than is needed. Aggressive research is wearing, but it's not intended to be a personal attack.

Heather, age sixteen, is a good example.

Heather has been asked repeatedly not to borrow her mom's clothing without permission, but Heather's mom has some really nice outfits that Heather really likes.

"Is that my new sweater?" asks Heather's mom as Heather dashes out the door for school. "You know you're not supposed to borrow my things without permission. Why are you deliberately disobeying me?"

"Why are you such a clothes nazi?" Heather snaps back. "I wasn't going to damage it. Can't you make an exception this time?"

"No!" says her mom. "What you did is deceptive and dishonest. Take it off and put it back where you found it. Next time, ask permission."

"You're so mean!" grumbles Heather as she takes off the sweater.

Heather's testing is not intended to be a personal attack upon her mom's authority. In fact, her testing is not about her mom at all. It's about Heather and how she learns. Like many strong-willed teens, she's an aggressive researcher and has to collect a lot of data in the form of experience before she's convinced that compliance with her mom's rules is required, not optional. Persistent testing is part of her normal learning process.

Heather's mom was right on track when she made Heather put back the sweater, but she turned an instructive guidance lesson into an unnecessary relationship conflict when she personalized Heather's testing. If you tend to personalize your teen's testing, try to hold on to the bigger picture. Aggressive research is normal behavior for many teens. Parents set themselves up for needless relationship conflicts when they personalize their teen's testing.

## Chapter Summary

Let's reflect upon the new tools you added to your toolkit so far. In Chapter 8, you learned how to give a clear, firm limit-setting message with your words. In this chapter, you discovered how to stop power struggles by not taking the bait and not allowing them to get started. You're as prepared as you can be with your words, but as you know, your words are only the first part of your overall message. If your teen continues to test, then it's time to act and support your words with instructive consequences. Consequences will speak louder than your words. It's time to get acquainted with your next set of tools.

CHAPTER 10

# Supporting Rules with Natural and Logical Consequences

Your words are only the first part of your overall limit-setting message. Your aggressive researcher may decide to test and challenge even your clearest verbal message, and when this happens, the time for talking is over. Now it's time to act and support your words with instructive consequences. Consequences are the second part of your overall limit-setting message. They speak louder than your words. This chapter will show you how to use these instructive tools in the clearest and most understandable way. Get to know them. Make friends with them. You'll need to use them frequently. They are the key to enforcing your rules and your ticket to credibility.

## What Are Consequences?

We've discussed consequences throughout the book. Now it's time to get a more precise handle on what they are and how they work. *Webster's Dictionary* defines a consequence as: "1.

That which logically or naturally follows from an action or condition, 2. The relation of a result to its cause, and 3. A logical result or inference." In the context of teen guidance and limit setting, *Webster's* definition captures all the key elements of the term as it is used in this book.

Consequences are essential to the teaching-and-learning process. On an intellectual level, they help teens make the cause-and-effect connection between their choices and behavior and the outcomes of those choices. On an experiential level, consequences operate like walls. They stop unacceptable behavior. They provide clear and definitive answers to teens' research questions, and they help strong-willed teens and many fence sitters learn rules the way they learn best—the hard way. Consequences are the "hard way."

What makes these guidance experiences so effective? Consequences hold teens accountable for their behavior and impact their lives in meaningful ways. Without accountability, rules carry little enforceability, and without enforceability, rules are not really rules at all. They're hopeful expectations. Consequences give meaning and strength to your rules. That's why teens take them seriously. So should you.

The consequences in this chapter fall into two general categories: logical consequences, which we can control to a high degree, and natural consequences, which we have limited or no control over. Both provide instructive learning experiences.

This chapter will show you how to use both.

Logical consequences, the ones we can control, are structured learning experiences. They are arranged by parents, experienced by teens, and logically related to the event or situation. For example, if your fifteen-year-old exceeds the minutes on her cell phone plan, you can arrange an instructive logical consequence by suspending her cell phone privileges until she pays for the overages. The message is clear: *Use your phone responsibly or lose it.*

Natural consequences, the ones we have limited or no control over, are arranged by the world or others, experienced by teens, and naturally related to an event or situation. For example, if your thirteen-year-old goes to school without his lunch money, he may have to forgo his lunch that day. Natural consequences occur in both low- and high-risk situations. Both lead to effective learning, but the lessons are sometimes enforced by those who don't love or care about your teen. Let's look at the range of possibilities in low-risk situations.

## Natural Consequences in Low-Risk Situations

Kellen, age seventeen, has a habit of staying up late and oversleeping in the mornings. He depends on his mom to get him up for school, but that's about to change. She's tired of this routine and decides to let him learn the lesson the hard way. When his alarm goes off at six thirty, Kellen turns it off and sleeps for another forty-five minutes. He arrives at the kitchen in a panic.

"I was supposed to be up an hour ago!" he exclaims. "You let me oversleep. I'm going to be late! I'm gonna miss part of my first-period class."

"When you oversleep, you risk being late for school," says his mom, matter-of-factly. "You'd better get going. I have to leave for work."

"But I need a ride," says Kellen, "or I'll miss all of my first-period class."

"Sorry, Kellen," says his mom. "I could have given you a ride thirty minutes ago. I can't be late for work. You'll have to take your bike."

Kellen's mom is letting the natural consequence of oversleeping teach her hard-way learner the lesson he needs to learn. Like many parents, she was probably tempted to say, "I told you so," give a lecture on the poor choice of staying up late and oversleeping, or possibly even rescuing him by writing him an excuse note and giving him a ride. But she realizes that any more words on her part might sabotage the real-life consequence Kellen is about to experience. Kellen will probably think carefully before he decides to turn off his alarm and oversleep on school days.

Natural consequences, as the name implies, follow naturally from an event or situation. They are nature's version of "learning the hard way." Natural consequences require little or no involvement from parents. A lecture, an "I told you so," fixing the problem, a rescue, or adding consequences can undermine the instructional value of the lesson. This is one lesson that teaches itself.

Some parents find natural consequences easy to use and welcome opportunities to allow their teen to learn from his or her poor choices and mistakes. For other parents, natural consequences are not easy to use. When something happens, they must resist the urge to intervene and do more than is needed. If this happens to you, practice limiting your involvement to restating the obvious facts of the situation: *When you stay up too late and oversleep, you risk being late for school.* Let's look at some of the low-risk situations in which you can use natural consequences.

## WHEN AN ITEM IS LOST, DAMAGED, OR STOLEN DUE TO CARELESSNESS

**Natural Consequence:** Don't replace or repair the lost or damaged item until enough time has passed for your teen to experience the loss.

Jordan, age thirteen, receives an expensive pocket-sized video game from his parents for his birthday. Within a few days of receiving the gift, he leaves it on a bench at a neighborhood park. When he returns to find it, it's gone. He complains to his parents, who promptly buy him another one.

The second video game lasts nearly two weeks before Jordan loses it again. Once again, he complains to his parents and pleads for another one.

His parents have learned their lesson, but not Jordan. When he begs for a new one, his parents propose a different plan.

"We'll contribute half toward the purchase of a new one if you save your money, pay for the rest, and present us with a good plan for taking care of it," says his father. Reluctantly, Jordan agrees. This time, Jordan also will do the learning.

## WHEN TEENS MAKE A HABIT OF FORGETTING

**Natural Consequence:** Don't remind them or take away their responsibility by doing for them what they should be doing for themselves.

Fifteen-year-old Kendra has a habit of forgetting her homework and lunch money in the morning. Each time, one of her parents makes the dutiful trip to school to drop off the forgotten item. Noticing the pattern, her counselor suggests her parents use a natural consequence to handle the problem. She recommends that they do not make any more trips to school for a full month. Kendra is a good student. If she misses three or four lunches or assignments, it won't hurt her. Kendra's parents agree.

On Tuesday of the first week, Kendra forgets her lunch money. When lunchtime arrives, she asks the office if her parents dropped off her lunch money.

"Not yet," the secretary replies.

That night, Kendra complains to her parents, "You forgot my lunch money! I couldn't eat lunch today."

"I'm sure you'll remember tomorrow," says her father, matter-of-factly. Nothing further is said.

Kendra did remember her lunch money, but on Thursday she leaves the house without her homework. As before, she checks with the office to see if her parents have dropped it off.

"Not yet," says the secretary. Kendra gets a zero on the assignment.

Once again, Kendra complains to her parents. "You forgot to bring my homework. I got a zero on that assignment!"

"You're a good student," says her mother. "I'm sure you'll remember tomorrow." She did.

## WHEN TEENS DAWDLE OR PROCRASTINATE

**Natural Consequence:** Let them experience the outcome of their dawdling or procrastination.

Sixteen-year-old Will had three months to prepare for the written portion of his driver's test, but devotes less than ten minutes the night before the test. He fails the written portion on his first attempt and complains to his parents.

"Why didn't you tell me it was going to be that hard?" he asks.

"When you don't put in much study time, it's hard to pass the exam," his father says, matter-of-factly. "You're bright. I'm sure you'll do better next time."

Will really wants his driver's license. He's not likely to repeat this hard-way learning experience.

## WHEN TEENS FAIL TO DO THEIR PART
**Natural Consequence:** Let them experience the result.

Serena, age fourteen, knows she's supposed to put her dirty clothes in her hamper and bring them downstairs on Saturdays to be washed, but that's not what really happens. Instead, she leaves them lying all over her bedroom floor, and her frustrated mother picks them up and washes them anyway.

Her mother decides it's time for Serena to handle the complete job on her own. The next morning at breakfast, her mother announces the new plan.

"From now on, if you want your clothes washed, you'll have to put them in the hamper and bring them downstairs on Saturdays," says her mother. "Otherwise, you'll have to wash them yourself."

*She doesn't mean it*, Serena says to herself. Two weeks pass before Serena discovers she's out of some necessary items.

"Mom, I'm completely out of clean socks and underwear," Serena complains one morning.

"I didn't see any in the hamper on Saturday," replies her mother. "If they're not downstairs in the hamper, they won't be washed. You'll have to wash them yourself." She does, and she doesn't like it. On Saturday, Serena's dirty clothes are in the hamper downstairs to be washed.

# More Examples of Natural Consequences in Low-Risk Situations

## WHEN TEENS LIE OR DECEIVE OTHERS
**Natural Consequence:** Loss of trust, damaged relationships.

## WHEN TEENS MISTREAT OTHERS
**Natural Consequence:** Damaged relationships, loss of friendships, estrangement, retaliation from others.

## WHEN TEENS SPEND MONEY IMPULSIVELY
**Natural Consequence:** Wasted money, debt, disappointment.

## WHEN TEENS HAVE POOR EATING HABITS
**Natural Consequence:** Poor nutrition, obesity, health problems, low self-esteem, social alienation.

## WHEN TEENS HAVE POOR PERSONAL HYGIENE HABITS
**Natural Consequence:** Health problems, social alienation.

## WHEN TEENS HAVE POOR WORK HABITS/ STUDY SKILLS
**Natural Consequence:** Poor grades, academic failure, missed opportunities, loss of employment.

## WHEN TEENS ARE CHRONICALLY LATE
**Natural Consequence:** Loss of dependability, school detentions, irritation from others, damaged relationships, loss of employment.

# Natural Consequences in High-Risk Situations

Natural consequences are easy to use in low-risk situations when the health, safety, and welfare of our teens are minimally affected. This changes in high-risk situations when the stakes are higher. Some natural consequences can be very painful. For example, if your sixteen-year-old son decides to drink and drive and gets caught, or worse yet, gets in an accident and gets injured, he will face a number of natural consequences that are beyond your control: expensive fines, a suspended driver's license, attorney fees, court fees, higher insurance rates, medical costs, or possibly worse.

Parents can prevent, or at least minimize, some of these painful learning experiences by being proactive and arranging logical consequences you can control. Let's look at some of the high-risk natural consequences you should help your teen avoid.

## WHEN TEENS PRACTICE UNSAFE OR UNPROTECTED SEX

**Natural Consequence:** Sexually transmitted diseases, emotional and psychological distress.

## WHEN TEENS EXPERIMENT WITH DRINKING

**Natural Consequence:** Arrests, accidents, injuries, alcohol toxicity, social embarrassment, or other emotional, psychological, or physical harm.

## WHEN TEENS PRACTICE UNSAFE DRIVING

**Natural Consequence:** Arrests, accidents, injuries, suspended license, attorney fees, fines, court fees, higher insurance rates, incarceration, lawsuits.

## WHEN TEENS EXPERIMENT WITH DRUGS

**Natural Consequence:** Arrests, school suspension/expulsion, physical or psychological harm, impaired functioning, relationship problems, incarceration, court fees, attorney fees, expensive rehab programs.

## WHEN TEENS USE VIOLENT OR AGGRESSIVE BEHAVIOR AT SCHOOL

**Natural Consequence:** School suspension or expulsion, injury, social alienation, possible arrest, legal problems.

## WHEN TEENS PRACTICE UNSAFE DATING OR PARTYING

**Natural Consequence:** Physical, emotional, or psychological injury.

## WHEN TEENS ARE TRUANT FROM SCHOOL

**Natural Consequence:** Academic failure, expulsion, social alienation, involvement with juvenile justice system.

## WHEN TEENS SHOW DELINQUENT BEHAVIOR

**Natural Consequence:** Involvement with juvenile justice system, incarceration, probation, legal expenses, social alienation.

# Logical Consequences: The Gold Standard for Guidance

Logical consequences are the gold standard for teen guidance. These instructive learning experiences are arranged by adults, experienced by teens, and logically related to an event or situation. They accomplish all of your guidance goals. They stop unacceptable behavior. They hold teens accountable for their poor choices and behavior, and they teach your rules in the clearest and most understandable way. Logical consequences are ideal for setting up readiness-testing experiments or for providing instructive guidance lessons when teens test, challenge, or violate your rules. Use them as often as needed. They are your ticket to credibility.

Some parents have difficulty using logical consequences, but those who do usually encounter two types of problems. They think too hard and try to come up with the perfect consequence for each situation; or they don't think enough, and react emotionally and apply consequences in a punitive or permissive manner. Logical consequences are easy to use if you think simply and logically and follow a few basic guidelines.

# Guidelines for Using Logical Consequences

If you're willing to take a little time and get to know these tools, you'll discover that logical consequences are easy to use. Almost anyone can use them. You don't have to think on your feet like a courtroom attorney, and you don't have to rack your brain to come up with the perfect consequence for each situation. All you have to do is follow a few simple guidelines.

## THINK LOGICALLY

When you think in simple, logical terms, an appropriate logical consequence usually jumps out at you. For example, most problem behaviors involve the following situations: teens with others, teens with parents, teens with possessions or items, teens with situations, and teens with privileges. In most cases, you can arrange a logical consequence by temporarily separating your teen from others, your teen from you, your teen from an item or possession, your teen from a place or situation, or your teen from a privilege. Ask yourself what's happening and select the corresponding consequence that's most instructive.

Our world is full of examples of logical consequences. When we fail to pay our phone bill for several months, does the phone company respond by shutting off our water? No. That would not stop us from using the phone without paying. Instead, the phone company does something meaningful and applies a logical consequence. It shuts off our phone service. This sends the right message about responsibility: Pay for the service if you want to use the phone.

Remember, punitive thinking is not logical thinking. It makes little sense to take away your teen's computer or TV privileges for the evening because he put his dirty shoes on your sofa. What do video games or TV have to do with making a mess on the sofa? Nothing. What are logical consequences for making a mess on the sofa? You ask your teen to clean up the mess and remove his shoes before he sits on the sofa. The message is clear and so is the rule behind it: Don't put your dirty shoes on the furniture.

If you've relied on punitive guidance practices in the past, you will have to guard against using logical consequences in a punitive manner. Punitive consequences may stop unacceptable behavior, but they seldom teach or inspire acceptable behavior. Why? Because teens perceive them as a personal attack, and that is where the lesson ends. Punitive consequences do not inspire cooperative, respectful relationships between parents and teens.

How do you know if you have punitive tendencies? Check your thinking. If your first thoughts are *What does my teen care about? I'll show him. I'm going to take it away,* then you have punitive tendencies. Punitive thinking is not logical thinking. If you're still in doubt, examine the types of consequences you use. Are they logically related to your teen's behavior or the situation? Is your goal to inspire cooperation or to inflict pain and show your teen who's boss? If your goal is to hurt, you're probably using a punitive consequence. Think it through, and try it again.

## BE MATTER-OF-FACT

Logical consequences are most effective when carried out in a matter-of-fact manner, with your normal voice. Anger, drama, or strong emotion on your part will sabotage the instructive value of your consequence and hook your teen on an emotional level. Remember, logical consequences are intended to stop unacceptable behavior and answer your teen's research questions, not to shame, blame, humiliate, or provoke your teen.

## KEEP THEM PROPORTIONAL

Consequences are most effective when they are proportional to the seriousness of the behavior. That is, not too much, not too little, not too long, and not too short. This concept is difficult to grasp for those who operate from the punitive or permissive models. Punitive parents usually err in the "too long" and "too harsh" directions, and permissive parents usually err in the "too short" and "not meaningful" directions.

Toby's father is a good example of someone who uses punitive consequences. When Toby arrives home twenty minutes late, his father goes ballistic.

"I told you to be home by five!" he shouts. "It's five twenty. You're grounded to the house for the next two weeks."

"But, Dad, that's not fair!" complains Toby. "I was only twenty minutes late."

"Don't argue with me," says his father sternly, "or I'll add another week."

Toby's father sincerely believes that if a little is good, then a lot must be wonderful. That's why he tends to go overboard with his consequences. Long, drawn-out consequences are almost always harder on parents than on teens. Why? Because parents have to live with an angry, resentful teen for the duration of the consequence. A proportional logical consequence, such as suspending Toby's after-school privileges for the next day, would have taught the lesson just fine.

Consequences applied in a permissive manner are even less

effective. Permissive parents tend to err in the "too brief" or "too little" direction. The consequences carry little enforceability because they lack accountability. Teens don't take them seriously. Tara, age seventeen, is a good example.

Tara has been asked repeatedly not to use her mother's makeup without asking but continues to do it anyway. Her mother intervenes.

"Tara, I've asked you repeatedly not to use my makeup without my permission, but you continue to disobey me," says her mother. "So I'm going to make it unavailable for the next two days."

*Two days! What a joke!* Tara says to herself.

Do you think two days without access to her mother's makeup will keep Tara from using it again without permission? Not likely. If Tara's mother wants her consequence to be instructive, she needs to keep her makeup in a locked cabinet for several months or more. Teens can think abstractly. They understand losing access to privileges and belongings for longer periods of time, particularly when those consequences are used in readiness experiments.

## USE THEM CONSISTENTLY

Trent, age thirteen, knows he's not supposed to leave the house after dinner on school nights, but he really wants to show something to his buddy down the street.

"May I go to Tom's house for a few minutes?" he asks. He hopes his mother will make an exception, but she holds firm.

"You can see him tomorrow," she says.

*Crap!* Trent says to himself. He decides to plead his case to his father, who also holds firm. Trent remembers what happened last time he decided to avoid his parents' rule and sneak out of the house after dinner. He lost all of his after-school privileges for three days. *I'll only be gone for a few minutes,* he says to himself. *They'll never know.* He sneaks out and gets caught. Once again, his parents suspend his after-school privileges for three days. Chalk up another hard-way learning experience for Trent.

Consistent consequences are vital to effective limit setting, but consistency has many dimensions. There's consistency between what we say and what we do, between one parent and another, and from one time to the next. All are important. The teaching-and-learning process can break down when we are inconsistent in any of these areas. Trent's parents were consistent in all of them. Trent receives a very clear signal from his parents about their rule and expectations.

## FOLLOW UP WITH FORGIVENESS

When a consequence is over, it should really be over. No debriefings. No lectures or inquisitions. No rubbing their noses in it or adding an "I told you so." Your teen has already collected the needed data. Allow the experience to teach the lesson, then let it go. You're not likely to achieve much more with your words. In fact, saying or doing more may diminish the instructive value of your consequence. If your teen has not completed his or her research and chooses to repeat his or her unacceptable behavior, then provide another instructive learning experience and repeat the consequence. Use logical consequences as often as you need them, but when each consequence is over, it should be followed with forgiveness and a clean slate.

# When to Use Logical Consequences

Logical consequences can be used in a wide variety of situations. The following are just some of the many possibilities to get you thinking in the right direction.

## WHEN TEENS MISTREAT OTHERS

**Logical Consequence:** Separate your teen from others temporarily.

Seth, age fifteen, and his younger brother, Paul, age twelve, are playing video games in their living room when Seth decides to give himself an extra turn after making a mistake.

"That's not fair!" shouts Paul. "You can't take two turns in a row."

"Shut up," says Seth. "You're such a baby! I can do what I want."

"You're cheating!" Paul protests and grapples for the controls. Seth gives him a push, but Paul hangs on tight. So Seth slugs him twice on the shoulder to try to loosen his grip. Their father hears the commotion, enters the room, and sees Seth getting ready to punch his brother again.

"That's not how we treat each other," says Seth's father, matter-of-factly. "Seth, you're done with the game for now. You need to leave the room and stay away from your brother for the next half hour. Paul can play on his own if he wants."

"Fine!" Seth grumbles, as he leaves the room.

**More Examples:** Bullying, put-downs, antagonistic behavior toward others, inappropriate behavior with others, extreme disrespectful behavior with others, profanity.

## WHEN TEENS MISTREAT OR DISRESPECT PARENTS

**Logical Consequence:** Separate your teen from you temporarily or separate yourself from your teen temporarily.

Regina, age fifteen, finishes her homework and asks her mom if she can visit one of her friends for a while.

"Sorry, Regina," says her mom. "It's too close to dinner. Maybe tomorrow."

"But Mom . . . you never let me do anything!" complains Regina. Her mom gives her an understanding look but holds firm. Regina tries another tactic.

"You let Evan visit his friends sometimes before dinner," says Regina. Evan, her eighteen-year-old brother, has been responsible about making it to meals on time.

"Your brother has his driver's license, so he's in a position to make quick trips," her mom replies. "When you get your license, things will likely be different."

"That's not fair!" protests Regina. "I'll be back in time. I promise."

"We're done discussing it, Regina," says her mom. Regina explodes.

"I'm not a little kid!" Regina shouts. "This is shit, and you're a shitty mom. I'm sick and tired of taking your crap!"

"It's time for you to leave the room," says her mom, trying her best to maintain her composure.

"Why do I have to leave?" asks Regina. "It's my house, too. Why am I always the one who has to go?" The bait is skillfully presented, but Regina's mom doesn't bite. Instead, she leaves the room, grabs a magazine from the coffee table, and locks herself in the bathroom.

"I hate you!" screams Regina. Her mom doesn't respond. With no one to fight with, Regina eventually leaves the room.

**More Examples:** Verbal abuse, name-calling, angry rants, tantrums, profanity, hurtful statements, yelling and screaming.

## WHEN TEENS MISUSE OR ABUSE POSSESSIONS OR THINGS

**Logical Consequence:** Separate your teen temporarily from the things they are misusing or abusing.

Marshall, age thirteen, knows he's not supposed to play on his PlayStation before doing his homework, but his parents allow him to keep it in his bedroom, where he does his homework. The temptation is hard to resist. He decides to take a chance and gets caught.

"Turn off the PlayStation and leave it off until tomorrow," says his mom, matter-of-factly. "Homework comes first before video games. You can use it tomorrow evening if your homework is finished. If this happens again, we're going to have to move the PlayStation out of your room." Marshall will probably think carefully the next time he tries to evade his parents' rule.

In a separate situation, sixteen-year-old Lena arrives home more than an hour late with the family car after she promised to return it by five. Her father missed an appointment.

"May I have your car keys, please?" says Lena's father. "They'll be off-limits for the next three days. When I say I need the car by five, that's what I mean."

"I'm sorry, Dad," says Lena, remorsefully, hoping for a reprieve. She wants to use the car again the next day. "It won't happen again, I promise."

"That's a good choice for next time," her father replies. "You'll have another chance in three days."

**More Examples:** Cell phones, computers, electronic games, skateboards, hats, motorcycles, pornography, jewelry, TVs, sound systems, and other belongings.

## WHEN TEENS MISUSE AND ABUSE PRIVILEGES

**Logical Consequence:** Temporary loss of that privilege.

Fifteen-year-old Krystal is allowed to carry a low-balance credit card for approved purchases and emergencies only, but each month her parents notice purchases for music downloads, apps for her cell phone, and fast-food items on her credit card bill.

Each time, Krystal apologizes and promises it won't happen again, but the pattern of expenditures is increasing, not decreasing. Her parents decide to take a stand.

"Krystal, your mom and I have decided you're not ready for the privilege of using a credit card," says her father, matter-of-factly. "We'll try it again in six months if you're willing to follow the ground rules." Krystal pleads for another chance, but her parents hold firm. "You'll have that chance in six months," says her father.

**More Examples:** Driving privileges, party privileges, 3–6 p.m. after-school privileges, unsupervised trips to the mall, curfews, cell phone privileges, video game privileges, computer privileges, dating privileges, sleepovers, TV privileges, home alone privileges, credit card privileges, school function privileges, visiting friends, using parents' tech equipment, etc.

## WHEN TEENS LOSE OR
## DAMAGE THINGS

**Logical Consequence:** Repair or replace the damaged item.

Seventeen-year-old Aldon borrows his father's expensive sunglasses and loses them. "I know it was an accident," says his father, "but you need to pay for half of the replacement cost."

"But, Dad, I don't have any money to pay for that," says Aldon.

"That's no problem," his dad replies. "I have some chores you can do to earn the money you need."

## WHEN TEENS MAKE MESSES

**Logical Consequence:** Clean it up.

Vinnie, age fourteen, arrives from school hungry. He heads to the refrigerator, grabs the leftover enchilada casserole from last night's dinner, and heads to the living room to eat it in front of the TV. The phone rings. He gets up to answer it. When he returns to the living room, he sees his dog, Barnie, finishing up the casserole, which is all over the sofa and carpet. Vinnie complains to his mom.

"That's too bad," she says, "but now you have to clean it up. I'll give you the fabric and carpet cleaner."

"But I didn't make the mess!" Vinnie protests. "Barnie did. I don't see why I have to clean up his messes."

"There wouldn't be a mess if you hadn't left it where Barnie can get it," replies his mom. "It's your job to clean it up. You won't be doing anything else until it's done. Is that clear?" she asks.

"It's not fair!" complains Vinnie. Reluctantly, he begins the cleanup.

## WHEN TEENS REFUSE TO PICK UP THEIR STUFF

**Logical Consequence:** Put it in the Saturday box and don't return the item until Saturday.

Danny, age sixteen, watches TV with his stuff spread out all over the family room. His mother enters the room. "Danny, it's time to pick up your stuff. Our guests will be arriving in twenty minutes. If it's not picked up, it goes in the Saturday box."

"Yeah, yeah . . . I will," says Danny, but he makes no moves to do so. After a while, he leaves the room but returns forty-five minutes later to retrieve his cell phone.

"Where's my cell phone?" Danny asks.

"I had to pick it up along with a lot of your other stuff," replies his mom. "You can have it back on Saturday." She knew he would probably search the house to find them, so she placed them securely in the locked trunk of her car.

"This really sucks!" complains Danny. He'll probably think carefully next time his parents ask him to pick up his stuff.

## WHEN TEENS HAVE MESSY BEDROOMS

**Logical Consequence:** Close the door or clean it up.

Your teen's bedroom takes on special significance during adolescence. It can be a place of refuge, retreat, and privacy. It can be a showcase for individual expression and personal identity, and it can be a platform for dissent and rebellion. The bottom line: your teen's bedroom is sacred ground, and many teens will tenaciously defend their right to keep it the way they want—clean, messy, or anywhere in between.

More often than not, the choice is messy. Why? Because most parents want it clean. Messy bedrooms send a message of independence and rebellion: *I'm me, not you. I'm different, and I'll keep my room the way I want.* The unmade bed, dirty clothes, mildewed towels, stinky socks, empty fast-food containers, candy wrappers, and schoolbooks scattered about are all part of the intended statement.

Realizing how much this issue means to your teen, do you really want to go to war over a messy bedroom? Fortunately, there are other options. One of the best things about bedrooms is that nearly all have doors that open and shut. The door is your solution. Simply insist that your teen keep the door shut whenever the room is messy. It's much easier to endure your teen's rebellion and self-expression when you don't have to look at it.

What happens when your teen doesn't comply and leaves the door open? Then support your rule with a logical consequence. Ask them to clean it up. No exceptions. The solution is a win-win for parents and teens. It meets your teen's need for self-expression and your need not to have to look at the mess.

Many parents find this solution a suitable compromise. I used it successfully with my two sons, but my wife and I had to add a few conditions to meet our comfort needs. We insisted that they change the linens on a weekly basis and that no friends were allowed in their rooms when they were messy. If they wanted a private retreat to visit with friends, then they had to clean it up first.

## WHEN TEENS LIE, STEAL, CHEAT, OR DECEIVE

**Logical Consequence:** Increase monitoring, checking, surveillance until trust is restored.

Trinity, age thirteen, tells her parents she's going to a girlfriend's house after school but decides to hang out at the mall instead with a rowdy group of her friends. A neighbor sees her and shares the news with Trinity's parents.

"Trinity, Allie Kim said she saw you and a group of friends at the mall yesterday after school," her mother begins. "You know the mall is off-limits unless you have our permission. You told us you were going to Katie's house. Your father and I need to be able to trust that you will be where you say you will be. I'm afraid some of that trust has broken down, and you're going to have to earn it back. For the next six weeks, you need to ask our permission before you go anywhere after school. When you do get our permission, we expect a phone number and address so we can get in touch with you if we need to. Is that clear?"

"I'm really sorry," says Trinity, "but is it necessary for me to give you phone numbers and addresses? That's so embarrassing! My friends will think I'm on a leash."

"I'm sorry, Trinity, but it is necessary for the next six weeks," replies her mother. "Your privileges are based upon trust. You need to earn some of that back by showing us you're trustworthy. If you deceive us again, your father and I will have to reexamine if you're ready for after-school privileges with your friends altogether. Is that clear?" Trinity nods. The seriousness of her untrustworthy behavior is beginning to sink in.

## WHEN TEENS WASTE YOUR TIME

**Logical Consequence:** They owe you the time they waste, which should come from their prime time (for example, their after-school free time, TV time, video games time, weekend time).

For several months Gavin's parents have planned a weekend family outing with some relatives, and they insist that their fourteen-year-old join them. Gavin prefers to stay home by himself and watch TV or play video games.

"Do I have to go?" Gavin asks, in a whiny voice.

"Yes, you do," says his father. "We planned this trip more than a month ago, and your relatives want to see you."

"Well, I don't want to see them," Gavin complains. "This is going to be boring. Why can't I stay home this time?"

"We're done discussing it," says his father, who leaves the room.

*I'll go if I have to,* Gavin says to himself, *but they'll wish I didn't.* He decides to make the trip miserable for everybody.

Gavin fusses and complains during the entire trip. He wears his headphones to avoid conversations, stays well behind everybody during their walks, and rolls his eyes with impatience when his parents ask him to catch up. Halfway through the trip, his father takes him aside.

"Gavin, I don't expect you to like our outing," his father begins. "But I do expect you to respect others and our time together. You've wasted the first three hours of our trip, and you owe us that time when we get home. It will come from your TV time or video game time. The clock is on. If you continue to waste our time, we'll add that to the time you already owe us. Is that clear?"

*Maybe my plan wasn't such a good idea,* Gavin thinks to himself. The thought of losing more time when he gets home is not very appealing. He decides to improve his attitude for the rest of the outing.

**More Examples:** Car trips, family outings, trips to the restaurant, shopping, rides to and from school, and special occasions.

## WHEN TEENS DISRUPT ACTIVITIES

**Logical Consequence:** Separate your teen from that activity temporarily.

Leah, age fifteen, wakes up grumpy and arrives at breakfast with a big scowl on her face. She complains that they never have anything good to eat, then picks a fight with her younger sister by criticizing her eye makeup and choice of outfits. Their mother intervenes.

"Leah, we all wake up in bad moods from time to time, but it's not okay to take it out on others," says her mother.

"But she looks like a clown!" says Leah, hurtfully.

"You can finish your breakfast at the coffee table in the family room," says her mother, matter-of-factly. "It's not okay to be unkind."

"Fine!" says Leah. "I'd rather eat by myself anyway." She finishes her meal at the coffee table. Her mother doesn't respond.

**More Examples:** Family gatherings, special occasions, family TV time, family games or conversations, school activities, community activities, sport events, parties, dances, concerts.

## WHEN TEENS NEGLECT CHORES AND HOMEWORK

**Logical Consequence:** Use Grandma's Rule: Work before play.

Chores and homework are the expected jobs of teens in most families. Both have valuable lessons to teach about responsibility and good work habits. Teens who do chores and homework on a regular basis make valuable contributions to their families and make better roommates, marital partners, and parents. Teens who do homework on a regular basis enjoy greater success at school and in the workplace.

But chores and homework can be a source of great conflict between parents and teens. Why? Because parents care more about these activities than teens do. Parents understand the necessity and importance of developing good work habits for their teen's future success.

Teens, on the other hand, live in the present. Many don't understand or care about the long-term benefits of these activities. From their point of view, chores and homework are an annoyance that interfere with the other more important things they want to do. If your teen repeatedly neglects chores and homework, he or she may need you to structure an instructive lesson.

Is there a solution to this complicated problem? Fortunately, there is. It's called Grandma's Rule, or Work Before Play. Here's how it works. You simply arrange for chores and homework to be completed earlier in the day before the "good stuff" (for example, friends, long chats on the phone, TV, video games, computer use, etc.). The good stuff is the paycheck your teen looks forward to each day. Chores and home-work are the work that earns the paycheck. Your job is to make sure the work is complete before allowing your teen to move on to the good stuff. You withhold or provide the paycheck and stay out of the power struggles.

For example, if your teen gets home from school by 3:30 p.m., then chores and homework should be the first order of business. You may need to collect cell phones and turn off the TV to minimize distractions. If you suspect your teen does less than a complete job, then you may need to check their work for completion.

What happens if your teen digs in his or her heels and refuses to do their part? Then withhold the paycheck for that day. It's just quiet time in the house with few privileges. If they change their mind and decide to comply, great. If not, let them experience the consequence and do the learning. Don't fight or coerce them. They'll have another opportunity the next day. Just take it one day at a time.

If you do have to withhold their paycheck for that day, expect the usual mumbling, grumbling, and complaints of unfairness. Hold firm. Loss of the paycheck was their choice, not yours.

## Chapter Summary

Consequences are the second part of your overall limit-setting message. They speak louder than your words because they provide the accountability and enforceability teens need to take your rules seriously. Without accountability and enforceability, your rules are, at best, only hopeful expectations or hypotheses about what you would like to happen. Consequences give your rules meaning and help teens complete their research.

The consequences you learned in this chapter fall into two general categories: logical consequences, which we can control to a high degree; and natural consequences, which we have limited or no control over. Both provide instructive learning experiences for teens, but logical consequences are the gold standard. They are arranged by parents, experienced by teens, and logically related to the behavior, event, or situation. Logical consequences help strong-willed teens and fence sitters learn rules the way they learn best—the hard way.

At this point, you've got all the basic tools in your toolkit. You know how to give a clear, firm message with your words. You know how to stop power struggles before they begin, and you know how to support your rules with natural and logical consequences when your teen chooses to learn your rules the hard way. Now you need to prepare for the next round of resistance you'll likely encounter.

## CHAPTER 11

# Managing the Resistance You'll Likely Encounter

What parent doesn't want their limit-setting efforts to go smoothly with as little upset as possible for both parents and teens? Learning the "easy way" is very appealing, but this isn't the way most strong-willed teens and fence sitters learn. They need to repeatedly experience the consequences of their poor choices and behavior before they'll accept our rules and authority. Hard-way learning is still good learning, but no matter how you cut it, the "hard way" is hard on parents.

When you begin supporting your rules with natural and logical consequences on a regular basis, you're not likely to hear comments such as *Gee, Mom, you handled that well!* or *Good job, Dad! You gave me some great consequences.* More likely, you'll hear complaints such as *You're mean!* or *You're not fair!* or *I liked you better the other way.* Don't expect it to be easy and don't expect them to like it. What should you expect instead? Resistance.

The resistance you'll likely encounter may take many forms and come from many sources: from your teen, from siblings, from other family members, and from within yourself.

This chapter will help you recognize the different forms of resistance you'll likely encounter, respond to it effectively, and move forward without collecting all the hurts and baggage that accumulate with unresolved conflict.

## What Is Resistance?

Frustration and upset are normal reactions when things don't work out the way we want, but some teens take these reactions to extreme levels. They can mount considerable protests and resistance. Expect them to turn up the volume and intensity level—more yelling, more screaming, more drama, and more hurtful statements. These are normal and expected forms of resistance from some teens.

Their tactics are dramatic and extreme, but don't be misled by the heightened drama and strong emotion. What appears like a whole new layer of conflict and obstacles is simply an extension of the limit-testing process you learned about in Chapter 5. This is still aggressive research. They still want answers to their most pressing research questions: What's okay and not okay? Who's in charge? How far can I go? What happens when I go too far?

The goal is to wear you down and get you to give in. That's why they're turning up the intensity level. They want you to react. The tactics are simply a means to an end, and the end goal is to get you to give in.

But the process can be exhausting and confusing for parents. On an intellectual level, you recognize that extreme limit testing is normal for some teens, but does resistance feel normal in the moment when you confront it? No. It seems extreme, and often, it brings out extreme reactions in us. If we act on these feelings, we're right back into the power struggles. Reacting doesn't require much impulse control, emotional maturity, or thoughtfulness. Reacting works for kids, not for parents.

## REACTING VERSUS RESPONDING

We can't control our teen's reactions to the consequences we use, but we can control how we respond to our teen's reactions. Reacting and responding are very different processes. One leads predictably to conflict, power struggles, and loss of control. The other defuses conflict and keeps us in control. Learning to respond, rather than react, is the key to managing resistance effectively.

Let's begin by defining terms. What is reacting? Reacting is a natural, automatic, and nearly reflexive process that isn't always within our conscious control. Anyone can react. It just happens—the first thoughts you think, the first feelings you feel when something happens to you. That's a reaction. Many teens do it naturally in response to their parents' limit-setting efforts. Compliant teens show mild reactions. Strong-willed teens show more intense and extreme reactions. Fence sitters do a little of both. Reacting doesn't require emotional maturity, impulse control, or thoughtfulness.

Responding, on the other hand, is a more thoughtful process that involves observing and being aware of how we react, then choosing how to respond. Responding requires patience, thoughtfulness, and emotional maturity. Adults are better equipped with the emotional and intellectual tools to do it. Responding allows us to stay in control.

Sure, responding sounds great on a theoretical level, but

how do we actually do it on a real-life level? How do we respond like mature adults when our teens try to get us to react like children? I'm certainly no expert on patience or composure. I've always considered my efforts to be a work in progress, but I'm happy to share what worked for me and thousands of other parents.

The process begins with awareness. First, we need to be aware of what resistance looks like before we confront it so we're not caught off guard and taken by surprise. This chapter will provide lots of examples to help you do that. Second, we need to give ourselves a "thoughtful moment" to respond.

When my son Ian was a teen, my "thoughtful moments" were simply attempts to buy myself a little time to cool down and put things into perspective. I'd begin by saying to myself, *I'm the adult. He's the kid.* This always seemed to help. Then I'd ask myself three questions: *What am I feeling? What's going on? What am I going to do about it?*

The first two questions were easy to answer. Usually, I was feeling angry, and usually, Ian was testing me in some extreme way. The third question helped me follow through with the appropriate logical consequence. As Ian got older and I became more patient, I condensed my thoughtful moment to saying my mantra—*I'm the adult, he's the kid*—then went directly to question number three: *What am I going to do about it?* That's when I realized I was responding on a routine basis, but the process took time and a lot of practice. I've taught this procedure to thousands of parents in my workshops and family counseling work. Let's see how Tony's dad handles a typical situation with his strong-willed son both before and after Dad learned to take a thoughtful moment.

Fifteen-year-old Tony finishes his snack in the kitchen and leaves an empty cereal box, carton of milk, bowl, utensils, and crumpled napkins strewn all over the counter. Then he returns to the living room to watch his favorite show. When Tony's dad enters the kitchen, he sees the mess and reacts.

"Damn it, Tony!" he shouts. "You are so inconsiderate! What the hell is wrong with you? You're always leaving messes for others to clean up, and I'm sick of it. Get your butt in here and clean up."

"I'll do it later," Tony replies.

"No, you'll do it now or you'll be sorry," says his dad, pointing a threatening finger.

"Oh, I'm real scared," says Tony, sarcastically. "What are you going to do? Take away my cereal privileges?" Tony rolls his eyes, gives his dad a look of disgust, and makes no effort to get up from the couch. His dad becomes even more enraged.

"You don't talk to me like that, young man!" says his dad. "If you don't clean up this mess this instant, I'll turn the TV off, and you won't be watching it again the rest of the evening." Tony doesn't like the sound of that. Reluctantly, he walks back to the kitchen to clean up his mess.

What convinced Tony to cooperate? It wasn't his dad's anger or drama. Tony chose to cooperate because he didn't want to lose his TV privileges for the rest of the evening. His dad's intense reaction just fueled their angry power struggle and made things worse.

Now let's replay the scene, but this time, Tony's dad exercises a different choice. He expects Tony to resist and chooses to respond, rather than react. When he enters the kitchen and sees the mess, his initial reaction is the same. He feels angry, but rather than explode, he takes a moment to put things into perspective.

*It's just a mess, not the end of the world,* he tells himself. Then he approaches his son in a more thoughtful and respectful manner.

"Tony, you need to clean up your mess in the kitchen before you do anything else," says his dad, matter-of-factly. No blaming. No anger. No drama.

"I'll do it later," Tony replies. He shoots his dad an irritated look and makes no effort to comply with the request. This is the resistance Tony's dad expected. He remains calm and doesn't take the bait.

"You can do it now or in the next ten minutes," says his dad, "but the TV will stay off until it's done." He walks over and turns the TV off.

"Okay," says Tony, reluctantly, "but I don't see what the big deal is." He gets up to clean up his mess so he can return to his show.

"Thank you, Tony," says his dad with an appreciative smile.

Isn't responding more effective and less stressful than reacting? Tony's dad accomplished all his goals with much less energy. He modeled respectful communication and problem solving. He gained respect for his rules and authority, and he managed Tony's resistance without getting hooked into a power struggle.

## FORGIVENESS VERSUS
## RECONCILIATION

Most of us can agree that resistance is hard on parents, but how do parents avoid collecting all the baggage, hurts, and disappointments that accompany the repeated resistance we encounter from our teens? How do we move past these unpleasant experiences without harboring negative feelings toward our teens? The answer is forgiveness. Forgiveness is liberating, and it's solidly within our control.

But let's be clear about what we're forgiving. We're not forgiving unacceptable behavior. Unacceptable behavior shouldn't be tolerated. That's why we're setting limits in the first place. What we should forgive is the teen doing the behavior. We need to separate the deed from the doer. This is an important distinction that makes forgiveness possible. We're rejecting unacceptable behavior, not the teen doing the behavior.

The message to the teen is this—I love you, but what you're doing is not okay. This message puts the focus where it belongs, on your teen's behavior, not on your teen's value as a person. When we forgive the person, we can move forward without harboring the burdens of anger and resentment that we would otherwise carry around with us.

Forgiveness is a one-way process that is solidly within your control. It's a choice. Forgiveness does not require your teen's agreement or acceptance or anything else from your teen. It's liberating for you and your teen every time you choose to exercise it. Just write your teen an imaginary forgiveness slip and let it go. Voilà! No baggage.

Some parents have difficulty with this concept of forgiveness because what they really want is reconciliation. That is, they want their teen to understand, accept, and agree with the parents' limits and guidance methods. Reconciliation is a two-way process that requires your teen's agreement. You can't control that; only your teen can. You can only control what you say or what you do. You can't control how your teen reacts to it. Reconciliation is not a realistic outcome of your limit-setting efforts.

What do you really want from your teen when you set firm limits? Do you want them to agree with you and like it? Or do you want them to cooperate? You're not likely to get both. If you can settle for cooperation, then you're in a position to forgive and move forward. The choice is yours. You can collect baggage that interferes with your relationship, or you can drop that burden and preserve a positive relationship with your teen while you set limits on his or her unacceptable behavior.

## Typical Forms of Resistance

You're as prepared as you can be to confront and overcome the resistance you're likely to encounter. You understand that resistance is simply an extreme version of the limit testing you learned about in Chapter 2 and Chapter 5. You recognize that responding thoughtfully, not reacting, will keep you out of power struggles and on the right track. Finally, you know that forgiveness will prevent you from collecting the baggage that wears you down and weakens your resolve. Now it's time to take a closer look at the typical forms of resistance you're likely to confront.

Resistance takes many forms and comes from many sources. Resistance from your teens may range from subtle protests to full-blown tantrums of defiance and all points in between. Don't be surprised if you also encounter resistance from unexpected sources such as other family members, and even from within yourself. Whatever form the resistance takes, recognize it for what it is, hold the firm line, respond to it thoughtfully, write your teen a forgiveness slip, and move forward in a positive direction.

## INCREASING THE DRAMA

When mild forms of protest and drama are not enough to wear parents down, often teens will turn up the volume and increase the drama to achieve their goal. Celia, age fourteen, is a good example.

Celia hates it when her parents cut off her disrespectful tirades and ask her to cool down. She mumbles, grumbles, and complains all the way to her room, and when she arrives, she usually shouts out something hurtful, such as "I hate you!" or "You suck!" then slams the door loudly in protest. Each time, Celia fully expects her parents to take the bait and yell at her for slamming the door, but this has been going on for two weeks, and nothing has happened. Her parents know that reacting will only prolong Celia's drama.

*I'll show them!* Celia says to herself. The next time Celia is asked to go to her room, she stands in the hallway, slams her bedroom door three times, and shrieks insults at the top of her lungs. Her parents don't respond, but Celia does not give up easily. Like many strong-willed teens, she tries this tactic half a dozen times before she finally cools down and regains her composure.

## HURTFUL STATEMENTS

Hurtful statements directed at parents are powerful tools in a teen's limit-testing arsenal, especially when parents take these comments personally. In most cases, the teen's goal is not to inflict emotional pain but to make you feel guilty or sympathetic, or to weaken your resolve. Yes, this is a form of emotional manipulation, but most teens don't do it maliciously or even consciously. They do it because it works. It's a means to an end. The behavior is their best attempt to control you and get you to do what they want. Consider the following.

Randal, age thirteen, refuses to pick up his stuff in the living room. In a calm, matter-of-fact tone, his mother says, "You won't be going anywhere or doing anything else until it's done." Randal tries to wear her down with some hurtful statements.

"You don't care about me, anyway," he says. "All you care about is your clean house. You're a slave driver! I wish I had a nice mother who really cared about her kids." His mother pauses a moment to put things into perspective.

*Wait a second*, she says to herself. *All I asked him to do is pick up his stuff, and he turns it into an issue about love and caring. This isn't about me, and I'm not going to take the bait.* She holds firm.

"I'm sorry you feel that way," says his mother, "but I love you too much to allow you to do less than your part. You still have to do what I asked, and you won't be doing anything else until it's done." She leaves the room. Randal is too smart to waste his precious free time. Reluctantly, he picks up his mess.

## REPEATING THE MISBEHAVIOR

When your teen repeatedly tests you, how far are you willing to go before you give up in frustration? That's what most strong-willed teens and many fence sitters are trying to figure out when they repeat their misbehavior. This is aggressive research, and it can be so exhausting that parents ask themselves, *Is this normal? Is this worth all the hassle? Maybe I'm doing something wrong?* I know. I've been there. Some teens require a lot of data.

In Chapter 1, I shared a personal example about my strong-willed son, Ian, and how far he was willing to push us before he accepted our rules. Often, Ian would test us five or six times in a row for the same issue before he would accept my rules and stop testing! His compliant brother, Scott, even tried to help Ian with his research by saying, "Mom and Dad really mean it." But Ian just ignored his brother. This was his research, not Scott's.

Does five, six, even seven times in a row seem like a lot to you? It did to me. That's a lot of forgiveness slips! I felt the same confusion and doubt many parents feel when they are tested further than they ever imagined. I even began to wonder if his behavior was normal or if I was doing something wrong. His testing seemed excessive.

But I held firm and trusted in the process. Sure enough, eventually Ian did the learning I wanted him to do, but I never would have imagined pushing my parents as far as he pushed me. I've heard this same comment from hundreds of parents.

## ESCALATING MISBEHAVIORS

Strong-willed teens are very skillful at wearing parents down. If one misbehavior doesn't work, they may try another and another until they achieve their goal. Escalating misbehavior is a common form of resistance parents need to watch for on their radar screen. Molly, age seventeen, is a good example.

"May I go to Serena's house before dinner?" asks Molly.

"You can if all your chores are all done," her mom replies. "Are they done?" Molly nods. "Let me do a quick check," says her mom, expecting testing.

"Well, most of it is done," says Molly. "I can finish it after dinner."

"You know the rule, Molly," says her mom. "Chores first, then friends."

"That's not fair!" protests Molly. "I won't have any time if I finish all of it. Serena's mom doesn't make her do chores before friends." Molly's mom can see where this is going and cuts it off.

"We're done talking about it," she says, matter-of-factly. "If you bring it up again, you're going to spend time by yourself."

"You're so mean!" Molly shouts. "What a bitch!" Her mom walks away.

Did Molly mount some serious resistance to her mom's rule about completing chores before playing? You bet. In the space of a few minutes, Molly tried deception, protesting, complaining, arguing, name-calling, defiance, and high-screaming drama to wear her mom down. But Molly's mom expected the resistance, kept her composure, and held firm. So can you.

## ACTING UNCONCERNED
## ABOUT CONSEQUENCES

Some teens will go to great lengths to give parents the impression that their logical consequences aren't having the intended effect. Joel, age thirteen, is a good example.

Joel and his younger brother play video games in the family room when his brother lets out a shout. "Hey! That's cheating! You just had a turn!" When Joel's father hears all the commotion, he comes over to investigate.

"I was just kidding," says Joel. He hands his brother the controller. His father doesn't get involved. The game continues for a few minutes, then Joel's brother shouts again, louder than before. Their father enters the room a second time.

"He did it again!" says Joel's brother. Their father announces the game is over.

"Okay, here's the controller," says Joel with a mischievous laugh, but it's too late. His father intervenes.

"You need to find something else to do, Joel," says his father. "Your brother can play by himself."

"I don't care," says Joel, acting unconcerned. "It's a stupid game anyway, almost as stupid as you." His father takes a few deep breaths to compose himself.

"It's not okay to talk to me or anybody else that way, Joel," says his father. "The game is off-limits for the rest of the week, and you need to spend some time by yourself." He sends Joel to his room for a fifteen-minute time-out.

"Fine," says Joel. "That doesn't bother me. I prefer to spend time away from you." The bait is skillfully presented, but Joel's father doesn't bite. "I'll see you in fifteen minutes," he says, matter-of-factly.

## PLEA BARGAINING

Strong-willed teens are masters at avoiding the consequences of their poor choices. Sixteen-year-old Arnie is a good example. It's Arnie's job to rinse the dishes and load the dishwasher each night after dinner. Some nights he almost throws the items into the dishwasher.

"Hey! Don't be so rough!" says his concerned mother, but Arnie doesn't even acknowledge the comment. He continues to fling the dishes into the dishwasher. Suddenly, there's a loud sound of shattering glass. When his mother investigates, she discovers two broken plates and a serving dish.

"You just broke about seventy dollars' worth of dishware," says Arnie's mother. "You'll need to replace those items with money from your allowance."

"Hey, that's not fair!" Arnie protests. "It was an accident."

"Not exactly," says his mother. "You were very rough with them and didn't heed my warning."

"I don't have seventy dollars," says Arnie. "That's a lot of money! Can't you give me a break? I didn't mean to break them." He pleads for a reduced consequence. "I won't do it again, I promise." His mother holds firm.

"That's a good choice for next time," his mother replies. "The money will come out of your allowance, or I can give you extra jobs to do to pay them off. What would you like to do?" No reprieves or second chances this time. She lets the consequence teach the lesson.

## NOT RESPONDING

Passive resistance can be a powerful form of persuasion for wearing down a worthy adversary. Let's see how fourteen-year-old Rhiana uses this strategy to avoid her mother's request. Rhiana arrives home from high school, drops her backpack next to the front door, eats a quick snack, and announces that she needs a ride to soccer practice.

"You need to put away your backpack before you go," says her mother. "You left it next to the door where others can trip on it." Rhiana pretends not to hear and heads for the door. Her mother intercepts her and checks in.

"Rhiana, what did I ask you to do?" Rhiana gives her mother an impatient look, rolls her eyes, but doesn't say a word or make any effort to comply. Her mom provides some choices.

"I'm not ready to give you a ride until you put your backpack away. What would you like to do?" Rhiana glares and doesn't say a thing. Her mother sees where things are headed. *No response is the same as a refusal,* her mother says to herself. *I think she's made her choice.* Rhiana's mother set her keys down on the counter and takes a seat. Rhiana recognizes her mother's resolve. Precious time is wasting.

"Okay, I'll put it away," says Rhiana, reluctantly.

"Thanks," says her mom.

## DISHONESTY AND DECEPTION

From time to time, nearly all teens are tempted to use dishonesty and deception to avoid taking responsibility for their poor choices and behavior, especially when parents don't witness the actual event. Consider the following.

Gina, age fourteen, and her acrobatic terrier, Tippy, love to play catch with the Frisbee. Her parents insist this is an outdoor game, but when they're not looking, sometimes Gina takes a few practice throws in the house. This is what her father suspects when he hears a loud crash in the living room. When he arrives on the scene, he sees Gina holding the Frisbee and a family portrait broken on the floor.

"Tippy did it," says Gina. "We were getting ready to play catch in the backyard. I guess he got excited." Her dad doubts the story.

"But the picture was on the table," says her dad. "Tippy doesn't usually get up on the table unless he's chasing something. Are you sure that's what happened?"

"I swear it," says Gina, with a sincere look on her face. Her story just doesn't check out.

"I could be wrong," says her dad, "but it looks to me like something else happened. You need to replace the broken frame with your own money, or I can give you some jobs to do to pay it off."

"But that's not fair!" protests Gina. "Tippy did it, not me." Her dad holds firm.

"We're done discussing it, Gina," he says. "I'll hold on to the Frisbee until you pay for the frame."

Would you give Gina the benefit of the doubt in her unlikely story? Many parents find themselves in the position of having to make guidance decisions based on incomplete or less than accurate information. All you can do is your best in these situations. You're a parent, not a police detective. You don't need video cameras or surveillance tapes to determine the veracity of your teen's stories. Use your best judgment.

Gina chose to use dishonesty and deception as a strategy to evade responsibility for violating her parents' rule and for the damage she caused. Did it work? No. Will she try it again? Maybe. This all depends upon how much data she needs to collect before she realizes that deception is a poor strategy for avoiding responsibility. If Gina's parents continue to use their best judgment in these situations, hold firm, and follow through with the appropriate consequences, Gina will learn the lessons they're trying to teach.

## RESCUING AND ENABLING: HELP THAT ISN'T HELPFUL

Did you ever imagine that compliant siblings and family members can be a source of resistance? In some families, it happens regularly and it's done with the best of intentions. Compliant family members have an underlying desire to please and cooperate. They dislike conflict and will go to great lengths to avoid confrontation and upset. When they see aggressive research in action, compliant family members will sometimes step in and try to help out, but the helping is anything but helpful. It actually rewards and encourages teens to be more persistent in their research.

How do parents handle the well-intended interference? They need to expect it and be prepared to prevent it when they see it happening. Let's follow a typical week in the home of one strong-willed teen to see how it's done.

Troy, age thirteen, is the second of three children and very strong-willed. His younger brother, Max, and older sister, Glenda, are both compliant. Max and Troy share a bedroom.

Each morning before school, the kids are expected to make

their beds before they leave the house. Who makes Troy's bed on a semiregular basis? Max. He hates all the commotion that happens when his parents make that last-minute bed check and inform Troy that he's not ready to leave the house until the job is done. Max also hates being late to school.

When it's time to get in the car, who gets the coveted spot in the front seat next to Mom? Troy. His siblings gladly give it up because Troy antagonizes them when he shares the backseat. Rides to school with Troy in the backseat are not fun.

When the kids arrive home from school, they're expected to do a few chores and finish their homework before playing. Who complains and avoids doing chores and dawdles during homework? Right again. Troy. Who does some of Troy's chores and homework for him when their mom isn't looking? Glenda. Why? Because she hates to hear Troy's fussing and see how frustrated her mom becomes when he doesn't do his part. Sometimes, their mom catches Glenda helping out and intervenes by saying, "That's Troy's job, not yours. He needs to do it himself," or "You'll be a great parent someday, Glenda, but disciplining Troy is my job." Troy enjoys the drama and thrives on all the negative attention.

Each Wednesday after school, their mom goes to the gym and their grandma helps out with child care. Who doesn't require Troy to do his chores and tolerates his disrespectful behavior? Grandma. Who ignores Troy when he antagonizes Max and Glenda? Grandma. Does any of this sound like your home? Can you see why rescuing and enabling by compliant family members makes your job more challenging?

## RESISTANCE FROM OTHER
## FAMILY MEMBERS

Spouses and other family members in positions of authority can be a great source of support when they're willing to back you up and a source of resistance when they don't. If your spouse or family member is a reluctant supporter, you might have to win him or her over by demonstrating your effectiveness. Role-modeling is a powerful tool of persuasion. Give them some time to see you in action and getting results.

Two effective parents working together is the best-case scenario, but don't become discouraged if this isn't the case in your home. One effective parent is an improvement upon two ineffective parents. Give your partner and other family members time and offer generous helpings of encouragement. The process may feel like taking two steps forward and one step backward, but you will be making forward progress.

## RESISTANCE FROM WITHIN YOURSELF

The biggest obstacle for most of us is not our relatives or even our resistant teens. The biggest obstacle comes from within ourselves as we struggle against our compelling desire to revert to our old habits and do things the way we always have. Old beliefs and habits feel comfortable and familiar and are hard to change.

If you've been permissive in the past, you'll have to resist your urge to talk your teen into cooperating, even though those methods haven't worked for you in the past. If you've been punitive or autocratic in the past, you'll have to resist your urge to intimidate, coerce, or force your teen into cooperating, even though this hasn't worked for you in the past.

If you've used the mixed approach in the past, you'll have to resist the urge to flip-flop back and forth between the two ineffective extremes.

The biggest source of encouragement you'll experience will likely come from the positive results you get from the new tools in your toolkit. If you stay on course, you will experience new levels of cooperation, but it won't come easy. You'll have to earn it with your consistent efforts.

## Chapter Summary

Resistance is a normal and expected part of the learning and behavior change process for all of us, but some teens take resistance to extremes. They can mount considerable protests when things don't work out the way they want. Don't be misled by the heightened drama and emotion. What appears to be a whole new layer of conflict and obstacles is simply an extension of the limit-testing process you learned about in Chapter 5. The game hasn't changed. The solutions are the same. Their goal is to wear you down and get you to give in. Your goal should be to hold firm, maintain your resolve, and work through this second wave of resistance. If this chapter has done its job, you should be in a better position to do this.

You have all the basic tools you need in your limit-setting toolkit. You know how to give a clear, firm message with your words when your teen challenges your rules and authority. You know how to end potential power struggles before they begin, and you know how to support your rules with instructive consequences when your teen chooses to learn the hard way. You've prepared yourself to recognize the second wave of resistance you'll likely encounter and how to weather the storm without collecting unnecessary hurt and baggage. You're as ready as you can be.

In the next four chapters, we're going to switch gears and apply the tools you've learned thus far to perhaps the biggest limit-setting issue of adolescence—determining your teen's readiness for more freedom and privileges.

## CHAPTER 12

# Patience:
# The Remedy to Anger

What do strong-willed teens do better than most teens? That's right. They test our limits, challenge our authority, and wear us down with formidable resistance when we try to guide them in the right direction. How do most parents feel when this happens? Angry? Impatient? Frustrated? Of course, and these intense feelings are some of the biggest obstacles to effective limit setting. They cloud our thinking, impair our judgment, make us overreact, and cause us to say and do things we later regret.

To further complicate matters, we live in an era that places high value on all things fast and convenient. We expect quick remedies and instant solutions to the obstacles we face. As a society, we've become less tolerant of the challenges in life that require patience, understanding, restraint, and big-picture thinking. Raising a strong-willed teen or any difficult teen is certainly one of those challenges. The expectation of a quick fix only intensifies our anger and impatience.

Many things can be remedied by cranking up the speed, but changing your teen's behavior isn't one of them. Parents today need a mind-set based on tolerance, restraint, understanding, and big-picture thinking. Patience is the remedy for anger and frustration. Fortunately, patience is a skill that can be taught and learned and applied directly to challenging situations. That's what this chapter will show you how to do. Patience is the key to preserving your sanity as you guide your teen through the challenges of adolescence.

## What Is Patience?

Patience is a term with complex meanings. *Webster's Dictionary* defines patience as the capacity of calm endurance, tolerance, capable of bearing delay. Other sources define it as the bearing of provocation, annoyance, misfortune, or pain, without complaint, loss of temper, irritation, or the like. Synonyms include: composure, stability, endurance, fortitude, steadfastness, calmness, and courage and strength of character in the midst of pain and suffering. Does this sound like the stuff we need when working with strong-willed teens? You bet.

Patience is the remedy for overcoming the intense feelings we feel when we encounter resistance from our strong-willed children. Patience provides us with an opportunity for responding, not simply reacting. Here's the best news. You don't need to be a saint to be patient. Patience is a skill that can be taught and learned by nearly anyone and applied in challenging situations.

My most instructive lessons in patience come from my wife, best friend, and longtime business partner, Lisa, whom I affectionately refer to as the "patron saint of special education." In addition to being a co-presenter at my workshops for parents and teachers for more than a dozen years, Lisa has been a distinguished special education teacher and recipient of countless awards for teaching and creative program development. Lisa must be to children what St. Francis was to animals. She has an amazing way with kids. I don't fully understand how she does it, but I'm sure patience and a solid command of effective limit setting have a great deal to do with it.

In the classroom, Lisa is unflappable. Nothing rattles her, and she works with the most difficult kids on campus, who do all the usual things difficult children do—test limits, tantrum, disrupt, dig in their heels, power struggle, defy adults, even lose emotional control and lash out physically. Lisa just maintains a steadfast calm, patient demeanor. She sets clear, firm limits when her students need them, and she *always* follows through with an appropriate logical consequence when they make poor choices. Lisa always keeps the big picture in view. She knows how to bring out the best in her students and the adults who work with them.

When I ask her how she maintains her calm, encouraging, and resolute demeanor in the face of such extreme and intensely emotional situations, Lisa always reminds me, "They need me to be that way. They're just kids trying to do the best they can. They need to be able to trust and depend on me no matter how bad things get. That's my job. I'm always going to be there for them."

In the classroom, Lisa doesn't need to take any special steps to thoughtfully reflect on what she needs to do. She's always in that moment. She keeps the big picture in view the moment she enters the classroom. She makes patience look easy.

When we get in the car to return home after a full day's workshop or training event, Lisa becomes more like the rest of us. She and I usually debrief about how the workshop went and about how we, or mostly me, can improve. We're close, and we can be honest with each other. On more than a few occasions, Lisa has pointed out my mistakes during our workshop.

"Slow down, Sparky," she often says. "You schedule things too tightly. It really bugs me when you rush people to get the points. You need to give more examples, provide more practice opportunities, and allow more time for questions." I know she's right, but I'm thinking, *Do you have to be so brutally frank? Where's your patience now?*

Probably most of us know someone who is extremely patient in some situations and less patient in others. Isn't this normal? I watch checkout clerks at the grocery store and marvel at how well they tolerate difficult customers. Most of us are capable of being patient in specific situations, but few of us can be patient in all situations. Here's some good news—you don't have to be, but you can learn to be patient with your challenging teenager.

## PATIENCE IS A TEACHABLE SKILL
Nearly anyone can learn to be patient in specific situations, but we shouldn't expect it to come as naturally or automatically as Lisa's experience in the classroom. You'll have to work at it. I've taught this skill to thousands of parents and teachers during my career, and I'm confident you can learn it if you are willing to practice a three-step process you'll learn in the next section. You don't need any special qualifications. All you need is a willingness to look at the triggers that hook your anger, then give yourself an opportunity to choose a different, more thoughtful response. Let's begin with triggers.

Each of us has our own special set of triggers when it comes to working with teens. Triggers are behaviors that really set us off and cause an intense emotional reaction. They're like fire alarms. When they go off, they get our quick attention and shock us into a reaction. At the moment, things seem bigger and more serious than they really are. In most cases, triggers are false alarms because there isn't any fire. They cause us to overreact to our teen's misbehavior.

Triggers are great for getting our prompt attention, but they cloud our thinking, impair our judgment, make us overreact, and cause us to say and do things we later regret. Angry triggers are big obstacles to effective limit setting.

What are your triggers? Whining? Fussing? Screaming? Refusals? Stalling? Arguing? Defiance? Challenging? Namecalling? Dishonesty? Tantrums? Eye rolling? Looks of contempt? All of the above?

Whatever your triggers may be, you need to recognize them as red flags or warning signals that you're about to lose your self-control. Awareness is the first and most important step in regaining your self control. This step begins with an observation. When you think your trigger is being pushed, observe your reaction and ask yourself, *What's going on here? What is my teen doing? What am I feeling?*

This can be your moment of opportunity or the beginning of a destructive dance. It all depends upon what you do next. If you recognize the warning signal and observe your anger without acting on it, you can interrupt the usual knee-jerk reaction and give yourself an opportunity to respond effectively. Or, you can simply react to the trigger, let your anger and frustration run its course, and risk saying or doing something hurtful to your teen or to your relationship.

Does recognizing the trigger make the reactive feelings go away? In most cases, the answer is no, at least not right away. When kids push our triggers, we react, almost automatically, on an emotional level, but we don't have to allow the intense emotions to take us over. Our moment of opportunity begins the instant we feel ourselves becoming angry or impatient. How long does that moment last? It lasts as long as it takes us to regain our emotional composure so we can respond effectively.

## Creating Your Own Thoughtful Moment

Most of us will need to practice three basic steps to create our own thoughtful moment, but how we go through these steps will vary from person to person. Let's look at each step to determine how this procedure will work for you.

### STEP ONE: OBSERVE WHAT'S HAPPENING

Step one is the important awareness step we discussed earlier. When you think or feel that your trigger has been pushed, observe your reaction and ask yourself some questions so you can become aware of what's happening in that moment: *What's going on? What is my teen doing? How am I feeling? Have we been through this before?*

In most cases, you'll discover that your teen is testing or resisting the way he or she always does, and you're feeling angry and frustrated the way you usually do. The questions won't make the feelings go away, but they will help you recognize what's really happening in that moment so you can begin to put things into perspective. In effect, the questions provide a moment of clarity so you can begin to change an emotional process that takes you out of control into a rational process that helps you recover self-control.

## STEP TWO: RECOVER SELF-CONTROL

Step two is a vital recovery step that permits you to follow through with your moment of opportunity. When you recognize that your trigger has been pushed and you're beginning to feel angry, this is the time to make a decision. You can step back and recover or proceed. Think of yourself as a train moving to a switching point that leads to two different tracks: an angry track or a controlled track. This is your opportunity to choose the right track because the train is not going to stop. It has too much momentum. If you're aware of the choice, you can make the right one.

This recovery step varies from person to person depending upon your reactivity to your triggers. If you tend to be highly reactive and can't restrain yourself from saying or doing something in anger, then you've already missed the signal and you're already on the angry track. You can still salvage the situation, but your moment of opportunity will have to begin with a cooldown or an apology of the sort we discussed in Chapter 9.

That's okay. Managing intense feelings is not easy. Learning to be patient takes time and practice. You can use breathing and relaxation exercises to keep you on the right track. You will need to discover for yourself the strategies that work best for you.

Recovering self-control was not easy for me. I have a quick temper and tend to be reactive. When my son Ian pushed my triggers, I reacted almost instantaneously. My face would flush with anger. My voice would get loud and stern, and I'd be ready for battle. When Ian was young, many of my thoughtful moments began with the words "Pal, I'm feeling really angry, and I need a few minutes to calm down. Have a seat on the couch. We'll deal with this in a few minutes." Then I would remove myself from the situation, take some deep breaths, and wait for my angry feelings to dissipate.

I found two strategies particularly helpful for restoring my self-control. The first involves a comforting phrase I repeated to myself that puts the big picture back into focus. When I felt like exploding, I would repeat to myself, *I'm the adult. He's the kid. I can handle this.* Other times, I found it helpful to separate the deed from the doer by saying to myself, *I love my son, but what he's doing is not okay.*

The recovery process gets easier with time. As Ian got older, and I got more practice, I discovered I needed fewer cooldowns and only an occasional apology. By the time he reached elementary school, I was able to start off in a calm, matter-of-fact manner most of the time. But learning to be patient has always been "a work in progress." I never really got good at it until Ian grew up and left the house.

Parents often ask, *Am I supposed to feel patient and composed when I'm trying to behave in a patient and composed manner?* No. The feeling of composure, serenity, or patience may develop over time, but it's not required to master the skill. I appreciate what parents mean when they inform me that they don't feel patient when they act patient. That's okay. Your teen is not likely to know your internal emotional experience anyway. All he or she knows is that you're behaving in a composed and under-control manner.

## STEP THREE: RESPOND THOUGHTFULLY

Steps one and two may seem like a lot to go through to simply to reach step three, but in real life, this whole process often takes place in a brief moment. Step three is the easiest part. Your feelings are under control. Your thinking is clear, and your judgment is good. Finally, you get the opportunity to use the skills you've been learning in this book. If things have already progressed to the point where you need to support your rules with consequences, you simply follow through with the appropriate logical consequence you learned in Chapter 10. Let's look at how several parents apply the three-step method to create their thoughtful moments.

## Patience with an Explosive Temper

Tony and his fourteen-year-old son, Marcello, are both strong-willed. Both have short fuses and explosive tempers. They adore each other, but in discipline situations, they are like charged particles in a reaction chamber. Tony came for counseling to learn better ways to manage his explosive temper.

"I don't know who explodes first, me or Marcello," says Tony. "I can't stop myself. I start shouting the moment I see him misbehave, and he starts yelling the moment he sees me coming. It's crazy! I feel terrible after it's over."

From his description, I could see that Tony was past the point of beginning at step one. He didn't recognize how far things progressed until he saw how upset Marcello became. Tony's first task was to learn to restore his self-control, then try to salvage his thoughtful moment. We practiced cooldowns and did some relaxation exercises, but Tony decided that what he really needed to do was give himself a five-minute time-out and follow up with an apology. Then he would try to respond thoughtfully and follow through with an appropriate consequence. Marcello liked the plan.

Tony had an opportunity to practice his plan the evening following our first appointment. "It's time to turn off the TV, Marcello, and get ready for bed," Tony announces. Marcello is so engrossed in his program that he doesn't realize how much time has passed. His father enters the room to check on his progress and explodes.

"Damn it, Marcello!" Tony shouts. "How many times do I have to tell you? This is the stuff that makes me so mad." Tony sees the tears welling up in his son's eyes and stops himself before he unleashes even more anger.

"Marcello, wait here. I need five minutes alone," says Tony. Marcello looks surprised and scared at the same time. Tony leaves the family room, sets the kitchen timer, and waits to regain his composure. When the timer goes off, Tony reenters the family room. Marcello still has an alarmed look on his face. To Tony's surprise, the TV is turned off.

"I'm sorry I yelled at you, Marcello, and thanks for turning off the TV," Tony says, matter-of-factly. "Will you accept my apology?" Marcello nods. "Thank you," says Tony. "It's time to get ready for bed." Tony had taken a big step toward learning to become more patient. He and Marcello had taken a big step toward interrupting their angry power struggles.

## Patience with Dawdling and Bad Attitude

Beth is a patient parent, but she also has her triggers. Dawdling and negative attitude really set her off. Chelsea, her strong-willed daughter, discovered the dawdling trigger about age three, but things didn't get ugly until Chelsea turned thirteen.

Each night after dinner, Chelsea knows it's her job to load the dishwasher and wipe off the counters, but she dawdles and avoids and waits until the last possible moment to get started. Their dance usually begins with a series of prompts.

"It's time to get started," says Beth, matter-of-factly.

"I will," Chelsea replies, but makes no move to do so. She knows what her mother will do next.

"We don't have all evening," says Beth, impatiently. "I'm getting upset!"

"Mom, I said I would do it!" Chelsea replies, with the same level of impatience, then rolls her eyes and gives Beth a look of contempt. This is when Beth loses her self-control and starts yelling, but not this time. She remembers the skill she's working on and recognizes her moment of opportunity.

*Oh no, she found my triggers. We're not going down this path again*, Beth says to herself. She walks into another room, takes a few deep breaths, and checks in with herself. *What's going on?* Beth recognizes Chelsea's usual dawdle and attitude routine for what it is. *How am I feeling?* Beth can see she feels angry and frustrated the way she always does in these situations. She takes a few more deep breaths, checks her composure, and returns to the kitchen.

"Chelsea, I love you too much to yell at you about doing your jobs," Beth says, matter-of-factly. "I know you can do a good job if you choose to, but you won't be doing anything else until the job is done. Let me know when you're finished so I can check it over." Beth gives Chelsea an encouraging look and walks out of the kitchen. No yelling. No screaming. No drawn-out power struggles.

*What happened to her?* Chelsea thinks to herself. *She's no fun.* Chelsea considers dawdling again to see if she can re-kindle the flames, but reconsiders the plan when she realizes that the time she's wasting is her own.

## Patience with Whining and Complaining

It's a beautiful Saturday morning, and Barry, age seventeen, wants to take off with his friends. Barry's mom insists that he put his laundry in the laundry room before he leaves the house. It's a two-minute job that Barry agreed to do weekly. Barry protests and complains, but his mom holds firm. He tries bargaining. "I'll do it as soon as I get back," he promises.

"You know our agreement," his mom says, matter-of-factly.

"Yeah, well it's a stupid agreement," says Barry, angrily. His mom doesn't react, so Barry tries the one thing he knows will drive his mom crazy. He starts to fuss in a whiny voice. Barry's mom reacts instantly, but she remembers what she read in the book, takes a few deep breaths, and holds on to her moment of opportunity.

"You can fuss and complain all you want, Barry," says his

mom, matter-of-factly, "but you're not going to leave the house until the job is done." She blocks his exit. *Aah, patience feels good,* she thinks to herself.

"This really sucks!" complains Barry. He knows he'll just delay his departure the more he protests. Reluctantly, he finishes his job.

## Patience with Untrustworthy Behavior

Natalie's parents are concerned. Lately, their bright, capable fifteen-year-old has been less than honest about her schoolwork. They've noticed the pattern in other areas, too. Natalie's grades have fallen from B's to C's in three subjects, largely because she doesn't complete or turn in her homework assignments on a regular basis. On the advice of her teacher, Natalie's parents implement a new homework routine to remedy the problem.

Each day after school, Natalie is supposed to complete her homework before she does anything else. Her mother checks it over for completion. If it's complete, Natalie is free to hang out with her friends.

"I'm going to Annie's house," Natalie announces, after arriving home from school. "Ceci is going to meet us there. We have something we really want to do."

"Is your homework done?" asks her mom.

"We don't have any tonight," Natalie replies. Her mom is suspicious. Trust and honesty are two of her biggest triggers.

"May I see your weekly assignment sheet?" she asks.

"Well, maybe I have a little," says Natalie, sheepishly, "but I can do it when I get back."

"You know our agreement," says her mom. "Homework comes first, then free time." Natalie heads to her room to finish up. Forty minutes later, she returns and passes over two pages of math and one page of writing for her mom's inspection. As usual, Natalie has done a fine job.

"Can I go to Annie's house now?" Natalie asks.

"Okay," says her mom, "but you need to be home by five thirty. Is that clear?"

"I will," says Natalie, as she heads out the door.

At 6:15 Natalie has not returned. Her concerned mom calls Annie's house and discovers the girls are not there. They went to the park but should have returned thirty minutes ago. Natalie's mom feels panicky. As she heads to the car to look for her daughter, she sees Natalie walking up the driveway.

"Where were you?" asks her worried mom.

"I told you. I went to Annie's house," Natalie replies.

"When I called Annie's mother at six fifteen, she said you girls met at the park. You didn't ask permission to go to the park, and you know your father and I don't like you there in the evenings." Natalie's face is flushed.

"Well, I didn't think it would hurt anything," says Natalie. Her mom is furious and about to explode but catches herself, takes a few deep breaths, and asks Natalie to wait in the house. Natalie begins to realize the seriousness of the situation.

"I need a few minutes, then we'll talk," says her mom, with tears in her eyes. She recognizes the serious trust, honesty, and safety issues she has to consider and wants to be sure she chooses the appropriate logical consequences with a clear head. Twenty minutes later, Natalie's mom approaches her daughter in the living room.

"What time did I ask you to be home?" asks her mom.

"Five thirty," replies Natalie.

"What time did you actually arrive home?" asks her mom.

"About six thirty," says Natalie, remorsefully.

"Natalie, the real issues here are about honesty and trust," her mom says. "You deceived me about your homework, where you went, and about what time you would be home. Your father and I must to be able to trust you if we are to give you the freedom and privileges you have. You need to earn back the trust that's been lost.

"I will continue to check your homework each day before you play, for the rest of the semester. You can have your friends come to our house after school, but you won't be permitted to go to their homes or anywhere else for the next four weeks. After that time, you can resume your play privileges at your friends' homes, but we will check to make sure you're really there. If you're not, this privilege will be suspended for even longer. If you want to go anywhere other than where we agree, you must have our permission. If you don't, we will suspend the privilege for even longer. When we say we want you home at a certain time, we mean it. If you show up late without notifying us, we will suspend this privilege for even longer. Finally, we love you. We won't take any chances with your safety. Is all this clear?" Natalie nods.

## Chapter Summary

The gift of patience is one of the greatest gifts you can share with your strong-willed teen—or any teen, for that matter. When you give your patience, you share your best inner qualities—your clearest thinking, your best judgment, your loving understanding, and your most thoughtful guidance. Fortunately, patience is a skill that can be taught and learned. You don't need to be a saint to be patient. In fact, you don't need any special qualifications at all. Nearly anyone can learn to be patient. All you need is a willingness to recognize your triggers and follow a simple three-step procedure: Observe what's happening, Recover your self-control, and Respond thoughtfully. What we do is what we teach. When you practice patience, you teach an invaluable skill that can be passed on to future generations.

At this point, you have all the basic tools in your limit-setting toolkit. You know how to give a clear message with your words when your teen challenges your rules and authority. You know how to end power struggles before they begin, and you know how to support your rules with instructive consequences when your teen chooses to learn the hard way. You're prepared for the second wave of resistance you'll likely encounter when you start using your new tools on a consistent basis. Finally, you know how to use patience to weather the storm without collecting unnecessary hurt and baggage. You're as ready as you can be.

In the next four chapters, we're going to switch gears and apply the tools you've learned thus far to perhaps the biggest limit-setting issue of adolescence—determining your teen's readiness for more freedom and privileges.

## CHAPTER 13

# Entitlement: How Teens Determine Their Readiness

Teens are eager to enjoy the freedoms and privileges of young adults, which they feel they're ready to handle. How do they signal their eagerness? They test their limits. Limit testing is their job. This is their way of saying, *I'm ready for the privileges of a young adult. I'm ready to date and drive and stay out late.*

Their requests don't seem much different from what they were asking for before: more freedom, more privileges, more independence, and more control over their lives. But teens want these changes to happen all at once. There's a sense of urgency and impatience that wasn't there before and a new way of thinking that drives parents crazy. It's time to get acquainted with teenage thinking of entitlement, where feeling ready and wanting to be ready are considered the same as actually being ready.

Fortunately, most parents have the maturity and experience to recognize the faulty logic. We know that "feeling ready" and "being ready" are two different things. We understand that there is no set standard for readiness based on age and ability, and it doesn't just happen overnight as the result of strong desires and compelling impulses. Most important, we recognize that jumping into new experiences without adequate preparation can be dangerous. In this chapter, we'll examine two very different ways of thinking, entitlement and readiness, so you can see what you're up against.

## The Thinking of Entitlement

*Webster's Dictionary* defines entitlement as "to furnish with a right or to provide a ticket for free admission." *Webster's* definition is not far from the thinking of most teens when it comes to having new freedoms and privileges. From a teenage perspective, freedom and privileges are a right, not something they should earn by demonstrating readiness. Kristy, age fifteen, is a good example.

Kristy is excited because her parents told her that when she turned fifteen she could go out on dates with boys who drive. Kristy is sure she's ready for the privilege. Some of her friends have been dating for almost a year. Kristy has been asked out to a movie Friday evening. Her parents review some ground rules.

"There are some things we need from you before we'll feel comfortable about dating," her father tells her. "First, we need to meet your date before you leave. Second, we need to know where you will be in case something comes up and we need to reach you. Third, we want you home by eleven fifteen p.m., and we expect a phone call if anything comes up that might change these plans. If you follow these ground rules and show us you can handle this privilege, we can discuss increasing your curfew later on. Can you agree to follow those ground rules?"

Kristy rolls her eyes, lets out a big sigh, and begins to protest. "I don't believe it! I'm fifteen, not twelve," she says. "This is so unfair! Why you have to meet my date before we go out. That's so embarrassing! My friends' parents don't make their daughters do that. And eleven fifteen p.m. is a complete joke. All my friends get to stay out to at least twelve. Jody's parents let her stay out until one a.m. or later. What's the big deal? Your ground rules are so old-fashioned. I thought you trusted me!" Sound familiar?

Kristy sees no point to her parents' ground rules and no need to demonstrate her readiness. In her mind, her readiness is an established fact, a foregone conclusion, and not even worth discussing. She feels ready. She believes she's ready, and she sees her friends already doing the things she wants to do. Therefore, she must be ready. Her definition of readiness requires no preparation or accountability.

How does this thinking develop? Remember in Chapter 2 when we discussed that big growth spurt during adolescence and how strong emotions and impulses make rational thinking nearly impossible? Kristy is a good example. Her impulses and desires are so strong that they overwhelm her rational thinking. All she knows is that she wants everything all at once and without any conditions. She doesn't consider that jumping headfirst into new privileges without preparation might be risky, even dangerous. That's why parents encounter so much resistance when we try to introduce some clear thinking and rationality into the process.

What other influences contribute to entitled thinking?

Peers and the media have to be at the top of the list. Peers are your teen's immediate and most influential reference group. Your teen is very aware of the privileges and freedoms his or her friends enjoy and is eager to point these out to you as evidence of his or her readiness. That's where the familiar statement *All my friends get to do it* comes from. Teenage logic goes like this: *If my friends are ready, then I must be ready.* No further evidence is required.

The media also have a strong influence. Turn on your television and watch nearly any program that caters to the preteen and teen demographic (12–17 years). What do you see? You see lots of preteens and teens dressing and acting like young adults and enjoying the freedoms and privileges of adults. Often, the adults on these shows are represented as bungling buffoons who are easily confused and manipulated by teens. What's the message to the teenage audience when they see other teens successfully manipulating adults and enjoying the privileges of adults? Of course, *If my teenage role models on TV are ready, then I must be ready.*

### Examples of Entitled Thinking
- "That's not fair! All my friends get to do that."
- "Why do I have to prove I'm ready?"
- "If I feel ready, then I must be ready."
- "I'm thirteen. I'm ready."
- "All my friends' parents let them do it."
- "I know I can handle it."
- "Other parents don't make their teens follow stupid ground rules."
- "Don't you trust me?"

- "You know I wouldn't do anything stupid."
- "I'm not a little kid anymore. I don't need any ground rules."
- "You know I can handle it."
- "We've already talked about this. I know what to do."

## The Thinking of Readiness

Most parents I see in my workshops and counseling want to extend new freedoms and privileges to their teens, but parents approach this issue with apprehension. Why? Because we recognize the risks and dangers involved in jumping into new experiences without adequate preparation. We remember how naïve and inexperienced we were as teenagers, and we want to minimize the risks and keep our teens safe. We want to feel confident that our teens are ready to handle their privileges safely and responsibly.

What is a parent's definition of readiness? Let's refer to *Webster's Dictionary* again for a little help. *Webster's* defines readiness as "being prepared or available for service or action." *Prepared* is the key word, and it implies having the skills, judgment, and maturity to successfully carry out a task. Preparation is a requirement for readiness.

Parents recognize that readiness is not an all-or-nothing issue (for example, either you're ready or you're not). There are degrees of readiness that vary from individual to individual. Some teens show full readiness for a new privilege, that is, they are able to demonstrate the skills, judgment, and maturity needed to successfully handle the privilege on a consistent basis. Other teens show partial readiness—that is, they show some, but not all, of the necessary skill preparation. They need more time to practice and develop their readiness. Some teens don't show any readiness at all. They lack the skills, judgment, and maturity needed to handle the privilege. They need time to mature. Your challenge, as the parent, is to determine where your teen is on the continuum of readiness and allocate privileges accordingly.

### *Examples of Readiness Thinking*
- "You're ready when you show us you're ready."
- "Privileges are not a right. You have to earn them."
- "Your words are encouraging, but your actions show what you can handle."
- "I'm interested in what you can handle, not your friends."
- "This is about you, not your friends or your friends' parents."
- "Show me you're ready, and we'll both know it."
- "This is not about trust. It's about readiness."
- "I love you too much to take risks with your safety."
- "Teens on TV do not determine the ground rules in our house."
- "I want you to be ready, and I hope you show that you are."
- "You'll have other chances later on to show you're ready."
- "This is not about fairness. It's about readiness."

How do parents approach the issue of readiness with their teens? You have several options. You can take the "permissive approach" and give your teen the privileges he or she demands without any conditions, and hope for the best. You can take the "autocratic or punitive approach," deny your teen privileges and opportunities to acquire them, and brace yourself for the protests and rebellion you're sure to encounter. Some parents flip-flop back and forth between these two extremes. Or you can use the democratic approach and set the question of readiness up as an experiment, test it out, and learn along with your teen what he or she is ready to handle. In Chapter 14, we'll examine the experiences of parents who tried each of these options. As you'll discover, readiness testing is by far the best way to go.

*Table 6 Readiness Versus Entitlement*

| *Readiness* | *Entitlement* |
| --- | --- |
| Freedom and privileges with accountability | Freedom and privileges without accountability |
| Testing within clearly defined boundaries | A learning opportunity without guidance or direction |
| Clear thinking based on sound logic | Thinking based on faulty logic |
| A tested hypothesis involving observation and measurement of performance | An untested hypothesis accepted as true |

| | |
|---|---|
| Results are reality-based, accurate statements of readiness | No demonstrated skills, judgment, or maturity required |
| A learning process for both parents and teens | No guidelines to measure success or failure |
| Provides protections and safeguards | Provides no protections or safeguards |

## CHAPTER 14

# Readiness Testing:
# How Parents
# Determine Readiness

How do you know how much freedom and how many new privileges your teen is ready to handle? Often, you don't know, and neither does your teen. This is uncharted territory for both of you. However, there is a simple and effective way to find out. You can set up the question of readiness as an experiment and test it out. Your teen's behavior will tell you what he or she is ready to handle. That's what this chapter will show you how to do. Limit testing is your teen's job. Readiness testing should be yours.

## Readiness Testing

On a conceptual level, determining your teen's readiness for new privileges is no more difficult than carrying out a fourth-grade science experiment. You begin with a hypothesis. You set up the conditions for the experiment. You test out the experiment, make observations, and measure the outcomes. Then you develop your conclusions. It's that simple. Anyone can do it. If you have any doubts, refer to the Question and Answer section at the end of the chapter. Welcome to readiness testing. Here's the four-step formula:

1. State your hypothesis (for example, my fifteen-year-old is ready for dating).
2. Set the conditions for the experiment (for example, establish ground rules such as transportation arrangements, curfew, acceptable attire, etc.).
3. Carry out the experiment, make observations, measure outcomes, and share outcome data with your teen.
4. Develop your conclusion about readiness (for example, fully ready, partial readiness, not ready).

How long should each experiment last? This varies with the privilege and your teen's capacity to handle it. Some experiments will be very brief and should be discontinued shortly after they begin, particularly when safety issues are involved. Most readiness experiments require four to eight weeks before parents have sufficient outcome data to arrive at a thoughtful conclusion. Some experiments, such as driving, avoiding drugs, dating, and staying out late, require many months of consistent performance before parents have sufficient evidence.

The bottom line is—there is no one right length of time for determining readiness. Readiness testing is a learning process for parents and teens alike. Outcomes vary from teen to teen. Most teens want the experiments to be very short so they can enjoy the full privilege right away. Parents want the experiments to be long enough to provide the readiness information they need. Your teen's behavior or performance will demonstrate how much time he or she needs to be fully ready.

During the readiness-testing period, I recommend holding family meetings with your teen on a weekly basis, if not more often, to share your observations. Regular feedback minimizes surprises and arguments later on. State your observations in a matter-of-fact manner. Specify where improvement is needed, and revise parts of the privilege if needed. You'll see examples in the vignettes to follow.

There are only three possible outcomes to a readiness experiment: full readiness, partial readiness, and not ready. When your teen successfully handles the privilege and fully meets the conditions of the experiment, then he or she is fully ready to continue with that privilege. I recommend holding at that level for at least eight more weeks to allow your teen to show consistent readiness before increasing the privilege.

If your teen meets some or most of the conditions of the experiment, then he or she shows partial, but not full, readiness for the privilege. Partial readiness is the most common outcome. This means your teen needs more time to practice before he or she is fully ready to handle the privilege. Repeat the experiment and work toward full readiness.

You can always increase or decrease the conditions of the privilege based upon what your teen demonstrates he or she can handle. For example, let's say your teen is trying to demonstrate readiness for a dating privilege. If he or she successfully handles most of the conditions of the dating privilege except the midnight curfew time, then I recommend finding the next level your teen can handle. Revise the curfew downward to eleven thirty for the next two to four weeks. If he or she fails to handle that curfew, revise the time downward by thirty minutes each time this happens until you find a time your teen can consistently handle for four weeks. This is a process. Eventually, your teen will discover that he or she controls the outcome.

When your teen is unable to handle most or all the conditions of the experiment or exercises such poor judgment that they are at risk, then their behavior is telling you that he or she is not ready to handle that privilege. Discontinue the experiment and allow at least eight to twelve weeks before attempting the experiment again. Your teen needs time to mature. Brace yourself for the protest that is sure to follow. No teen wants to hear this conclusion, but it's good information for both teens and parents.

Remember, readiness varies from teen to teen. There is no universal standard, although your teen will do his or her best to convince you otherwise. Let your teen know that they will always have another chance to demonstrate their readiness at some future date.

## Topics for Readiness-Testing Experiments

Readiness is a topic that comes up repeatedly during adolescence whenever your teen presses you for more freedom and privileges. The following are some of the many possible topics for setting up readiness experiments with your teen:

- Driving privileges
- Dating privileges
- Party privileges
- Participation in extracurricular activities
- Car care
- Appropriate personal hygiene
- Balancing commitments (for example, friends, chores, school, extracurriculars)
- Sleepover privileges
- Curfews
- After-school unsupervised time (for example, 3–6 p.m.)
- Unsupervised time during weekends
- Cell phone privileges
- Computer privileges
- Credit card privileges
- Video game privileges
- TV privileges
- Bedtimes
- Spending time at the mall
- Attending concerts

## Brett: An Example of Freedom Without Limits

Now, let's see how readiness testing works in real life. We discussed the options available to parents when approaching the issue of readiness. Brett's parents chose option #1, "the permissive approach." Brett, age sixteen, believed he was ready for new privileges, and his parents believed it, too. He had always been responsible at home and at school. He did his chores without reminders, maintained a B-minus average, and hung around with friends who also seemed responsible. His parents trusted him, and, because they did, they extended many liberties and privileges.

Brett was permitted to have friends at the house when his parents weren't home. He didn't need to check in after school, and he wasn't required to tell his parents where he was going when he went out on weekends as long as he returned by twelve thirty. They even bought him a new car for his sixteenth birthday and gave him a credit card for gas.

Shortly after Brett turned sixteen, his parents noticed a change. He spent more time with his friends away from home. He showed up late for dinners on a regular basis, and he often arrived home well after his twelve-thirty curfew on weekends.

At first, his parents didn't think anything of it. *This is probably normal teenage behavior,* they thought. *He seems to be doing okay.* They didn't suspect that doing nothing was a tacit green light for more testing.

When they asked him how his schoolwork was going, Brett said, "Everything is good." He said he liked doing his homework at the public library better than at home. It was quieter.

Brett's parents got their first clue that everything wasn't fine a few weeks before the end of the semester. They received a deficiency notice in the mail that said Brett's grades had dropped below a C average (1.4 GPA). When they asked Brett about it, he said he had a few outstanding papers to complete and that his grades would be above a 2.0 by the end of the semester.

The next clue came on the weekend, when Brett announced, "I'm taking Curt and John to a party tonight."

"Don't forget about your twelve-thirty deadline," his father had reminded him, but it is nearly two in the morning when Brett's car rolls up in front of the house. He fumbles with his key in the door lock. When his father comes to investigate, he sees Brett is so drunk he can barely get his words out.

"We'll talk in the morning," says his father.

When Brett arrives for breakfast, he can see the anger and disappointment in his parents' faces. "I guess I really screwed up," says Brett.

"You sure did," replies his father. "How did Curt and John get home?"

"I drove them," says Brett.

"Do you realize the danger you put them and yourself in by driving that way?" asks his father. "What do you think would have happened if you had been pulled over or gotten into an accident?"

"I didn't think about it," says Brett contritely.

"Why didn't you call me or make some other arrangements to get home safely?" inquires his father.

"I knew I would get in trouble if you found out," says Brett. "Besides, I thought I could make it home all right, and I did."

"Yes, luckily you did," says his father, "but you were willing to risk your life, your friends' lives, and a drunk-driving charge to pull it off. Unbelievable!" The seriousness of Brett's poor judgment is beginning to sink in.

"Where did you get the liquor?" asks his father.

"At the party," Brett replies.

"Were there any adults there?" inquires his father. Brett just shakes his head.

"Look, Dad," says Brett. "I know I messed up big-time, but I promise it won't happen again. I promise."

"You're right about that," says his father angrily, "because you no longer have a car to drive or any evening privileges to abuse. May I have your keys, please? Your privileges are suspended until further notice. You can take the bus to and from school, but other than that, you're grounded to the house."

As bad as things seemed, they got worse. A week later, Brett's grades arrived in the mail along with a letter from the high school attendance office. He finished the semester with a 1.4 GPA. The letter from the attendance office was of greater concern. Brett had six truancies during the semester. Six excuse notes with his parents' forged signatures were attached to the letter.

"Is there anything more I should know about?" Brett's father asks that night after dinner. He noticed the credit card he provided Brett for gas had out-of-town addresses on it.

"No, that's all," says Brett dejectedly.

"How do you explain the gas charges in Rocklin and Auburn on school days?" asks his father. "May I have the card, please?"

*Oh shit!* Brett says to himself. *I didn't think about that.* He looks embarrassed as he hands his father the card.

"Where were you when you weren't in school?" asks his mom.

"We went to the park and downtown, and sometimes we took short trips to other towns. Most of the time, we hung out at John's house while his parents were at work." His mom just shakes her head with disappointment.

This is where things remained for the next eight weeks. Brett went to and from school, but other than that, he was grounded to the house. No car. No trips to the library. No party or evening-out privileges. His friends were allowed to visit on weekends only.

Brett and his parents did their best to avoid one another. He didn't speak much to them, and they didn't speak much to him. The only bright spot was Brett's mid-semester progress report: all B's and C's. His grades were coming up again. That's when Brett's father decided to make an appointment.

"I really don't know what to do," his father admitted after he shared what had happened. "We've lost a lot of trust in Brett, but we can also see he's making an effort. I don't know if he's even ready to handle the privileges we gave him, but we can't keep him locked up in the house forever, either. This isn't doing anybody any good. He's miserable, and so are we."

Both parents recognized the need to restore some of Brett's privileges, but they didn't know how to begin. Their confidence had been shaken, and they were uncertain about how much freedom Brett was ready to handle.

Brett, on the other hand, was eager to have his privileges restored and to have another opportunity to show he was trustworthy and capable of handling things more maturely. His mistakes had taught him some painful lessons. He knew that regaining his parents' confidence would take time.

We spent most of our first two sessions discussing the usual teen issues: limit testing, limit setting, responsibility, trust, and how to use logical consequences to support ground rules.

On the third session, I shared the simple four-step formula for determining Brett's readiness for each of the privileges he abused. Brett's parents had some new tools in their guidance toolkit. They were ready to give Brett another opportunity to show what he could handle. That night at dinner, Brett's parents introduced a new plan.

"Brett, let's talk about getting some of your privileges back," his father begins.

"Does that mean I can use my car again and go out on weekends?" Brett asks in a hopeful tone.

"Yes," says his father, "but this time we'll know if you're really ready for these privileges." He reviews the ground rules for successfully handling each of the privileges. "If you're willing to follow our ground rules and do your part, you can earn back the privileges you've lost. Your part means maintaining at least a C average, attending school regularly, and staying away from drugs and alcohol. If you follow those rules, we'll know you're ready to have some of your privileges back, such as using your car for trips to and from school, to the library in the evenings, for errands, and to your friends' houses after school if there's a parent there. We expect you home by six p.m. in time for dinner. We also expect you to keep us informed when you go anywhere other than school. Are you willing to follow those ground rules?"

"Well, yeah," says Brett, "but why are they so tight? I didn't have to leave notes or make phone calls before. None of my friends have to do that. It doesn't seem fair."

"Those are the ground rules we need to feel comfortable for now," Brett's father replies. "We need you to show us that you will be where you say you'll be. If you show us you can follow those ground rules, we can discuss changing them later on. We'll meet at the end of each week to discuss how things are going."

"What happens if I mess up or forget?" asks Brett.

"That all depends upon how much you mess up or forget," says his father. "If your grades drop below a C average or if you have any unexcused absences, then we'll know you're not ready to use the car for school transportation. Your driving privileges will be suspended until your next report card shows a C average and regular school attendance. If there is any more drinking and driving, the car will be off-limits for much longer than one quarter. If you neglect to keep us informed when you go anywhere other than to school and back, then each time that happens the car will be off-limits after school hours for one week," says his father.

"Can I go to dances and parties again?" asks Brett. "And can I use my car when I do?"

"Yes, on both," says his father, "if you're willing to following the ground rules. You'll have to be home by twelve midnight. If you're not, we'll try eleven thirty and see how that works out. If you come home drunk, dances and party privileges will be suspended for an academic quarter each time that happens, and you'll lose your driving privileges altogether for a full semester. But, if you follow our ground rules and everything works out fine, we can talk about increasing your curfew to twelve thirty again. Does that sound reasonable?"

"I can understand the twelve time," says Brett, "and the consequences for not following the ground rules, but I don't understand why I have to phone or leave a note when I go somewhere after school or on weekends. I'm not a little kid anymore. I didn't have to do that before. I feel real stupid doing that."

"I understand," says his father, "but that's what we need to feel comfortable. If you do your part consistently, we can discuss relaxing this requirement. Our ground rules may seem strict to you right now, but we love you too much to make the mistakes we made before. We'll review how things go at the end of each week. When we see you're living within the ground rules we've agreed upon, we may be ready to drop that requirement. Are you willing to go along with these arrangements?" Brett nods. The new ground rules went into effect the next day.

The experiments for determining Brett's readiness were set up. I continued to meet with Brett and his parents twice monthly for the next six months. How did things go? As expected, Brett tested some of the ground rules, and when he did, his parents followed through with a logical consequence and adjusted his privileges accordingly. Both Brett and his parents were discovering what privileges he really could handle.

During the first eight weeks, Brett arrived home late from weekend dances and parties on three occasions. Each time, his curfew was revised to a half hour earlier. He complied with the revised times on a few occasions and continued to test on others. During one of their weekly meetings, Brett's parents decided to suspend all of his evening-out privileges for four weeks because he didn't consistently follow the ground rules. He begged for another chance. Reluctantly, his parents agreed to try a ten-thirty curfew for four weeks. Then things improved.

Brett was not good about keeping his parents informed

about his comings and goings. There were many instances of forgotten notes and phone calls during the first three months. Each time this happened, Brett lost his car for after-school use for five days. He complained, and on one occasion he decided to take it anyway, got caught, and lost it for two more weeks. When Brett finally realized there was no way around the rule, he started keeping his parents better informed.

Brett didn't test the ground rules for the privileges that mattered most. He kept his grades above a 2.0 and attended school regularly. There were no further incidents of arriving home intoxicated. Although he repeatedly tested his curfew, Brett never fully lost his weekend privileges or the privilege of driving his car to and from school. He was showing his parents he could live within most of the ground rules and handle most of his privileges responsibly. Six months after we started, Brett had earned back most of his privileges.

## Whitney: An Example of Limits Without Freedom

Teenage "early bloomers" present a special set of challenges for parents. Their demands for freedom and new privileges come on suddenly and can be overwhelming. That's how it felt for Whitney's mom, a single parent, when her fourteen-year-old started pushing hard against the walls. But each time Whitney pushed, all she got was a lot of yelling, screaming, arguing, angry lectures, and stronger walls to discourage her testing. The harder Whitney pushed, the more her mom resisted and the deeper the two became stuck. When I first met them, things had deteriorated into all-out rebellion.

Whitney had all the usual teenage complaints: "My mom treats me like a little kid. She won't let me do anything. Her rules are stupid. She won't let me go to my friends' homes after school, and now she says I can't have anybody over to our house. When I try to talk with her, she won't listen. She tries to control everything I do. She won't even let me stay out past ten o'clock. What a joke! All my friends get to do that. Our high school games and dances aren't even over until nearly eleven."

Translation: Whitney wanted the things other teenagers want: more freedom, more privileges, more independence, less time at home, more time with friends, and more input into decision making. She felt she was ready for a major overhaul in the ground rules at home, and she was probably right.

In the past, Whitney had always been responsible at home and at school. She did her chores, completed her schoolwork, got acceptable grades, and was trusted to be on her own until her mom arrived home from work. Whitney was even permitted to have friends at the house when her mom wasn't home, a privilege that wasn't abused.

When Whitney turned fourteen, however, many things began to change. Physically, she was "an early bloomer," very developed, and very attractive. She spent more time with her friends and less time with her chores and homework. Her bedroom looked like a disaster area. Household chores were often neglected, and her grades slipped from B's to C's. She was on her cell phone or at her computer constantly.

But Whitney's mom was most alarmed about the steady

stream of friends, both male and female, who visited the house after school. There were messes. On several occasions, the house smelled like cigarettes. The house was declared off-limits to all of Whitney's friends. When Whitney insisted she was ready for this privilege, her mom said "absolutely not" and ended the discussion.

"I don't understand why she is doing this to me," complained Whitney's mom. "She has never openly defied my rules before."

Whitney's mom and I spent several sessions discussing the process of adolescence. We discussed limit testing, limit setting, how to support rules with logical consequences, and readiness testing. It was reassuring for her to hear that the behavior she considered abnormal and disturbing was normal for most teens.

I was curious why she took such a hard-line stand on increasing Whitney's freedom and privileges, when she had always demonstrated responsibility in the past. "She's not ready!" her mom insisted, then shared her real fears.

"I was an early bloomer like Whitney when I was her age. My parents gave me a lot of freedom, and I got pregnant when I was fifteen. It was probably the most painful experience of my life." She was determined not to let this happen to Whitney, but she faced a dilemma because she could also see that protecting Whitney from the pain of poor choices was making matters worse. It was time to revise their ground rules and increase her freedom and privileges. They had a talk the next evening.

"Whitney, I can see now that I haven't been giving you many opportunities to demonstrate your readiness for new privileges," her mom begins. "I think it's time we talked about changing some of the ground rules we've been fighting over." Whitney nearly falls over when she hears these words.

"Are you serious?" asks Whitney.

"I sure am," says her mom. "I'm done with all the yelling, screaming, arguing, and lectures. I trusted you before, and I think you're probably ready to handle more privileges now." She explains the four-step readiness-testing formula to Whitney. "Let's just go down the list and see what we can work out. Would you like to begin with Friday and Saturday nights?"

"May I stay out until eleven?" asks Whitney.

"I'm ready to try eleven for school events such as sports and dances as long as you ask several days in advance and parents do the driving. You need to be home by eleven and not later. If anything comes up that might affect that, I expect a phone call so we can decide what to do. Can you agree to that?"

"Of course!" Whitney replies, pleased with her new freedom and privilege.

"Good," says her mom. "We'll try it out for a few months and see how it goes. If you follow the ground rules, we'll stay with eleven. If not, we'll return to ten. If you're late on a regular basis, we'll both know you're not ready to handle this privilege yet. We can try this experiment again later on.

"Now, let's talk about doing your part at home," says her mom. "This means doing your chores regularly, following my rules about having friends to the house, and limiting your time on the phone."

"Does that mean cleaning my room, too?" asks Whitney. "Aren't I old enough to keep my room the way I want it?"

"You are," says her mom, "but up to a point. I don't want

to have to look at that mess every time I walk by your room. That's not fair to me."

"What if I just keep the door shut so you don't have to look at it?" Whitney suggests.

"I can go along with that," says her mom, "but if you leave the door open, you're going to have to clean it up. Also, I'm not comfortable with you having friends in there when it's a mess, so there won't be any sleepovers unless it's cleaned up. If you can live with that, so can I." Whitney nodded.

"Good," says her mom. "We'll add your room to the list of experiments. Let's try it out for a month and see how it goes."

"May I go to my friends' homes after school and have my friends over to our house again?" asks Whitney.

"Yes," her mom replies, "if you're willing to follow the ground rules. You can go to your girlfriends' homes and have your girlfriends visit our home after school if your chores are done and if you call me at work so I know where you'll be or who will visit our house. No boys are allowed in the house when I'm not home, and you're not allowed to be with boys in your girlfriends' homes unless a parent is there to supervise. No exceptions. You need to be home by six p.m. on weeknights. If I notice any cigarette odors, you will lose this privilege for two weeks each time it happens. If it happens repeatedly, I'll suspend the privilege for two months. Can you agree to that?"

"Yeah, but what happens if I forget to call or return home on time?" asks Whitney.

"If you forget to call or forget to return home by six, you'll lose that privilege for three school days each time it happens," says her mom. "We'll just try it again three days later. If you forget regularly, we'll know you're not ready to handle that privilege. Understand?" Whitney nods.

"I know I can follow your ground rules," says Whitney, "but I'm not sure my friends can. What happens if they mess up?"

"Then we'll know they're not ready to handle that privilege," her mom replies. "The friends that make messes can't be here when I'm not home. Agreed?" Whitney nods.

"The last big issue we need to talk about is the phone," says her mom. "You're on it all the time."

"I can't predict when my friends will call," says Whitney, "or how long they want to talk."

"But you do have control over when you call and how long you talk," says her mom. "I'm concerned because your grades have been slipping and your chores have been neglected. Homework and chores need to be completed each night before you use the phone. You usually finish your chores and homework by seven thirty. Tell your friends not to call until before seven thirty."

"What happens if my friends call before that time?" asks Whitney.

"Don't answer," her mom replies, but Whitney cannot imagine not answering her phone. "Can you agree to those ground rules?"

"I guess so," says Whitney reluctantly.

"If you don't follow those ground rules, then your phone privileges will be suspended for three days at a time each time it happens," says her mom.

"Three days!" Whitney protests. "Why so long? That seems so unfair!" Whitney's mom holds firm.

"You'll have another chance three days later," says her mom. "If this becomes a regular problem, I'll hold on to your phone each night until your chores and homework are done." Whitney does not like the sound of that.

The readiness-testing experiments were all set up. Each side had moved in the other's direction. Whitney was happy to have opportunities to get what she wanted, and her mom was happy to have a way to determine Whitney's readiness without all the angst and power struggles. The battles were over, at least temporarily. Whitney still had to demonstrate she could handle her privileges successfully.

What were the outcomes of the experiments? As expected, there was testing and the usual ups and downs. Whitney claims she just forgot, but she didn't arrive home from a friend's house until 6:45 one night.

"I'm sorry, Mom," says Whitney as she walks through the door. She pleads for a second chance, but her mom sticks to their agreement.

"You'll have another chance in three days," says her mom, matter-of-factly.

So Whitney decides to make the most of it. She invites several girlfriends over each of the three days. Her mom is apprehensive, but everything goes smoothly. Whitney follows the ground rules and so do her friends. No messes. No cigarette odors. *She's really trying,* her mom thinks to herself.

The following week, Whitney receives a phone call from one of her friends early in the evening. It is only six thirty, and she hasn't started her homework.

"It's only six thirty," says her mom. "Time to get off the phone."

"I will," says Whitney, but when her mom returns in thirty minutes, Whitney is still on the phone. When Whitney sees her mom, she hangs up quickly, but it's too late.

"May I have your phone, please?" says her mom, matter-of-factly. "You can have it back in three days."

"That's so unfair!" Whitney protests, but the rule is not negotiable. Reluctantly, she hands over her phone, and stomps off to her room. She's frustrated, but she knows it was her decision that lost the privilege.

Three months after the experiments began, Whitney continued to demonstrate her increasing readiness. Sure, she tested from time to time, particularly with her phone privilege and after-school return times, but each time she did, her mom followed through with the agreed-upon consequence to help Whitney stay on track. She never tested the conditions for the privilege that mattered most: the eleven o'clock curfew for school dances and sports events. At the end of our four-month follow-up session, Whitney's mom agreed to revise her weekend curfew to eleven thirty.

## Chapter Summary

Teens need freedom to test and explore, but they also need clear, firm limits to guide their exploration and discover their readiness. Autocratic approaches based on overcontrol (limits without freedom) and permissive guidance approaches based on undercontrol (freedom without limits) fail to provide the learning opportunities and outcome data parents need to discover their teen's actual readiness.

Whitney's mom took the "autocratic or punitive approach." What happened when she provided too many limits and too little freedom for Whitney to test and explore? She inspired her daughter's resentment and rebellion.

Brett's parents took the "permissive approach." What happened when they provided too much freedom and too few limits to guide Brett's exploration? He tested for the walls. Without solid walls to guide his exploration, he got into trouble.

Readiness testing (freedom within limits) strikes the desired balance between the two extremes and is ideally suited for teens. It provides opportunities for testing and learning within clearly defined limits that parents can control. It teaches responsibility because teens are held accountable for their choices and behavior, and it provides the outcome data parents need to determine their teen's readiness. The outcome of each readiness experiment is simply a factual statement of what your teen is capable of handling at a specific point in time. Brett's and Whitney's parents discovered a safe and reliable way to determine their teen's readiness without all the angst and power struggles. So can you.

### Questions and Answers About Readiness Experiments

*Question:* How do I set up a readiness experiment?
*Answer:* Three factors deserve your thoughtful attention:

1. Clearly state your hypothesis in measurable terms (for example, Is Tony ready to handle the privilege of driving to and from school each day?).
2. Clearly state the conditions or ground rules for the experiment in measurable terms (for example, Tony needs to obey traffic safety laws, arrive at school on time, take care of the car, and ask for permission before taking the car anywhere other than to and from school).

3. Clearly state the time frame for the experiment (for example, one month, one academic quarter, one semester, etc.).

*Question:* What is the recommended time frame for each readiness experiment?

*Answer:* The most important thing to remember is that readiness testing is a learning process with ups and downs, successes and failures. The goal is readiness preparation, not immediate success. You'll need to allow your teen sufficient time to demonstrate what he or she can do. For experiments involving dating privileges, party privileges, and unsupervised time, a 10–12-week time frame is a good starting point.

Experiments that involve safety issues (such as unprotected sex, drug or alcohol use, driving, high-risk activities) should be brief. Discontinue the experiment when your teen shows a complete lack of readiness with the understanding that he or she can try it again at some future time (for example, 12–16 weeks).

*Question:* Is a perfect outcome or 100 percent compliance a realistic expectation for readiness experiments?

*Answer:* In the vast majority of cases, the answer is no. I rarely see full readiness right out of the starting blocks. Most readiness experiments involve a lot of ups and downs, successes and failures. You should expect good weeks and bad weeks. The goal is improvement that leads to readiness, not perfection. Partial readiness is a typical outcome of many readiness experiments, and I consider that to be a successful outcome. It means your teen is heading in the right direction but still has more work to do.

The exception, of course, is experiments that involve safety issues and permit little margin for error. When the initial outcome of these experiments shows a complete lack of readiness, then discontinue the experiment. Your teen can always try it again at some future point in time when he or she has acquired more maturity.

*Question:* How many times should parents repeat a readiness experiment when the outcome shows only partial readiness?

*Answer:* Repeat the experiment as often as needed or until your teen shows complete readiness. Readiness varies from teen to teen. There is no one time frame that fits all. If your teen shows partial readiness, that's a good thing! It means the experiment is working and that readiness preparation is occurring. Consider it "a work in progress." Partial readiness is partial success.

*Question:* What are some dos and don'ts regarding sharing observations and conclusions with your teen about his or her readiness?

*Answer:* There's a lot riding on these experiments for your teen, so the atmosphere is likely to be tense and emotionally charged. With this in mind, the following tips should help. Let's begin with the dos.

THE DOS:

1. Accurate data collection is an important part of any experiment. I recommend you write down your observations when they occur, note the time and date, and save your observations and progress notes in a binder or notebook. Don't rely on your memory alone. This opens the door to subjectivity, arguments, and disputes.

2. Make an appointment with your teen to meet on a weekly basis while the experiment is in progress to review your observations and discuss progress toward the readiness goal. Arrange an appointment at the end of the experiment to share your conclusions based upon the data you've collected. There are only three outcomes: full readiness, partial readiness, and not ready.

3. Share successful observations before addressing failures or setbacks.

4. State your observations and conclusions in a matter-of-fact manner. When the conclusion of the experiment is "not ready," specify a time to repeat the experiment so things end on a hopeful note.

THE DON'TS:

1. Don't rely on your memory to keep track of events, observations, and progress.

2. Don't point out your teen's failures before addressing his or her successes.

3. Don't shame, blame, criticize, or express disappointment about your teen's efforts or lack of progress. The experiment is not about you. It's about your teen. Let the factual data speak for itself.

4. Don't argue with your teen about your observations or conclusions.

*Question:* When is professional help needed?

*Answer:* Seek professional assistance in the following situations:

1. When communication has completely broken down between you and your teen.

2. When you suspect a mental health issue might be contributing to your teen's lack of progress.

3. When safety or legal issues are involved.

## CHAPTER 15

# The Trust Bank Account

All teens share a Trust Bank Account with their parents. Teens make deposits and withdrawals from this account, and those transactions determine the balance of trust in the parent–teen relationship. What is a typical deposit? Teen deposits are simply the things teens do to build trust, demonstrate their trustworthiness, and show good character, such as honoring a curfew or helping out at home. Withdrawals are the things teens do that break down trust and erode trustworthiness, such as showing up two hours late or neglecting school responsibilities.

Your shared Trust Bank Account shows a positive balance when your teen's deposits outnumber withdrawals, but the account can become overdrawn and show a negative balance when withdrawals outnumber deposits. The balance fluctuates with the normal ups and downs of your teen's deposits and withdrawals.

The Trust Bank Account is an effective procedure for measuring your teen's readiness and character development. The procedure works hand in hand with the readiness testing experiments you learned about in Chapters 13 and 14. I recommend introducing both procedures to your teen at the same time.

Managing your shared bank account is no more difficult than managing a checkbook, and you're going to have to teach your teen to do this at some point anyway. Teens earn privileges and trust by making regular deposits, or they can lose privileges and trust by making withdrawals. Your job is to help your teen pay attention to the balance in the account, conduct regular reviews of the balance statements, and adjust freedom and privileges accordingly. That's what this chapter and the next will show you how to do. You're about to add a valuable new tool to your parenting toolkit.

## Why Trust Is So Important

The Trust Bank Account takes readiness testing to a deeper level and gets to the core of what's really going on between you and your teen. Readiness testing is about behavior, what your teen does or does not do, on the surface level of everyday life. Honoring curfews, keeping up with schoolwork, and driving safely are typical examples. The outcome of each experiment is simply a factual statement about what your teen can do at a particular point in time.

The Trust Bank Account, on the other hand, is about feelings and beliefs. The balance statement reveals how you much confidence you feel and where you and your teen stand on the important issues of readiness and trust at a particular point in time. A positive balance statement provides us with the confidence we need to know that our teen is ready for more freedom and privileges.

See how neatly the two procedures fit together? Readiness

leads to trust, and trust leads to increased freedom and privileges for teens. The sooner your teen learns this, the farther along he or she will be toward accomplishing that search for an individual identity we discussed in Chapter 2.

Identity is about character development and finding answers to the question *Who do I want to become?* It's a process of trying on different hats and appearances, exploring different ways of behaving, and testing out different values and beliefs to discover which ones fit best and feel right.

## What Trust Means to Parents and Teens

Trust means different things to parents and teens because we view the issue from such different perspectives. Teens tend to view trust from the perspective of a child. They see it as a right, something that should be freely given, with no strings attached, much like the unconditional love that exists between a child and his or her parents. The logic goes something like this—*You should trust me unconditionally because you love me unconditionally.*

Most parents, on the other hand, view trust from the perspective of an adult. We recognize that the love we have for our teen may be unconditional, but trust is not. Trust is fragile. It can't be turned off and on like a faucet. Trust must be earned through consistent, trustworthy behavior. Mature adults understand this. Most teens don't. That's why their deposits are so important. We need their regular deposits to develop the confidence that our teen is ready for more freedom and privileges.

To complicate matters, teens don't want to confront the issue of trust in a lecture format or well-intended heart-to-heart discussion with parents. Teens don't want to be told about trust. They want to experience the lesson firsthand for themselves. That's why the Trust Bank Account is such a wonderful tool. It's not about talk. It's about action. Teens get to actually experience what trust and trustworthiness are all about.

## Character Matters to Teens

Here's a jaw-dropper: character matters to teens. Contrary to popular belief, the biggest influence in shaping your teen's character and core values is not your teen's peer group, the mass media, or pop culture. The research shows that the biggest influence is you, the parent. You are the measuring stick or reference point for your teen's character development. For better or worse, the behavior you role-model sets the standard for acceptable adult behavior.

Surprised? Many parents are. This isn't exactly the message we get when we look at our teens' spiked hair, multiple earrings, pierced body parts, and see them talking nonstop on a cell phone with music blasting in the background. But the research evidence is clear. Our parental values matter most to our teens. If we were successful in role-modeling the values, morals, and ethical standards we hoped to pass on to our kids during their early- and middle-childhood years, then the lessons we taught were learned by our kids. Without realizing it, we've already made our biggest deposit in our kids' lives, and that deposit is securely in the bank.

Then why do teens go to such great lengths to tune us out and disregard our guidance about their character development? It's not that teens don't want to hear about character development. They just don't want to hear it from us. From their point of view, the lesson has already been taught. They already know our core values. They're ready to take the next step and test out those values against other values in their world.

Let me illustrate this point by referring back to the teen TV shows I disparaged in Chapter 13, the ones where preteens and teens regularly enjoy adult privileges, where teens are smarter and more capable than most of the adults, and where adults in positions of authority are often represented as clueless, bungling buffoons. Embedded in most of these shows is some moral or lesson about character. How do these teens typically learn these lessons? Not from lectures from adults. Teens learn the lesson through their interactions with other teens, and often there is some caring and understanding adult in the background who tacitly nods his or her approval of the lesson. These are the lessons that matter most to teens, and this is the way they want to learn them.

## Teen Deposits and Withdrawals

Now that we can appreciate what's really going on between teens and parents on a deeper emotional and psychological level, let's return once again to the surface of day-to-day life and examine the typical deposits and withdrawals teens make from their Trust Bank Account. I divided the deposits category into two subcategories, minor deposits and major deposits, to reflect the relative significance of each type. I divided the withdrawals category in the same way. Major teen withdrawals often require professional help.

The following categories are arbitrary, not research based, and reflect my value system and the values of parents I see in my counseling work. You may want to add items to each list or switch some deposits or withdrawals into the other subcategory, depending on your value system. That's okay. Let's take a look at some typical teen transactions.

### *Minor Deposits*
- Using basic courtesies (for example, "please," "thank you")
- Being punctual
- Practicing good personal hygiene
- Following basic family rules
- Handling chores and household responsibilities
- Complimenting others
- Expressing appreciation
- Showing trustworthy behavior
- Unsolicited hugs, kisses, and expressions of affection
- Showing respect for other family members
- Showing respect for teachers
- Remembering special occasions
- Handling money responsibly
- Showing good table manners
- Taking care of belongings
- Keeping parents informed
- Any unsolicited act of respect or kindness
- Showing good judgment on any minor issue

*Major Deposits*
- Attending school regularly
- Following school rules
- Achieving at or near potential
- Avoiding drugs and alcohol at parties and events
- Driving safely and responsibly
- Safe and responsible sex practices
- Being honest and truthful
- Using cell phone and computer responsibly
- Remembering birthdays, Mother's Day, Father's Day
- Handling credit card privileges responsibly
- Showing compassion for others
- Honoring commitments
- Showing loyalty to friends and family members
- Managing strong emotions
- Showing respect for self and others
- Showing good judgment on any major issue

*Minor Withdrawals*
- Disrespectful behavior
- Profanity
- Put-downs, hurtful statements
- Minor lies and deception
- Neglecting chores
- Neglecting homework and school responsibilities
- Experimentation with drugs or alcohol
- Experimentation with pornography
- Neglecting sleep requirements
- Occasional incidents of sneaking out at night

- Playing music with sexually abusive or violent themes
- Isolated incidents of shoplifting
- Missing curfews
- Abusing minor privileges (for example, cell phone, Internet, after-school privileges)
- Minor acts of defiance (for example, refusals to do chores, join family outings)
- Carelessness with money or possessions
- Holding a party when parents aren't home
- Consistent tardiness
- School suspension
- Poor personal hygiene habits
- Bullying siblings
- Occasional thefts from parent's purse or wallet
- Minor acts of untrustworthy behavior
- Minor incidents of poor judgment

### Major Withdrawals (often requires professional help)

- High-risk or unsafe sexual behavior
- Self-destructive behavior (for example, cutting, self-mutilation)
- Unsafe or reckless driving
- Driving under the influence of drugs or alcohol
- Repeated school truancies
- Substance abuse
- Major incidents of extreme poor judgment
- Repeated defiant behavior toward parents and teachers
- Running away

- School expulsion
- Repeated acts of bullying or violent behavior
- Repeated lying, deception, or untrustworthy behavior
- Participating in gang activities
- Sexual harassment
- Repeated thefts from parents (for example, money, credit cards)
- Major abuses of cell phone or computer privileges
- Repeated illegal activities (for example, vandalism, thefts, drug sales)

## Mason's Trust Bank Account

Mason's parents arrived alone for their first counseling appointment because their sixteen-year-old refused to accompany them. His parents took away his computer and cell phone six weeks before. Since then, Mason refused to cooperate with most everything his parents asked.

"Mason is the black sheep in our family," his mother began. "His older bother and sister are outgoing and athletic. They enjoy the outdoors, camping, and skiing. Mason is the complete opposite. He's introverted, a couch potato, dislikes sports and the outdoors, and avoids social activities at school. He spends nearly all of his free time playing computer games or talking about them with a few close buddies on his cell phone. When we go camping or skiing, Mason spends his time in the tent or in the lodge playing his electronic games. He's a whiz at anything electronic."

"We've never had any problems with Mason before this fall," his father chimed in. "He's bright, has excellent grades, and gets along well with his siblings. Until recently, he did his chores without complaint. He's never deceived or defied us before. That's why we're so concerned. He's acting very strange."

Mason's temperament and adolescent experience sounded quite different from that of his siblings, but he seemed like a great kid. He did his part at home and school and got along well with most of the important people in his life—that is, until recently. There was no previous history of adjustment difficulties.

"What do you think is going on?" I asked.

"We don't know, but we're worried about him," said his mother. She shared a list of things that concerned her.

"Mason has always been responsible, and we give him many privileges," she began. "He drives our old Dodge pickup truck to and from school and around town. We bought him a nice laptop computer for schoolwork and a cell phone so we can stay in touch. We even gave him a low-balance credit card so he can pay for gas and emergencies. Since school began this fall, Mason has repeatedly exceeded the minutes on his cell phone plan, made unauthorized purchases with his credit card, and ignored the warning light in our pickup for two weeks, which caused major engine damage. One of the things that bothers me most," his mother continued, "is his lack of attention to his grooming and personal hygiene. He leaves the house looking like he just rolled out of bed." Mason's father nodded in agreement.

"When did the defiance begin?" I asked.

"Six weeks ago, when we took away his computer and cell

phone," his father replied. "He's not interested in dating, but he and his friends are very interested in sex. They visit porn sites regularly when they're not playing computer games. We told him we didn't approve and tried to block him from these sites, but he always finds a way around our rules. So we took his computer and cell phone away."

"How did he respond?" I asked.

"He refused to do any chores or homework until we return them," said his mother. "So we stopped giving him an allowance. We've been at an impasse for the last six weeks. That's why we're here. His grades are dropping in all of his classes."

"He's only hurting himself," his father said, but I could see from the look on his face that that wasn't true. Mason's defiant behavior was beginning to make sense.

Mason's parents and I spent the rest of the session discussing his temperament, the temperaments of other family members, and their previous experiences with adolescence. It was clear they had an easy time with their other two teens. Mason was different, and the old tools in their toolkit were not working.

Their limit-setting methods, in particular, were not helping matters.

I showed them how to use logical consequences rather than lectures, complaints, and drawn-out punitive consequences. Then I introduced readiness testing and the Trust Bank Account and suggested a plan to help Mason earn back his privileges. His parents liked the plan. I listed Mason's withdrawals on my whiteboard and scheduled another session two days later to set up some readiness experiments.

*Mason's Withdrawals*
- Neglected grooming and personal hygiene
- Abused computer privileges
- Abused cell phone privileges
- Abused credit card privileges
- Neglected basic car maintenance
- Refused to do chores and homework

When we examined Mason's list of withdrawals, we could see that chores and homework didn't require experiments. His refusal was simply retribution for losing his computer and cell phone. We went down the list and developed readiness experiments for all the other issues. "What do you need from Mason to show that he's ready to handle his grooming and personal hygiene responsibly?" I asked.

"He needs to shower, brush his teeth, comb his hair, and wear clean clothes when he leaves the house each day," said his mother. "If that's not done, then he's not ready to leave the house."

"And he's not ready to use the truck," his father added. "He can walk the three miles to school if he wants to look like a bum."

*That was easy,* I said to myself. I summarized what I heard. "Mason is not ready to use the car if he's not clean and groomed." His parents agreed. The first experiment was complete. "What does Mason need to do to show he's ready to use his computer privileges responsibly?" I asked.

"Stay off porn sites," said his father. "Each time he decides to use his computer to watch porn, he loses his computer for a week." Experiment #2 was complete. I posed the same question to Mason's parents about his cell phone privileges.

"He needs to honor the minutes on our plan and stay off porn sites," said his father. "If he exceeds the minutes on our plan, then he loses his cell phone until he pays for the overage with his own money. If he uses his phone to access porn, then we'll eliminate Internet access from his cell phone. We bought him the phone for making calls, not watching porn." Experiment #3 was complete. We turned our attention next to his credit card.

"We gave him the credit card to buy gas and handle emergencies, not to purchase music or computer games," said Mason's mother. "If he uses his card for anything other than the intended purpose, then we'll take the card until he reimburses us with his own money. If this happens repeatedly, we'll know he's not ready for a credit card." Experiment #4 was complete.

"What does Mason need to do to show you he can handle basic car maintenance with the pickup?" I asked. This issue was a sore subject with his father.

"We spent nearly eighteen hundred dollars to repair the engine when Mason ignored the red warning light for more than two weeks," his father reported. "Since that time, he and I discussed the maintenance manual and the importance of responding to warning lights. I'll check the truck once a week. If this issue comes up again, we'll know he's not ready to operate the car responsibly and postpone that privilege for a full semester to give him time to mature." All five experiments were complete. We were ready to include Mason in our next session.

When his parents told him they were working on a plan to restore his computer and cell phone privileges, Mason was willing to join them at their next appointment. He arrived looking like he just got out of bed. His shirt was dirty. His hair was disheveled, and he had a distinct adolescent aroma. I introduced myself, discussed privacy and confidentiality issues, then listened as his parents brought Mason up to date on the readiness experiments we developed. Next, they explained how the Trust Bank Account worked. Mason was attentive and respectful.

"So, when do I get my computer and cell phone back?" he asked.

"We're ready to give them back tomorrow," said his father, "but whether or not you get to keep them is up to you. You'll have to show us you're ready to use them responsibly."

"How do I do that?" asked Mason.

"We've developed some readiness experiments to help us find out," replied his father. "Are you ready to see them?" Mason nodded. I displayed the five experiments on my whiteboard for Mason to see.

*Mason's Readiness Experiments*
Experiment #1: Is Mason ready to handle his grooming and personal hygiene?
Experiment #2: Is Mason ready to handle his computer responsibly?
Experiment #3: Is Mason ready to handle his cell phone privileges responsibly?
Experiment #4: Is Mason ready to handle his credit card privilege responsibly?
Experiment #5: Is Mason ready to handle basic maintenance with the truck?

"I can do all of those things already!" Mason insisted.
"Yes, you're capable of doing them," said his father, "but

you don't do them regularly. We need to see some regular deposits before we can be confident you're ready for these privileges now." I asked Mason's parents to describe the ground rules for each experiment so he understood what his father meant.

"Let's start at the top of the list," his mother began. "When we tell you it's not respectful to others to leave the house looking dirty and poorly groomed, you ignore us. Starting tomorrow, if you're not ready to leave the house, then you're not ready to use the truck. The keys stay with us until you are ready?" Mason nodded.

"The computer issue is even easier to solve," said his father. "Pornography is not okay in our house or on your computer. If we see evidence of pornography on your computer, you will lose your computer for one week each time it happens. If it happens repeatedly, then we'll know you're not ready to use your computer responsibly, and you'll lose that privilege for a full semester. We can try the experiment again later."

"Why are you guys are so bothered about it?" said Mason. "It doesn't hurt anything. Darren's and Jeff's parents don't care."

"Our values and our rules are different," said his father. "We need you to respect them."

"I like their rules better," says Mason.

"When you're an adult, you may choose to do things differently," says his mother, "but you're living here now. Are our ground rules clear?" Mason nods.

"The same consequence applies to your cell phone," adds his father. "If you have porn on your cell phone, then you'll lose your cell phone for one week each time it happens. If it happens repeatedly, we'll delete Internet access from your phone plan. If you exceed the minutes on your phone plan, then you'll lose your phone until you pay for the overages. Now let's talk about the credit card.

"The credit card is for gas and emergencies only," his father continued. "If you use it for other purposes, you need to reimburse us at each billing period. If you don't, we'll know you're not ready for a credit card. Is that clear?" Mason agreed. "Good," said his father. "Let's talk about the truck.

"Using the truck is a privilege," his father continued. "It's an old truck, but repairs are still expensive, and we expect you to let us know if anything is going on with it. I'll check it on weekends. If we discover that you're ignoring warning lights or basic maintenance, then we'll discontinue the privilege of using the truck for a full semester and try it again later. Is that clear?"

"No problem," said Mason.

Mason and his parents agreed to start the experiments the next day and to run them for eight weeks. They also agreed to review the balance statement each weekend. Mason's parents felt confident they could manage the experiments on their own but wanted to check in with me at the midway point and once again at the follow-up conference. I encouraged them to expect the usual ups and downs, stay positive, and try not to overreact to individual withdrawals.

"If you hold firm and follow through," I said, "you'll get the answers you're looking for."

Let's fast-forward to week four of the experiments. When Mason arrived with his parents he was wearing a clean shirt. His hair was combed. His father was upbeat, but his mother looked tired.

"How did it go?" I asked.

"You were right about the ups and downs," Mason's father replied, "but things are much better than they were four weeks ago." He smiled in Mason's direction. "Mason made a lot of deposits in some areas, and we're gaining the confidence we need." Mason's mother tried to be positive but looked drained.

"Other areas are works in progress," she added. "On the whole, I think we're moving in the right direction."

When I asked Mason how things were going, his response was brief. "Okay, I guess. Could be better."

I asked them to review the list of experiments, beginning with the most successful ones, and bring me up to date. His father went first.

"Experiments 2 and 5 have gone great since day one," said his father. "Nothing but big deposits! Mason has honored all of our requests. He does his chores and homework without complaint. We're very pleased."

"Good job, Mason!" I said. I suspected he might risk losing his computer over porn he could still enjoy at his friends' homes. "How did the other experiments go?" I asked.

"Experiments 3 and 4 are works in progress," said his mother. "Mason exceeded the limit on his cell phone plan last month and continues to make nonessential purchases with his credit card. The big difference is that he pays off the balance with his own money when the bills arrive at the end of the month. He's doing what we asked," she conceded.

"Experiment number 1 has been the most difficult and contentious of all of them," said his mother. "Mason doesn't consider his appearance until we point it out to him. When we do, he complains and tries to argue with us. We always hold firm, tell him what he still needs to do, and don't turn over the keys until he looks presentable. Mornings are miserable!" Mason scowled. His mother looked discouraged. She'd lost some perspective.

"He's been late to school eight times during the last four weeks," his mother complained. "When he arrives late, he gets a tardy slip. After three tardy slips, he has to serve one hour of after-school detention."

*Great!* I thought to myself. *The tardy slips and detentions were natural consequences that added weight to our experiment.*

I summarized what I heard to put things into perspective. "It sounds like you've experienced the usual ups and downs," I began. "There have been lots of deposits in some areas and withdrawals in other areas, but Mason is working within the ground rules and making good progress. Everyone is doing their part, although it may not feel like it at times. You're all on course with four weeks to go." We scheduled the follow-up session for the end of week eight.

I received a call from Mason's father a few days later. "We've had a major setback," he said, "and we don't know how to handle it." We scheduled an appointment for the next day.

Mason parents arrived looking angry and upset. Mason looked downcast. "Mason has been suspended from school for five days," his father announced, angrily. "He was caught showing pornographic photos to his friends on his cell phone during lunch break. We grounded him to the house during the five days of his suspension, but we feel like we should do more. We're considering taking away his phone and computer for a full semester." Mason sank into his chair.

"Did he misuse his computer, too?" I asked.

"No, just his cell phone, but this is serious," said his father.

"And upsetting," I added, "but Experiment 2 is going well. Is he following all of your ground rules?"

"Well, yes," said his father, who realized he had overreacted and lost perspective.

"Then why should we change something that's working?" I asked. "What happened is about his cell phone, not his computer. Perhaps we should focus on Experiment 3," I suggested.

"You're right," said Mason's father. "I'm so angry! I just feel like we should do more."

"It's hard to think clearly when we're upset," I agreed, "but it appears that most of his consequences are already in place. Mason is suspended for five days. He has a week of schoolwork to make up. All of his friends and many of his classmates know what happened. In addition, he's grounded to the house for a week and will likely lose his cell phone privileges for at least a week."

I tried to shift our focus to Experiment #3. "What did you say you would do if he violated the ground rules for using his cell phone?" I asked.

"We said we would take it away for one week if there was evidence of using it for pornography," said Mason's mother, "but he also continues to exceed the limits on his plan," she added. "I'm not sure he's ready to handle his cell phone responsibly." Mason's father agreed.

"I'm sure he's not ready to handle the responsibility of having Internet access on his cell phone," said his father. "At the very least, we should take his phone for a week and replace it with one of those inexpensive phones that can only send and receive calls." His mother nodded. They agreed to cancel his cell phone plan and replace it with an inexpensive phone. The immediate crisis was over. We agreed to meet again at the follow-up conference.

Let's fast-forward another four weeks. Mason and his parents arrived for the follow-up conference in good spirits. Mason wore a clean T-shirt. His hair was combed, and he was wearing an aftershave. He sat straight, not slumped, in his chair. *That's different*, I thought to myself. Mason's mother looked more upbeat.

"How did the experiments go?" I asked. "Let's start with the good news first."

"There's a lot of good news," Mason's father began. "He made a lot of deposits since the last time we were here, and he has earned back a lot of our trust." I gave Mason a high five, then asked his parents to review the experiments and share their conclusions. His father took the lead.

"Experiments 2 and 5 have been great since the beginning," he reported. "Many deposits and no withdrawals. He consistently followed our ground rules regarding his computer and the truck. We feel he's fully ready to continue to enjoy these privileges provided nothing new comes up. If it does, we know what to do."

"How did things go with the cell phone?" I asked. His mother responded.

"Experiment 3 changed after the school incident, when we decided he was not ready for Internet access," she said. "Now he can only make and receive calls. We'll continue with the new phone until the end of the year, then repeat the experiment next year." We shifted our attention to the two remaining experiments.

"Experiments 1 and 4 show partial readiness," said Mason's mother, "but we're definitely making progress. He still complains and tries to argue with us when we point out he's not ready to leave the house or use the truck, but he always goes back and finishes what he needs to do. It's a work in progress. The credit card experiment also has been full of ups and downs. He continues to make nonessential purchases, but he also pays them off with his own money at the end of the month. We'll repeat these experiments until the end of the year."

"Partial readiness is partial success," I added. "It shows things are moving in the right direction." I congratulated them all on their hard work.

The initial round of readiness experiments had been a success. Mason's parents got their answers and left the session with a restored confidence in their son and a positive balance in their Trust Bank Account. More important, they left with some effective new tools in their toolkit. I was confident they could manage the next round of experiments on their own.

## Trust Is a Two-Way Street

It wouldn't be right to conclude this chapter without acknowledging that trust is a two-way street. The focus thus far has been on helping teens to earn privileges and build trust by making regular deposits and fewer withdrawals from their Trust Bank Account, but the same principles apply to parents. What we do is what we teach. The balance of deposits and withdrawals we make in our daily lives sets the standard for our family's values, morals, and ethics.

It's not realistic to expect more from your teen than you

are willing to do yourself. Teens can see through the hypocrisy of *Do as I say, not as I do.* Your efforts to get your teen to follow higher standards of behavior will ring hollow if you're not willing to follow those standards yourself.

Take a minute to inventory the deposits and withdrawals you make in your own family and carefully examine the balance statement in your account before introducing Trust Bank Accounts to your teen. If you discover you need to put your own house in order, it's best that you do so before discussing your teen's account. Otherwise, you're likely to encounter a lot of resistance. The following is a list of typical parent deposits and withdrawals to help you with your inventory.

### Parent Deposits

- Attending your teen's extracurricular activities
- Expressing love and concern when your teen messes up
- Role-modeling good grooming and health habits
- Holding a firm line regarding teen responsibilities at home and school
- Listening without comment or lectures when your teen is upset
- Giving regular and unsolicited apologies when you mess up
- Laughing at your own foibles, shortcomings, and imperfections
- Admitting fault when you mess up
- Role-modeling good table manners
- Observing your teen's birthday and special occasions

- Being available when your teen needs support and guidance
- Routine gestures of affection (for example, hugs, kisses, compliments)
- Showing patience when your teen is confused
- Keeping your composure when your teen loses hers
- Teaching by example, not lecturing
- Allowing your teen to learn some lessons the hard way
- Exercising good moral judgment
- Daily acts of integrity
- Handling crises without freaking out
- Role-modeling tolerance and acceptance of different values
- Role-modeling patience and forgiveness

*Parent Withdrawals*
- Role-modeling cheating or untrustworthy behavior
- Using hurtful, profane, or disrespectful language
- Demanding affection or respect because "I'm your parent!"
- Poor listening skills
- Neglecting daily gestures of respect and affection (for example, greetings, hugs)
- Overlooking your teen's birthday or special occasions
- Telling your teen that his thoughts or feelings are stupid
- Arguing with your teen
- Role-modeling poor driving skills

- Drinking to the point of drunkenness in front of your teen
- Role-modeling intolerance
- Role-modeling poor judgment
- Overinvolvement in your teen's life
- Abusing prescription medications
- Failing to follow through on promises and commitments
- Raging back when your teen rages at you
- Solving problems with hurtful or violent behavior
- Practicing infidelity
- Giving "the cold treatment" when your teen messes up

## Chapter Summary

The Trust Bank Account is a wonderful tool for measuring your teen's readiness and character development. Teens like it because it provides them with a fresh opportunity to restore, and eventually increase, their freedom and privileges. Parents like it because it helps them determine what their teen is and is not ready to handle and begin to rebuild lost trust and confidence. I like it because it helps parents preserve their clear thinking and hold on to the big picture of what's really going on between parents and teens during a tumultuous learning process. Adolescence is an emotional roller-coaster ride for parents and teens alike. The Trust Bank Account helps parents hold on to their seat and endure the ups and downs of what often seems like a crazy learning process.

# Trust Bank Account: Questions and Answers

*Question:* Is it easy to conduct readiness-testing experiments and manage your teen's Trust Bank Account at the same time?

*Answer:* Yes and no. Let me clarify. These are two different procedures that challenge parents on two different levels: the intellectual level and the emotional level. On an intellectual level, conducting readiness experiments is easy. Most fourth graders can do it. Readiness testing is about behavior: creating a hypothesis about your teen's behavior, observing your teen's behavior (the evidence), and arriving at conclusions based on what you observe.

Managing your teen's Trust Bank Account is about feelings: how you honestly feel about your teen's deposits and withdrawals. This part can be difficult and stressful. Why? Because you are emotionally invested in the experiments and their outcomes. You want them to go well and often feel discouraged when they don't. The Trust Bank Account helps you view your teen's ups and downs through a wide-angle lens and maintain a clearer perspective, but I wouldn't describe this as easy.

*Question:* I consistently overreact to my teen's withdrawals, then my teen reacts to me, and we're off to the races. What do you recommend?

*Answer:* Join the club! Overreacting is the single most

common problem reported by parents when they attempt to manage their teen's Trust Bank Account. Chapter 17 may help you get past this hurdle. If not, you may need some professional help.

*Question:* My teen and I are barely on speaking terms. Do you think we can use the Trust Bank Account procedure without professional assistance?

*Answer:* Possibly. Give it a try. If it doesn't work out, Chapter 11 was written for you.

*Question:* Are there readiness experiments for parents for managing their teen's Trust Bank Account?

*Answer:* Yes. It's called trying it on your own. All you can do is your best. Remember, partial success is still success. You'll get better with practice.

*Question:* When we review the balance statement with our teen each week, he tries to argue with us. How should we handle this?

*Answer:* You can minimize arguments by keeping accurate records of your teen's deposits and withdrawals during the experiment. Relying on your memory of events alone is an invitation for trouble. It brings too much subjectivity into play and increases the likelihood your teen might challenge or argue with your evidence. Keep a journal or notebook with dated entries. When you review the balance with your teen, stick to the facts of what you observed and share your honest feelings about those facts (for example, I feel encouraged, confident, more trust, etc.). Don't share your conclusions about readiness until the end of each experiment. The exception, of course, is cases where safety or legal issues are involved. If it's clear your teen is not ready, discontinue the experiment and allow sufficient time for your teen to mature before trying it again.

*Question:* After reading the last section in your chapter, I realize that I role-model many of the things I tell my teen not to do. Can I still set up readiness experiments in those areas?

*Answer:* Possibly. Honesty is the best policy. If you share this observation openly with your teen, your courage and honesty will give you big credibility points. By acknowledging your flaws and shortcomings you're giving your teen an opportunity to take stock of his or her flaws and shortcomings.

You can create a level playing field with your teen by conducting readiness experiments for you and your teen simultaneously. You research your teen, and your teen researches you. You review his balance statement, and he reviews yours. Your willingness to change and make new deposits will increase your teen's willingness to do the same.

## CHAPTER 16

# How to Fix an Overdrawn Account

Some Trust Bank Accounts become so overdrawn that parents lose hope, feel desperate, and consider drastic corrective measures. That's what happened to Stephanie's parents when I first met them. They could barely stand to be in the same room with their rebellious, strong-willed daughter. They were well beyond the point where they could solve the problem on their own. They needed professional help. You might need the same help if you find yourself in a desperate situation.

Fourteen-year-old Stephanie had spiky black hair with reddish streaks, heavy mascara and eye shadow, and rows of earrings on both ears when she arrived at my office with her parents for their first appointment. She agreed to accompany her parents to avoid being sent to one of those private schools for troubled teens in some remote part of Utah.

"We're at the end of our rope, and we don't know what to do," her father begins. "We've lost all trust in Stephanie. She's been nothing but trouble since she started hanging around with her new 'skater friends.' Her grades have dropped. She won't follow our rules at home, and she does risky things that scare us to death."

"My friends have nothing to do with it," interrupts Stephanie. She rolls her eyes and shakes her head.

"Well, that's the way it looks to us," says her father. He continues to share his concerns. "We can't even trust her to get to school and back on her own. She's had five truancies already this semester, and she was caught shoplifting with her friends during one of them. Her mother has to drop her off and pick her up from school each day so we can be sure she's actually there. The car rides are unbearable! Stephanie constantly changes radio stations and blasts the music much too loud. My wife has to take two hours off work each day because Stephanie can't be trusted to be home unsupervised after school. We've caught her using marijuana and having sex on several occasions."

"Oral sex is not really having sex," interrupts Stephanie again. "You can't get pregnant! And marijuana is practically legal. All my friends smoke weed. It's safer than the wine you have with dinner."

"We're not here to argue about what's really sex and what's really drug use," says her frustrated father. Stephanie's mother looks agitated. Stephanie just shakes her head and stares at the floor. Her father continues.

"At home, she refuses to do the few chores we ask of her each evening and spends nearly all her time in that disaster area she calls a bedroom room listening to music or talking with her friends on her cell phone, that is, when she's not sneaking out. We've caught her sneaking out late at night on three occasions."

"Since you put me on lockdown, that's the only way I get to see my friends outside of school," snaps Stephanie.

"Yes, we've tried grounding her to the house," says her

father, "but that's just one of many steps we've taken. We took her to our family physician when we suspected drug abuse, and she tested positive for marijuana and several other drugs. We also took her to see the pastor of our church, but she refused to talk with him and insisted she wanted a real counselor. So, that's why we're here. If this doesn't work, we've found a private school out of state that looks like a good fit."

"You mean you found a prison," interrupts Stephanie. "They just call it a school so parents won't feel bad about locking their kids up."

"Some kids need to be locked up when they're out of control," says her father angrily.

"Well, I'm not one of them!" shouts Stephanie.

Her father was about to shout back when I suggested we take a few minutes to cool off. The surface issues were out on the table. Clearly, Stephanie had run up an impressive list of withdrawals from her Trust Bank Account, but why? I spent the remainder of the session meeting with Stephanie and her parents separately, collecting background information, and looking for clues.

Her mother provided the first big clue when she said, "Stephanie has always been difficult, stubborn, and a challenge to raise, but nothing like this. Everything changed at the beginning of eighth grade." *Sounds like a strong-willed teen,* I said to myself.

When I explored how she was doing prior to eighth grade, Stephanie's life sounded fairly normal. She lived in a stable home with a compliant younger sister and two very busy, hardworking professional parents who put in long hours. Stephanie got above-average grades, did her chores most of the time, and played competitive soccer year-round on two teams that occupied a lot of her free time. To her parents' dismay, Stephanie chose to give up soccer at the end of seventh grade and began hanging out with a different group of friends, whom her parents called "skaters."

When I asked Stephanie why she gave up soccer, her response was revealing. "After sixth grade, my parents rarely went to my games on weekends and never on weeknights. They were just trying to keep me busy so I wouldn't be a problem for them."

*Soccer is about parental attention,* I thought to myself. *Who says parents don't matter?*

As it turned out, Stephanie's "new skater friends" were not really new at all. She had known most of them since elementary school, and, like Stephanie, most had opted out of their previous extracurricular activities. They all had a lot of free, unstructured, and unsupervised time to spend together. They shared something else in common: they all lived in busy homes with parents who worked long hours, had high achievement expectations for their kids, but had little free time to spend with them.

Stephanie's acting out was beginning to make sense. On the surface, she was saying, *I'm angry. Get out of my life!* But on a deeper level, she seemed to be saying, *Pay attention to me. Get in my life!* If this was Stephanie's attempt to get her parents more involved, it seemed to be working.

The puzzle pieces were falling together. Readiness testing and the Trust Bank Account would be important interventions for addressing many of the surface issues and some of the deeper ones, but this family needed more. Their communication had completely broken down. They were stuck. The anger and tension level was so high they could barely sit in the same room together without ripping into one another. We spent the next full session working on basic communication skills and trying to bring the tension level down to a manageable level. Finally, we were ready.

I could see that her parents' limit-setting practices were not helping their cause, so I showed them how to support their rules with logical consequences, rather than punishment. You learned to do the same thing in Chapter 10. Stephanie's parents responded the way many parents do. "Logical consequences make a lot more sense than what we were doing," her father exclaimed.

Next, I introduced the Trust Bank Account and explained how it works. Stephanie and her parents caught on quickly to all the concepts: deposits, withdrawals, and the balance statement. Most important, they all recognized how the account pertained to them.

"My account is way beyond overdrawn!" observed Stephanie. "Can I cancel the old one and start a new one?" I appreciated her humor. Even her parents smiled at the thought. It was clear they all realized how severely trust had broken down and where they really stood with one another.

"Yes, you've put together an impressive list of withdrawals," I replied. "We can't erase the old account, but we can certainly change it and improve it. Are you ready to get started?" They all nodded. "Then let's set up some readiness experiments," I said.

Readiness testing is a good place to start in situations like this. Teens like it because it provides them with a fresh opportunity to restore, and eventually increase, lost privileges. Parents like it because it helps them determine, in a safe context, what their teen is and is not ready to handle and begin to rebuild some trust. The procedure provides a starting point for moving forward.

I introduced the four-step readiness-testing formula and explained how it worked. "Each successful outcome during the experiment adds a new deposit into your account and sets up a chain reaction—the more deposits, the better the balance statement, the quicker we build trust, and the sooner parents feel comfortable restoring privileges. Withdrawals set up the opposite chain reaction. If you're uncertain where you stand, you can check the balance statement at any time. It never lies. I recommend you check it regularly." I pulled out my whiteboard with the list of Stephanie's withdrawals and said, "Are you ready to develop a readiness experiment for the withdrawals on the list?" They all nodded.

*Stephanie's Withdrawals*
- Unprotected sex
- Experimentation with drugs and alcohol
- Sneaking out at night (on at least three occasions)
- Five school truancies
- Abusing unsupervised after-school privileges
- Shoplifting incident
- Dropping grades at school
- Neglected chores
- Radio aggression during car rides
- Trashed bedroom
- Isolated from family

When we surveyed her withdrawals, we could see that many of the issues could be addressed under the same experiment. For example, the issues of unprotected sex, experimentation with drugs and alcohol, the shoplifting incident, sneaking out at night, and abuse of unsupervised time could all be included in a single experiment under the hypothesis: Is Stephanie ready to handle her unstructured, unsupervised time responsibly?

The five school truancies and falling grades could be included in a single experiment under the hypothesis: Is Stephanie ready to handle her responsibilities at school? The neglected chores and trashed bedroom could be included in an experiment under the hypothesis: Is Stephanie ready to handle her responsibilities at home? The radio aggression issue required its own experiment. I noted the four experiments with their corresponding hypotheses on my whiteboard.

> Experiment #1: Is Stephanie ready to handle her unstructured and unsupervised time responsibly?
> Experiment #2: Is Stephanie ready to handle her responsibilities at school?
> Experiment #3: Is Stephanie ready to handle her responsibilities at home?
> Experiment #4: Is Stephanie ready to handle her radio privileges in the car?

Stephanie protested as soon as she saw the list. "I'm fourteen, not five," she said. "You know I can do all that stuff."

"We know you're bright and capable," said her father. "The experiments are not about what you can do. At some point, we know you'll be able to do all of this stuff. The experiments will tell us what you're ready to handle now." Stephanie understood what he was saying, but she didn't like it.

Next, I asked Stephanie's parents to draw upon their understanding of logical consequences and set the conditions or ground rules for each experiment. We began with Experiment #1.

"We already know the answer to this experiment," says her father. "She's not even close to being ready. Her list of withdrawals speaks for itself. I love her too much to take chances with her safety." I liked the way he said that. So did Stephanie.

"What would it take to get her ready?" I asked. Stephanie's mother responded first.

"She needs to show us she can handle her structured, supervised time responsibly before I'll have enough confidence to give her unstructured, unsupervised time." Stephanie's father agreed.

"Okay, we can revise the hypothesis for Experiment 1. The new hypothesis is: Is Stephanie ready to handle her structured, supervised time responsibly? What do you need from her to show you that she can do that?" I asked.

"She needs to come home directly from school," said her mother. "Then she's free to listen to music or call her friends. But as far as I'm concerned, she's still grounded to the house." Stephanie's father nods in agreement. "If she does that for eight weeks without any drug or alcohol use, risky behavior, or sneaking out at night, we're willing to recognize her big deposit by restoring some of her free, unsupervised time. If there are more major withdrawals, then we'll extend the grounding period for another eight weeks each time it happens."

"Great!" said Stephanie sarcastically. "Eight more weeks of lockdown."

"Or eight more weeks to freedom," I said. "Can you do that?"

"I guess I'll have to or face prison in Utah," Stephanie replied.

"There's one more thing we need," said her father. "We've made arrangements with our family doctor to have screenings for drugs and alcohol every two weeks. If you can't stay away from that stuff during your supervised time, then your mother and I have little confidence you're ready to avoid that stuff during your unsupervised time."

"Great!" said Stephanie sarcastically. "Now I have to pee in a bottle while I'm in lockdown."

"This may seem extreme to you," said her mother with tears in her eyes, "but your father and I are scared. We love you too much to take chances with your safety. Clean drug tests are the kind of deposits we need to be confident you're ready to handle freedom on your own." Her mother's message came from the heart and hit home. Stephanie also had tears in her eyes.

The first readiness experiment was difficult to set up because so many emotionally charged issues were involved. The three remaining experiments would be easier. We turned our attention to Experiment #2. "What do you need from Stephanie to know she's ready to handle her responsibilities at school?" I asked. Her father responded first.

"Stephanie has always been a strong student, with mostly A's and B's, not C's and D's like she had the last two semesters. I expect her to work to her potential, which means mostly

B's. I also expect her to arrive at school on time, attend school every day, attend all of her classes, avoid being tardy to her classes, and to be where she's supposed to be when her mother arrives to pick her up. If she does that for the rest of the semester, then we're willing to consider allowing her to go to and from school on her own again, provided everything goes well with Experiment 1." Her mother nodded in agreement. Experiment #2 was complete. We were ready for Experiment #3.

"What do you need from Stephanie to know that she's ready to handle her responsibilities at home?" I asked. Her mother responded.

"I need her to pick up her room and do the few chores we ask after school and on weekends before she talks with her friends on her phone," her mother began. "I'll hold on to her cell phone until she does. During this grounding period, she's welcome to have her friends visit her at home after her chores and homework are done if they respect our ground rules. If they don't, then we're not ready to have them visit."

"How does that sound to you, Stephanie?" I asked.

"I want to see my friends outside of school," Stephanie responded, "but I should get to choose when I do my chores and homework, and I should be able to keep my room the way I like it, messy or not. I'm almost fifteen."

"You can choose when you do your chores and homework," her mother insisted. "But I'm holding your cell phone until your chores are done, and your friends are not welcome until your homework is done. I'm also willing to give you some leeway on your bedroom. If you want to keep it messy most of the week, that's up to you, but you have to keep the door closed so we don't have to look at it. If the door is open, and the mess is visible, I expect you to clean it up, and you may not have friends in your room unless it's clean. Also, I expect you to clean it once each week on weekends." Stephanie seemed satisfied with the compromise. We were ready for the final experiment.

"What do you need from Stephanie to be convinced she's ready to handle her radio privileges in the car?" I asked. Once again, her mother responded.

"The car radio is an issue that drives me absolutely crazy!" said her mother. "I don't mind if you listen to music as long as you keep the volume at a reasonable level, and I'll determine what 'reasonable' is. If we can't agree on the volume, then the radio stays off. I hate it when you constantly change stations to find songs you like. You can change stations three times each car trip. If you exceed that, the radio goes off." I watched Stephanie do a big eye roll, so I decided to check in with her.

"Does that sound reasonable to you?"

"Whatever," said Stephanie, shaking her head. I waited for a more definitive response. She nodded her agreement.

The four readiness experiments were set up. Stephanie and her parents agreed to start them the next day. I agreed to meet with the family once a week for the next eight weeks to monitor their progress, review the balance statement in their account, and continue to work on communication and relationship building.

How did things go? Things seldom go from bad to good, or very good, in a short period of time. Sometimes there's an initial "honeymoon period" where things go smoothly for a few weeks before teens return to their old patterns. I expected the usual ups and downs, successes and setbacks. Stephanie was no exception.

Stephanie took immediate advantage of her parents' offer to have friends visit after school provided her chores and homework were completed. Her girlfriends visited three times the first week. They hung out and listened to music in Stephanie's bedroom, which had to be clean. *She's making an effort,* her mother said to herself. *Her room hasn't looked this good in months.*

Stephanie also made some minor withdrawals during the first week. She argued about the car radio, which had to be turned off on two occasions, and she got caught lying about completing her chores on another occasion. Her friends were asked to wait in the living room until she finished up. Stephanie and her mom also had some arguments over Stephanie's definition of "clean." Otherwise, her deposits far outweighed her withdrawals. She seemed to be doing her homework after school each day. Her parents would know for sure when progress reports arrived in three weeks. Stephanie's balance statement for week one was encouraging.

Week two was less encouraging. There was an incident that nearly resulted in an extension to her eight-week grounding period. One of Stephanie's "skater friends," Justin, arrived after school for a visit. Stephanie's chores and homework were done, and her room was picked up.

"Come on, Justin, I want to show you something in my room," says Stephanie.

"Justin can wait for you downstairs," says her mother.

"Mom, my room is clean. We'll only be a minute," says Stephanie.

"Well, okay," says her mother reluctantly. Five minutes go by. *Things sound pretty quiet up there,* her mother says to herself. *I should check on them.* When she arrives at Stephanie's bedroom, she sees the two of them locked in an embrace. Stephanie's pants are unzipped, and Justin has one hand down her panties.

"It's time for you to leave, Justin," says Stephanie's mother. "If you don't respect our rules, you're not welcome in our home." Justin hurries out the door.

Our next counseling session was lively. Based on the incident, Stephanie's parents wanted to extend the grounding period another eight weeks but decided instead to limit after-school visits to girlfriends only. "Stephanie has shown us she's not ready for male visitors," said her mother.

Other than the incident with Justin, the rest of the week went well. Stephanie did most of her chores and all of her homework with minimal complaints and followed the ground rules for using the car radio. Things seemed to be going well at school. Her first drug and alcohol screening was clear. For the second week in a row, her balance statement showed more deposits than withdrawals. Let's fast-forward to week four.

Week four was an important week. Stephanie's mid-quarter progress report showed B's or better in all of her classes, and her second drug screening was clear.

"This is her best effort in well over a year," remarked her pleased father. "I'm gaining some confidence." His appreciation was heartfelt, and Stephanie knew it. There were the usual ups and downs during the week with chores and the car radio, but most of the experiments showed encouraging signs of readiness. Stephanie was building a positive balance in her account.

Week five was a setback. Although things went well with the car radio and two after-school visits with her girlfriends, Stephanie was caught lying about completing her chores on two occasions. On one of these occasions, her mother confiscated the phone. Stephanie snuck it out of her mother's purse, got caught, and lost it for the next two days as a consequence.

The most concerning incident during week five, however, involved a call to Stephanie's parents from the school vice principal, who reported that Stephanie was on the athletic field during lunch with two boys who were smoking marijuana. Both boys were suspended for one week. Although Stephanie was not observed smoking, the concerned vice principal thought her parents should know.

"Looks like we're back to square one," said Stephanie's father. "I'm ready to consider that school in Utah once again." He shot a disgusted look in Stephanie's direction. The atmosphere was extremely tense.

"I didn't do anything wrong. I didn't smoke any weed, and I'm not in trouble with the school," Stephanie insisted. Her father shook his head.

"We want to believe you," said her mother, "but these are the kinds of incidents that shake our trust."

"I was just hanging out with my friends," said Stephanie. "There's no law against having friends who smoke weed. They're not bad people."

"Well, there are laws against using drugs at school," said her father, angrily, "and you're choosing to hang around with people who are breaking the law."

"You can't choose my friends!" Stephanie shouted.

"You're right! But we can choose which school you attend," said her father. "If these are the kinds of friends you choose, then this may not be the right school for you." I asked everybody to take a brief cooldown, then tried to summarize the facts to add some perspective to the discussion.

"Let me see if I understand what took place," I began. "What I heard is that Stephanie was standing on the athletic field during lunch next to two boys who were observed smoking marijuana. Both boys were suspended. Stephanie was not observed smoking, and no disciplinary action was taken. The vice principal called to express his concerns, and you're very upset. Is that accurate?" I asked.

"Well, those are the facts," said Stephanie's father, "but it sounded much more serious when the vice principal called, and we don't know for sure that she didn't smoke anything," he added.

"You will next week when she's screened by her doctor," I said. "Are you willing to give her the benefit of the doubt until then?" I asked. He nodded. I could see he was beginning to calm down and get some perspective.

I like to share this story because it illustrates how easily we can overreact and lose perspective when emotions run high. Stephanie's father is a very bright guy, but his thinking was clouded by his strong emotions, and he knew it. This can happen to anybody. It's so easy to lose the big picture. When we examine the complete balance statement in our teen's account, it's easier to view individual withdrawals from the proper perspective. What seemed like a major withdrawal to Stephanie's father was possibly quite minor.

Other than the incident at school, there were only a few minor withdrawals during the rest of the week: one lying incident about completing chores, and the failed attempt to recover her phone from her mother's purse. Sure, there were the usual mumblings, grumblings, and complaints about fairness, but other than these two withdrawals, Stephanie honored the ground rules for most of the experiments. Most of the car rides to and from school went well. She continued to make more deposits than withdrawals, and her balance statement continued on a positive trend.

Stephanie's biggest deposit took place in week six, when her drug screening turned up clear. She'd been telling the truth the whole time. Her parents offered their apologies for doubting her, and Stephanie accepted them graciously.

"I understand why you guys don't trust me," she said. "I've lied to you more than I've been truthful." Everyone got teary-eyed and hugged. After the hug, we reviewed the rest of her balance statement. Everyone agreed it had been a good week. Many deposits. Few withdrawals. Trust was on the mend. Before they left, Stephanie's mother made a surprising disclosure.

"I never thought I'd say this, but I really like your girlfriends," her mother said. "They're good kids." Stephanie was probably fighting back the urge to say, *I told you so.*

For six weeks, Stephanie's home had become the main hangout spot for her and her girlfriends. They usually arrived about an hour after school, and Stephanie's mother usually offered warm chocolate-chip cookies and other treats. The girls were always polite and thanked her. Sometimes they would share things about their families and give Stephanie's mother a glimpse into their lives. They were a lot like Stephanie. Let's fast-forward to week eight.

Week eight was a major milestone. Stephanie's semester grades arrived. She had B's and A's in all of her classes. She also had another clear drug screening. We reviewed her progress with all four experiments, then had a frank discussion about the balance statement in her Trust Bank Account.

"We're so proud of you," said Stephanie's father. "You've earned back a lot of our trust." Her mother nodded her agreement.

"Does that mean I can have some of my privileges back?" asked Stephanie.

"Yes," said her father. "We're ready to talk about some changes. Let's just go down the list." He began with Experiment #1. "You've made enough deposits to give us the confidence that you can handle your structured time responsibly. Now we want to see if you're ready to handle your unsupervised time responsibly. Do you think you're ready for this?" Stephanie nodded.

"Good," said her father. "You can go to and from school on your own each day and visit your girlfriends after school, provided your chores are done and you've asked us in advance. All the old ground rules still apply. We'll continue to check your chores for completion and have drug screenings every two weeks. If you handle this new experiment successfully for another eight weeks, we can discuss adding more privileges. If not, we'll be returning to our old experiment with more supervised time." Her father continued down the list of experiments.

"Experiment 2 is a complete success," said her father. "You've done a great job. We have full confidence you're ready to handle your school responsibilities on your own unless we see a progress report or report card that changes our minds." Stephanie looked relieved.

"Experiments 3 and 4 are partial successes," her father continued. "You've made a lot of deposits, but you continue to make regular withdrawals. We need to continue both of these experiments for another eight weeks, then reevaluate. We're heading in the right direction." Everyone left feeling encouraged.

I continued to see Stephanie and her parents twice a month for the next semester and intermittently during her sophomore year due to boyfriend issues. How did things go during the second semester? The revised Experiment #1 was full of ups and downs, but all of the withdrawals were minor. She neglected to notify her parents when she visited her girlfriends after school on many occasions and lost that privilege for two days each time it happened. One weekend, Stephanie told her parents she was going to a girlfriend's house but went to the mall instead and arrived home three hours late. She lost her weekend visitation privileges for the following two weekends.

Stephanie's chores and bedroom continued to be a sore spot. She dawdled, avoided, and complained about her chores on a regular basis and only completed them to get her cell phone back. The bedroom continued to be a disaster area. She only cleaned it when her friends visited or as required on weekends.

Despite these minor withdrawals, Stephanie continued to make consistent deposits in all of the other important areas. Her grades were good. Her drug screenings were clear. No more truancies. No more sneaking out at night or unprotected sex. There were only occasional hassles over the car radio. At the end of the semester, her parents had enough confidence to discontinue the drug screenings and discuss adding more privileges.

## Chapter Summary

When Stephanie and her parents began counseling, their Trust Bank Account seemed beyond repair. Emotions ran high. Communication had completely broken down. Her parents had lost all perspective. This can happen to anyone, especially when high-risk behavior, safety, and legal issues are involved. Some problems are too complicated to solve on your own.

With professional help, Stephanie and her parents were able to put their Trust Bank Account back in balance. I've seen many other parents do the same thing. Recognizing that this option is available can save you and your teen a lot of grief and financial expense. I encourage you to take advantage of the resources in your community. Counseling with a good adolescent therapist is much less expensive than tuition fees for private schools, hospitalization, attorney fees, court costs, and all the grief and hassles that come with navigating through the juvenile justice system.

## CHAPTER 17

# When Professional
# Help Is Needed

Firm, respectful limit setting will help any teen navigate through the challenges of adolescence, but limit setting is not a remedy for all teen problems. Some teens need more. Stephanie in the last chapter is a good example. I like to share her story because it illustrates the importance of parent–teen relationships as a starting point for resolving teen acting-out issues. As you recall, Stephanie was a bright, capable, strong-willed, and very angry teen in the throes of a very stormy adolescence. Her parents were so overwhelmed with Stephanie's acting out that they had lost perspective. Communication, trust, and respect had completely broken down. Their relationship was in such bad shape that they couldn't move forward without professional assistance. This can happen to anybody.

When emotions run high and perspectives are clouded, it's difficult, if not impossible, to see your teen's behavior realistically and to decide what's normal and what's not. Little problems seem like big problems, and big problems seem catastrophic. How do you know when normal acting-out behavior crosses the line into something more serious, and where do you look for help when this is the case? This chapter will help you answer these questions.

## Evaluate the Status of Your Relationship

The research shows that your relationship with your teen is the single most important factor in helping your teen get through adolescence without serious problems. It's also one of the most important factors to take into account when considering whether to seek professional help. Take a moment to reflect on the following questions: Is there mutual trust and respect between you and your teen? Are you able to communicate without things breaking down into an argument or power struggle? Is your own house in order? Are you able to muster enough patience to keep your emotions in check and hold on to the big picture? Are there stressors other than your teen that strain family relationships?

When parent–teen relationships are in good shape, parents have a much better chance of resolving normal teenage acting-out behavior without professional assistance. When the parent–teen relationship is not good, however, even normal acting-out behavior is more likely to escalate into something more serious.

Where do you stand with your teen? Is your relationship in good shape? If so, you're in a better position to weather the ups and downs of normal teen acting out. If your relationship is in bad shape and you suspect your teen's acting out may be serious, I encourage you to get some help. If your suspicions are correct, you'll know you acted in a timely manner. If the acting-out behavior proves not to be serious, you'll have the peace of mind that comes with that perspective. A positive, respectful relationship with your teen is your best insurance against more serious acting-out behaviors down the road.

You've assessed the status of your relationship with your teen; now let's try to distinguish between normal teenage acting out and behavior that is potentially more serious. Throughout the book, we've looked at teen behavior that falls at or near the extreme end of normal. When your reference point for normal is this skewed to begin with, how do you distinguish between normal acting out and something more serious? This is not an easy call to make.

## Normal Acting Out

Most teens act out in ways that seem shocking and extreme to their parents at some point. Brett and Whitney in Chapter 13 and Mason in Chapter 14 are typical examples. All enjoyed loving relationships with their parents, but trust and communication had broken down, and their parents had lost some perspective.

What are the typical things teens do that seem extreme to their parents? Here's a sampling of the things I hear from parents.

### Normal Acting-Out Behaviors
- Extreme clothing and hairstyle choices
- Disrespectful behavior (for example, eye rolling, murmuring, looks of disgust)

- Profanity
- Put-downs and hurtful statements
- Minor lies and deceptions
- Neglecting chores
- Neglecting homework and school responsibilities
- Experimentation with drugs or alcohol
- Experimentation with pornography
- Neglecting sleep requirements
- Abusing after-school privileges
- Occasional incidents of sneaking out at night
- Playing music with sexually explicit or abusive themes
- Isolated incidents of shoplifting
- Missing curfews
- Abusing minor privileges (for example, cell phone, Internet, credit cards)
- Minor acts of defiance (for example, refusal to do chores or join family outings)
- Holding a party when parents aren't home
- Consistent tardiness
- Occasional thefts from parents' purse or wallet
- Poor personal hygiene habits
- Poor judgment while using the car

Do these incidents feel normal when they're taking place? No. Does this mean they're abnormal? Not necessarily. You'll be relieved to know that in most cases, what appears to be extreme acting out is simply your teen's limit testing or attempt to express his or her independence with dramatic but misguided antisocial behavior or protest. There is no manual for how to go about this. As extreme and shocking as these incidents feel at the moment, most still fall in the range of normal teenage acting out. What seems unusual for your teen and what's unusual for all teens are often two different things. You may need some help to see your teen's behavior from a broader and more realistic perspective. Consider the following example.

Ryan's parents made an appointment to discuss what they considered to be "very disturbing behavior" from their college-bound son. On the surface, he appeared to be a model teenager. He had many friends, got excellent grades, had a part-time job, and hung around with other seemingly well-adjusted kids. His teachers, neighbors, other parents, and his employer all sang his praises on a regular basis. He even got along well with his fifteen-year-old sister. Neither of them opted to express their individuality or independence through clothing, hairstyle, or "in-your-face music choices." They sounded like great kids. Until recently, there had always been lots of trust, respect, and good communication in their family relationships.

So what did Ryan do that was so disturbing? When he turned fifteen, Ryan had his first steady girlfriend. The two were inseparable. Ryan spent most of his free time hanging out at his girlfriend's house. When he was home, he retreated to his room, did his homework, and talked for hours on the phone with his girlfriend. His parents thought this was excessive and felt left out.

When Ryan's parents asked him how things were going with his girlfriend, he acted guarded and secretive and insisted the matter was private. If they pressed him for more information, he became angry, disrespectful, and resentful. Respectful conversations quickly deteriorated into arguments. When the arguments became too heated or personal, his parents would end them. Ryan always interpreted these outcomes as "victories." The pattern persisted for nearly two years.

The precipitating event occurred when Ryan's parents discovered an empty box of condoms in his bedroom. When his parents confronted him, a heated argument erupted. Ryan clenched his fists, shouted angrily at his dad, and gave him a slight shove when he stormed out of the room. That was the final straw. This was not the son they knew. His distressed parents made an appointment the next week.

Ryan's parents shared their heartfelt belief that something was terribly wrong. "Ryan has never acted like this before," they insisted. "We're worried sick about him." By all accounts, his behavior seemed very different from anything he'd done before. Clearly, this behavior was unusual for Ryan, but was it unusual for all teens?

When I explored how Ryan's life was going outside the home, the answers were consistently positive. He did great at school, on the job, in the community, and with his friends. There was no family history of mental health problems, and no evidence of drug or alcohol use or high-risk behavior. His teachers, employer, and other parents continued to sing his praises. Sure, there was a lot of drama, strong emotion, and lots of fireworks, but no red flags. Ryan's antisocial behavior was directed at his parents and no one else.

*Sounds like a typical case of normal adolescent acting-out behavior,* I thought to myself. When I shared this perspective with Ryan's parents, they seemed surprised and relieved.

"I guess we're so wrapped up in what's happening at home

that we lost sight of how well things are going in other important areas of his life," Ryan's father said. They could see he was just exercising his independence and trying to grow up. Their job was to weather the storm.

If you're caught in the storm of your teen's acting-out behavior and question whether it's normal, I encourage you to invest a few hours of your time to consult with a qualified helping professional. A neutral third party can be a valuable resource for helping you see your teen in the proper perspective. Your peace of mind will be worth it.

# Red Flag Acting-Out Behaviors

When does teen behavior cross the line between "normal acting out" and a more serious problem? Most of the red flags fall into two general categories: red flag situations and red flag behaviors. The need for professional help is indicated in the following situations:

### Red Flag Situations
- When trust, respect, and communication between parents and teens has broken down for extended periods coinciding with incidents of extreme acting out
- When health, safety, or legal issues are involved
- When high-risk behavior is involved
- When your teen is not functioning well (for example, neglecting friends, schoolwork, personal hygiene)

- When mental health problems are suspected (for example, depression, trauma, excessive worry and anxiety, poor impulse control, compulsive behavior, obsessive behavior, disorganized thinking, extreme poor judgment, extreme mood changes)

### Red Flag Behaviors
- Repeated school truancies
- High-risk or unsafe sexual behavior
- Self-destructive behavior (for example, cutting, self-mutilation)
- Suicidal talk
- Unsafe or reckless driving
- Driving under the influence of drugs or alcohol
- Substance abuse
- Extreme neglect of personal hygiene
- Major incidents of extreme poor judgment
- Repeated defiant behavior toward parents and authority figures
- Running away
- School expulsion
- Repeated acts of bullying or violent behavior
- Repeated lying, deception, or untrustworthy behavior
- Participation in gang activities
- Sexual harassment
- Repeated thefts from parents and others (for example, money, credit cards)
- Major abuses of cell phone or computer privileges
- Repeated illegal activities (for example, vandalism, drug sales)

- Repeated aggressive behavior toward parents or sibs (for example, abusive behavior)
- Repeated incidents of unusual eating behavior (for example, purging or gorging)
- Extreme weight loss or weight gain
- Violence or cruelty toward animals
- Obsessions with weapons or violence

## Where to Seek Professional Help

Once you've made the decision to seek professional help, an entire new set of questions confronts you: Where do you look for services? Will your health insurance cover the services? What type of help do you need? What licenses and credentials should the helping professional have? How do you know who's good? Let's tackle these questions one at a time to get you pointed in the right direction.

Where do you look for services? Professional help for adolescents usually falls under two areas: public and private. Public or community resources include: community mental health centers, social service agencies, state and federal assistance programs, religious organizations, and services through the public school system. Most are low cost or free. The yellow pages or Internet should provide a full menu of offerings. The credentials and licensing requirements of the service providers vary widely, as does the quality of the services, so be sure to ask around.

Private practitioners are the next category of services. These include: licensed counselors, licensed therapists, licensed psychotherapists, licensed clinical social workers, licensed psychologists, and psychiatrists. All of these individuals must meet strict requirements for education, training, licensing, and ongoing professional development. Private services are expensive; check with your health-care provider or insurance plan to see what specific services for adolescents are covered under your plan. Depending upon coverage, costs, availability, and "the fit" between the service provider and your teen, the private route might be the best way to ensure a high quality of service.

Remember, you're a consumer. You want to make sure that the service and service provider you select are a "good fit" for you and your teen. Don't be shy about checking them out and asking the tough questions about background, licensing, years of experience, or anything else that concerns you. If your teen is willing, involve him or her in the initial interview and ask them how they feel about the provider. The relationship is important. If the relationship doesn't feel like a good fit, I encourage you to shop around for one that is.

What type of service do you need? The answer depends upon the presenting issues or concerns. If the presenting issue is an emergency (for example, drug or alcohol overdose, suicidal talk, self-harm, etc.), then a 911 call or a trip to the emergency room at your local hospital is your best option. They are ready to assist your teen with the appropriate level of medical or psychiatric support.

If the health or mental health issues are not life threatening, your primary care physician is a good starting point. Ask what services are available for adolescents within your health-care package and who works well with teens and teen issues. Most primary care physicians are skilled at matching the appropriate service or service provider to the needs of their clients, particularly when psychiatric treatment or medications are involved.

If private mental health services are unavailable or not an option, check out the menu of public services in your community. The important thing to recognize is that you may not have much say in the training, experience, or "fit" with the provider who is assigned to your case. However, there's nothing to lose by asking the tough questions and trying to be a savvy consumer.

If the primary concern is educational or school related, then your teen's school guidance counselor is a good place to begin. Guidance counselors confront a wide range of teen issues on a regular basis. Many are knowledgeable about services available through the school and in your community.

If the primary concern is a legal issue that might involve the juvenile justice system, an attorney might be the best starting place. Ask trusted friends or colleagues for references. Private attorneys can be quite expensive, but the emotional costs to you and your teen may be greater without them.

## Chapter Summary

The decision to seek professional help can be difficult for many parents. An entirely new set of questions confronts you. Is this normal acting-out behavior or red flag acting-out behavior? What type of service provider do I need? Where do I go for services? Does my health-care package cover these services? What credentials should I look for in a service provider? How do I know if this person is a good fit for my teen?

This chapter provided some guidelines for helping you

decide what's normal and what's not. The type of service you need depends upon the type of problem your teen presents. Your teen's school guidance counselor or your primary care physician is a good place to begin your inquiry. Services for teens fall into two basic categories: public and private. Public services can be quite helpful, but the quality of services varies tremendously in quality. Private services usually ensure a higher quality level, but the fit between the provider and your teen is always an important factor. If the fit isn't right, shop around for one that is.

# Getting Started with Your New Toolkit

You're probably eager to start trying out the new tools in your toolkit. Eagerness is a good thing, but eagerness before readiness is not. I want you to be as prepared as you can be before you launch from the starting blocks, so let's take a moment to assess your actual readiness. Consider the following questions.

Do you recognize the limit-setting approach you used prior to reading this book? Did you tend to be permissive? Punitive? Or use the mixed approach? If you're unsure, I encourage you to go back and review Chapter 6. It's essential that you recognize the difference between your old approach and the democratic approach to limit setting. Without this awareness, you're likely to repeat many of your old mistakes with the new tools. You can't change old bad habits when you're not aware of them.

If you used the permissive, punitive, or mixed approach in the past, then you used soft limits that were unclear, inconsistent, and invited testing. Do you understand the concept of a clear, firm limit? Do you know how to give a clear limit-setting message with your words? If not, you're not ready to launch. Go back and review Chapter 8. This is where most of our limit-setting messages break down.

Do you know how to stop power struggles before they begin by using the check-in procedure, cutoff, cooldown, and limited choices? Do you understand the difference between attitude and unacceptable behavior? Do you know what to do when your teen tries to hook you with a negative attitude? If not, go back and review Chapter 9. With the right tools, you can avoid these stumbling blocks to the limit-setting process.

Do you understand how to support your rules and expectations with logical consequences? If you had punitive tendencies in the past, you'll have to resist the urge to take away your teen's favorite belongings and privileges (cell phone, computer, access to the car, curfews, etc.) when you confront unacceptable behavior. Punitive consequences are not logical or very instructive. If you had permissive or mixed tendencies in the past, you'll have to resist your urge to give warnings, second chances, lectures, or argue, bargain, and negotiate. These soft limits will sabotage your limit-setting efforts. Effective consequences are the key to the enforceability of your rules. If you're unsure about how to use them, you're not ready to launch. Go back and review Chapter 10.

If you tend to be reactive and become easily hooked by your teen's dramatic emotional displays, negative attitude, and limit testing, then you probably have a tough time starting off in a calm, matter-of-fact manner and thinking clearly when emotions run high. This can happen to anybody. If it happens to you, I encourage you to review Chapters 11 and 12 for support. Practice the skill of responding, rather than reacting, by giving yourself a thoughtful moment to clear the cobwebs and start off under control. If managing your anger is your most challenging issue, I encourage you to work on the important skill of patience. Patience is the remedy to anger.

If you answered yes to most of the questions above, you're ready to get started. I've included a suggested schedule for adding new skills to your teen guidance toolkit. People learn at different rates. You may want to add new skills to your repertoire at a slower or faster rate. That's okay. Choose a pace that is comfortable for you. For some, this may mean adding one or two new skills a week after the first few weeks. Others may want to add three or four new skills a week. I caution you against trying to go too fast. Change, even positive change, is stressful.

Expect to make mistakes when you begin using your new skills. The democratic approach to limit setting is very forgiving as long as you keep your limits firm and support them with instructive logical consequences. Work for improvement, not perfection. The more you practice, the faster you'll learn, as long as you maintain a comfortable pace. If you're experiencing difficulty with a particular skill, refer back to the pertinent chapter for assistance. Note the specific language used to carry out the skills in the examples. Enjoy setting limits.

## Suggested Schedule

| | | |
|---|---|---|
| *Week 1* | Be clear with your words | Chapter 8 |
| | Check-in, cutoff, cooldown | Chapter 9 |
| | Give limited choices | Chapter 9 |
| | Ignore attitude | Chapter 9 |
| | Support rules with logical consequences | Chapter 10 |
| *Week 4 or 5* | Practice responding, not reacting | Chapter 1 |
| | Practice forgiveness | Chapter 11 |
| *Week 6 or 7* | Practice patience | Chapter 12 |
| *Week 8 or 9* | Add readiness-testing experiments | Chapter 14 |
| | Add Trust Bank Account | Chapter 14 |
| *Any time you feel overwhelmed* | Manage resistance | Chapter 11 |
| | Practice patience | Chapter12 |
| | Fix an overdrawn Trust Bank Account | Chapter 16 |
| | Consider professional help | Chapter 17 |

UNDERSTANDING ADOLESCENCE

Bradley, Michael J., Ed.D. *Yes, Your Teen Is Crazy: Loving Your Kid Without Losing Your Mind.* Gig Harbor, WA: Harbor Press, 2003.

Erikson, E., *Childhood and Society.* 2nd ed. New York: Norton, 1963.

Kohlberg, L. *Stage and Sequence: The Cognitive Developmental Approach to Socialization.* In D. A. Goslin, ed., *Handbook of Socialization Theory and Research* (pp. 3478–80). Chicago: Rand McNally, 1966.

Piaget, J., and B. Inhelder. *The Psychology of the Child.* New York: Basic Books, 1969.

Riera, Michael, Ph.D. *Uncommon Sense for Parents with Teenagers.* Rev. ed. Berkeley, CA: Celestial Arts, 2004.

Siegel, Daniel J., M.D., *Brainstorm: The Power and Purpose of the Teenage Brain.* New York: Tarcher Press, 2014.

Steinberg, Laurence, Ph.D. *You and Your Adolescent: The Essential Guide for Ages 10–25.* New and revised edition. New York: Simon & Schuster, 2011.

Wadsworth, B. J. *Piaget Theory of Cognitive and Affective Development.* 4th ed. New York: Longman, 1987.

## INDIVIDUAL DIFFERENCES IN TEMPERAMENT

Chess, S., M.D., and A. Thomas, M.D. *Know Your Child.*
New York: Basic Books, 1987.

Rothbart, Mary K., David E. Evans, and Stephan A. Ahadi.
"Temperament and Personality: Origins and Outcomes."
*Journal of Personality and Social Psychology* 78, no. 1 (2000):
122–35.

Thomas, A., and S. Chess. *Temperament and Development.*
New York: Brunner/Mazel, 1977.

Turecki, S., and L. Toner. *The Difficult Child: A Guide for
Parents.* Rev. ed. New York: Bantam Books, 1989.


## YOUR CHANGING ROLE AS A PARENT

Bradley, Michael J., Ed.D. *Yes, Your Teen Is Crazy: Loving Your
Kid Without Losing Your Mind.* Gig Harbor, WA: Harbor
Press, 2003.

Phelan, Thomas W., Ph.D. *Surviving Your Adolescents: How
to Manage and Let Go of Your 13–18 Year Olds.* Glen
Ellyn, IL: Child Management, 1997.

Riera, Michael, Ph. D. *Staying Connected to Your Teenager:
How to Keep Them Talking to You and How to Hear What
They're Really Saying.* Cambridge, MA: Da Capo Press,
2003.

———. *Uncommon Sense for Parents with Teenagers.* Rev. ed.
Berkeley, CA: Celestial Arts, 2004.

Wolf, Anthony E. *Get Out of My Life, but First Could You
Drive Me & Cheryl to the Mall.* New York: Noonday, 1991.

## COMMUNICATION AND PROBLEM SOLVING

Bradley, Michael J., Ed.D. *Yes, Your Teen Is Crazy: Loving Your Kid Without Losing Your Mind.* Gig Harbor, WA: Harbor Press, 2003.

McMahon, Tom. *Teen Tips: A Practical Survival Guide for Parents with Kids 11–19.* New York: Pocket Books, 1996, 2003.

Riera, Michael, Ph.D. *Staying Connected to Your Teenager: How to Keep Them Talking to You and How to Hear What They're Really Saying.* Cambridge, MA: Da Capo Press, 2003.

Rosemond, John. *Teen Proofing: Fostering Responsible Decision Making in Your Teenager.* Kansas City: Andrews McMeel, 2001.

## PATIENCE AND FORGIVENESS

Das, Lama Surya. *Buddha Is as Buddha Does.* New York: Harper One, 2007.

Luskin, Fred, Ph.D. *Forgive for Good: A Proven Prescription for Health and Happiness.* New York: Harper One, 2002.

# ACKNOWLEDGMENTS

Special thanks go to all those who supported my workshops in major ways and to those who contributed to the writing of this book.

To my wife and best friend, Lisa MacKenzie, for your assistance and support during the duration of this project. Everything you've done is deeply appreciated.

To my dear friends, P. J. and Brigette Foehr, for reviewing the manuscript and for your thoughtful suggestions.

To Professor Dale Russell, chair of the Clinical Social Work Department, Sacramento State University, for reviewing the manuscript and being a reliable sounding board when I needed it most.

To Dr. Stewart Teal, Department of Psychiatry, University of California, Davis, Medical School, for your invaluable feedback, particularly with the chapters on readiness testing and the Trust Bank Account.

To Nathan Roberson, editor at the Crown Publishing Group, for helping me launch this project, and your steady support.

To Duane Newcomb, literary consultant, for teaching me nearly everything I know about writing books of this sort.

To all the parents and teens I've seen over the years in my counseling work. Your experiences helped many of the ideas and methods in this book to take shape.

# Move Beyond Traditional Methods That Wear You Down and Get You Nowhere

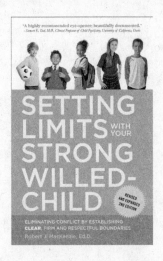

This revised and expanded edition offers the most up-to-date alternatives that zero in on what really works so parents can use their energy in more efficient and productive ways. Explore these time-proven methods for dealing with misbehavior and create positive, respectful, and rewarding relationships with children who are prone to acting out and disobedience. This is an invaluable resource for anyone wondering how to effectively motivate strong-willed children and instill proper conduct.

AVAILABLE NOW WHEREVER BOOKS ARE SOLD

**HARMONY**

BOOKS · NEW YORK

ISBN 978-0-7704-3659-9
US $15.00 | CAN $18.00